My accident defined who I am now and if it weren't for the accident I would not be the person I have become. Whatever I do with my life now has not yet been written. Maybe I am supposed to go out into the world and right the wrongs of mankind, or maybe I am just supposed to rest and take it easy... after all, I have died already! Whatever I do, you can be sure that I'll do the best that I can – I will not waste this second chance that I have been given. However, what I do is not important, the main thing is that I am here and I am happy.

Flight of a Lifetime

Flight of a Lifetime

Philip Watling

Dear Emma

I loved going shopping with you

Philip x

ATHENA PRESS
LONDON

ISBN: 978 1 84748 307 2

First published 2008 by
ATHENA PRESS
Queen's House, 2 Holly Road
Twickenham TW1 4EG
United Kingdom

Printed for Athena Press

To my friends and family, but mostly my parents.
Sure, I lived,
but what kind of life would I have had
if I were not surrounded by those who love me?

ACKNOWLEDGEMENTS

With a work of such magnitude, obviously there are many people who made it possible. Can I thank all my friends, family and neighbours who have been wonderful and aided where needed? The staff, helpers and riders at Penniwells and Digswell Place Riding Stables have been very supportive, helping me get back to the person I was before. My parents have been outstanding, even if only for providing a roof above my head, and my brother was superb, helping rebuild my sense of humour in the early weeks.

Can I thank Sarah Mawdsley, Alison Berry and Tony Joslin for their computer excellence; Mo Price and Jonathan Evans, who helped immensely in proofreading this short history; Alastair Wilson, staff at The Royal London Hospital and Richard Ranshaw, who helped with my research. Thanks also go to Milton Keynes Parks Trust for use of their computers and photocopier; the manufacturers of the various drugs used to fend off my death and preserve my life; and to Shotton Paper Co. Ltd in helping organise the finished product by providing the paper for many of the manuscripts.

Special thanks must go towards the nurses and therapists at my three hospitals who provided the tools to help me return to a former life. My love and thanks go to Sonja Downey and Jo Fresson, as they allowed me to return to life in the first place.

All their help was only possible because of one thing, and it is to this that my book brings honour and praise. *The HEMS helicopter saved my life*, an event I cannot stress enough. Without its unique talents – its speed and the presence of a doctor – I would not have had much of a life to return to and there would have been little for all these wonderful people to work their miracles on.

Ten years on, help was received from Headway (Milton Keynes) and the Community Head Injury Service (Aylesbury), both of whom helped get my mental faculties in some semblance of order. Last, but by no means least, a big hug goes to Caroline Fesharaki for giving me a kick up the backside and making me look for a publisher!

THE MIRACLE WORKERS

THE ACCIDENT

Gary Plowman – Bus Driver
Louise Dunn – District Nurse
PC Giovanna Richards – PC178, Sydenham Police Station
PC Roger Cook – Police Constable
Bill Brooks QAP – Paramedic, Lee Ambulance Station
Glynn Harris QAP – Paramedic, Lee Ambulance Station
Richard Ranshaw – Station Rep, Lee Ambulance Station

THE ROYAL LONDON HOSPITAL

TRAUMA

Alastair Wilson FRCS FCEM OBE – Clinical Director (A&E)
Dr Phil Hajimichael – HEMS doctor
Gareth Hughes – HEMS paramedic
Captain Ian Field – HEMS pilot
Dave Gurney BSc – HEMS co-pilot
Julie Baldry Currens – HEMS Rehabilitation Coordinator
Sonja Downey – Trauma Unit nurse
Jo Fresson – Trauma Unit nurse

ROYAL WARD

Chris(tine) Reavely – Nursing Sister
Doug Jones – Staff Nurse
Alan Tate – Nurse
Ros Wade – Senior Physiotherapist

Jackie Newitt – Physiotherapist
Jane Manners – Physiotherapist
Jacqui Hester – Speech Therapist

THE LISTER HOSPITAL

Josh Brombecker – House Doctor
Sharon Denham – Nursing Sister
Heather Brent – Staff Nurse
Karen Warn – Staff Nurse
Kate Morrisey – Physiotherapist
Nicola Russell – Physiotherapist
Audrey Canadas – Speech Therapist
Sue Fields – Speech Therapy student
Kathy Freedman – Head Occupational Therapist
Michelle Hamilton – Occupational Therapist
Georgia Donovan – Occupational Therapist
Tony Coxall – Technician
Don Bissett – Porter
Clea Fletcher – Fellow patient
Helen Allardyce – Fellow patient
Lisa Stringer – Fellow patient

NORTHWICK PARK HOSPITAL

Dr Natasha Hoddle – Staff Grade Medical Officer
Antonia (Toni) Christos – Staff Nurse
Grace Bentley – Staff Nurse
Linda Ryan – Staff Nurse
Mandy Spencer – Staff Nurse
Elaine Gates – Physiotherapist
Maria Purl – Physiotherapist
Theresa Heyward – Physiotherapist

Cath Badler – Physiotherapy helper
Sarah Ward – Junior Physiotherapist
Mary Oliver – Head Speech and Language Therapist
Barbara Kane – Speech and Language Therapist
Fran Jackson – Speech and Language Therapist
Rachel Halifax – Speech and Language Therapy student
Debbie – Speech and Language Therapy student
Samantha Eaton – Occupational Therapist
Jessica Johnson – Occupational Therapy student
Carol Lee – Therapy assistant
Clare Owen – Senior Psychologist
Anna Janes – Psychology student
Kelly – Health Care assistant
Matt Demus – Technician
Sarah Hayes – RDA riding instructor
Anita Stratford – Fellow patient
Arthur Yettigoda – Fellow patient
Chris Hyde – Fellow patient
George Vella – Fellow patient
Kelvin Connett – Fellow patient
Melvyn Plumb – Fellow patient
Norman Bembrick – Fellow patient
Stanley Lyon – Fellow patient

FRIENDS, RELATIVES AND HANGERS-ON

Nigel Watling – Father
Rosemary Watling – Mother
Simon Watling – Brother
Claire McDermott – Brother's future wife
Gordon and Marie White – maternal grandparents
Jane Watling – paternal grandmother

Brian and Ruth Salter – Uncle and Aunt

Lara Salter – Cousin

David and Carrie Ross – Uncle and Aunt

Andy White – Uncle

Colin and Laura White – Uncle and Aunt

Lavinia, Natacha and Antonia White – Cousins

Cynthia and David Matthews – Family friends

Peter and Jenny Hume – Family friends

Sarah and Alison Hume – Family friends

Becky Teacher and Jim Webb – Friend and her stepfather

Colin Zealley – Friend

John Nippress – Friend and ex-landlord

Lucinda Dymoke White – Friend

Rosalind Gill – Friend

Sam Selvadurai – Friend

Jan Massey, Mr and Mrs M – Owners of Willowtree

Catherine Fewell – Colleague from Willowtree

Julie Herbert – Colleague from Willowtree

Karen Newlyn – Colleague from Willowtree

Jane White and Sammie-Jo – Colleague from Willowtree and daughter

Leigh Fellerman – Colleague from Willowtree

Alison Berry – Friend from Willowtree

Brenda Aldis – Friend from Willowtree

Claire Barnsley – Friend from Willowtree

Danny Davies – Friend from Willowtree

Debi White – Friend from Willowtree

Fiona and Melissa Price and Mrs P – Friends from Willowtree

Hilary Kouriakous – Friend from Willowtree

Karen Lawley – Friend from Willowtree

Niki Kimm – Friend from Willowtree

Sheila Sproul – Friend from Willowtree

Vicki Blake – Friend from Willowtree

Ann Birkenhead – Parents' neighbour

Anne and Mike Styles – Parents' neighbours

Eileen and Steve Conley – Parents' neighbours

Innes Garden – Parents' neighbour

Dr Michael Croft – Family doctor, St Albans

Alan Soloman – Father's old school friend

Monica King – PEACE Founder

Paul Rudd – Production and IT Director, the Daily Express

Peter Felgate – Manager, the Bradbourne Group

Liz Turner – The Bradbourne Group volunteer

Val Payman – Post-adoption worker

Sir Richard Branson – Himself

Thinking

If you think you are beaten, you are;
If you think you dare not, you don't;
If you think to win, but think you lost
It's almost sure you won't.
For out in the world we find,
Success begins with a person's will
It's all in the state of mind.
Life's battles don't always go
To the stronger or faster man,
But sooner or later the man who wins
Is the man who thinks he can.

Walter D Wintle *

---

* Though the title 'Thinking' applies to the poem by Walter D Wintle, this poem could have been 'The Victor' by C W Longnecker, or even written by Norman V Peales in his book *The Power of Positive Thinking*. Poetical authenticity has never been accurately established.

FOREWORD

The 'golden hour' is a term in the medical profession used with particular reference to life-threatening injuries. This is a yardstick time from the moment of the accident to arrival in a hospital appropriate for the patient's injuries, which gives the best chance of survival and recovery. In a large number of cases this is hard to achieve by road ambulance because of road conditions or distances involved and because of ambulance protocols, which dictate that patients are taken to the nearest Accident and Emergency hospital. Protocols also determine the use of HEMS – the Helicopter Emergency Medical Service. They allow the London Ambulance Service to identify accidents where life-threatening injuries have or may have occurred. This tasking is done by one of the Helicopter Paramedics in the LAS Control Centre. However, the paramedic has to rely on reasonable accuracy in reporting by the general public, and sometimes the serious nature of injury may not be appreciated until the road ambulance arrives on scene.

This is what happened with the accident to Philip. The ambulance crew requested that HEMS be sent, having made their examination of Philip after arriving on scene. The aircraft was alerted seventeen minutes after the accident was first reported and the HEMS doctor was by Philip's side six minutes later. Those six minutes included the start-up of the helicopter on the helipad of the Royal London Hospital in Whitechapel, the flight to Catford five miles to the south, and then the landing close to the scene.

Many people believe that HEMS is trying to beat the road ambulance to an accident. This is not the case. The helicopter is the most effective vehicle for the whole of London for carrying a doctor and a paramedic who are skilled at dealing with trauma to serious accidents. It is the most effective vehicle for transporting patients from the accident scene to an appropriate hospital, where it can be seen to be quicker than by road. In Philip's case the major injury was to his head, so he was quickly intubated and ventilated, and twenty-five minutes after the helicopter's arrival at Catford he was airborne in the aircraft and taken to the Royal London Hospital, arriving there fifty-two minutes after his accident; so the golden hour rule was 'observed' for him. I have always likened HEMS to a system that takes the hospital to the accident scene, and I firmly believe having flown a few thousand missions and witnessed the skills and dedication of the HEMS teams that the golden hour criterion ends with the arrival of HEMS.

I am convinced after reading this book and talking to some of the staff involved that Philip would not have survived without HEMS and the Royal London Hospital. But that element is only part of his story. His recovery has been a long, painful and exasperating process. He has had to relearn all the basic functions of speech, walking, eating, vision and all those everyday tasks we take for granted. It must be difficult to master those basic skills as an adult using another part of your brain. A great number of people have helped Philip in his recovery in the time after he landed on the helipad on that fateful day in December 1994. Doctors and nurses in the Resuscitation Room, the staff in the Trauma Unit and on the wards, physiotherapists and occupational and speech therapists and many more professional people in several hospitals. Then again there is the support of parents, relatives and friends. All have played an important part, but what comes over in this book is Philip's determination to make the best recovery possible. He was obviously a strong and self-confident character before his accident. Without these traits I doubt his recovery would have been so quick or as successful. It was a long hard road, and one he never flinched from following.

Flight of a Lifetime gives a very detailed insight into the lengthy treatment and rehabilitation after a serious head injury. It shows the skills of the medical profession and the loving support from parents, relatives and friends. But most of all it shows the courage and determination of the patient himself in never giving up during the dark days of his recovery. This book is a definitive record of that recovery and of the rebuilding of a personality.

Alan Rock

ALAN ROCK – CHIEF PILOT, HEMS 1988–1998

'I've treated patients trapped in cars, in the process of dying: I know for a fact these people would have died if it had not been for the aircraft.'

Gareth Davies – Emeritus HEMS Registrar,
Newsroom South-east, June 1997

Contents

Prebirth

Bang! The car hit me. Quite what happened nobody knows; my memory appears to have stopped the night before the accident, though that whole week may be lost in the mists of time. I feel certain that whatever small part of my brain, enrolled to remember the days surrounding my accident, was expelled – burnt up like a Christian worshipper at a satanic cookery school as my brain cells fried.

'You're lucky,' I was told. 'You don't want to remember what happened.'

Like turning off a computer before a file is saved, the brain shuts down in moments of intense stress, erasing the events that caused the catastrophe from any hope of recall. Yet I was on a bus, and I never travelled on buses around London. This coincidence, so close to my accident, is one too many. I want to remember.

It is a cliché that is told by parents to their children to make them wear clean underpants: 'If you get knocked down by a bus tomorrow…' The trouble was, it happened… It happened to me… It could have happened to anyone…

Most children hate school; they are told to make the most of it, as school would be the best years of their lives. They are traditionally told this by adults as they complain about having to go to the local educational nut house. As these children grow and the time between birthdays seems to shorten – time apparently speeding up in its endless rush towards destruction – as they mature and gain both confidence and knowledge, they begin to understand the meaning of what they had been told. By middle age, when their wisdom has increased to the level where they see themselves as leaders, be it in industry, politics, and the army or simply as parents, these children have long since become adults and finally agree with the statement, to the point where they pass on the message to their children. This handing down of information transfers from one generation to the next our cumulative gathering of wisdom so that it is not lost to our people.

I loved school. Like my peers, though, I should have messed around and caused havoc; I should have bunked off lessons and run riot around the town centre. As each generation appears, we see this more and more: parents gradually begin to lose control, letting go of the tenuous hold they have on their children. These wild tearaways gradually become delinquents and the world turns into one of anarchic disruption, where pupils kill their teachers and children divorce their parents.

This was not the life for me. I treated school in the way that it should be and maybe once was. I could see before me a golden opportunity to learn things and have a childhood without suffering the stresses of being an adult. Certainly I had to attend lessons and partake in exams, but that is the price you pay when you do not have to earn a living. Looking at the world the way it is today, I realise that we need to have a firmer hold on our children, with a greater understanding. I sometimes think we should revert to sending children of four and five years old up chimneys to clean out the soot.

Only sometimes, though. In truth, I dread to think what would happen if we went back to a Victorian way of life. That said, there is no reason why we cannot still prize some of those values that were the foundation stones of our once great civilisation. Certainly, we have at long last broken free of the shackles of colonialism, dictatorships (mostly), communism and apartheid, but that does not mean to say we should forget everything that we have learnt. I felt I was mature enough to realise this and thought that I showed wisdom that was far beyond my years; an intelligence founded in common sense learnt throughout my short lifespan, developed in childhood and painstakingly gathered through my teenage years, adolescence and into adulthood. Maybe I was even old before my time.

In fact, in my early childhood at Bath I never seemed to fit into my peer group – I was always a bit of an outsider. I had friends, but tended to keep a handful of close friends, whereas most children my age 'knew everybody'. If ever I went out it was with my close set of friends, and I avoided large groups. These were only generally encountered when my brother and I went out with our friends or when my parents held a party for their friends. It was at these I really shone. I got on with everyone there and was able to converse intelligently and maturely; at long last I seemed to have found somewhere I fitted in! I grew up early and strived to break out of the pool of immaturity I was paddling in and climb onto the cliffs at the edge where maturity reigned.

At school, especially, I was viewed as being a little bit odd. Even the teachers failed to understand me, telling my parents that I was stupid and was always messing around. Could I help it? After five minutes I had solved the problem everybody else took half an hour to complete. Being a very quiet and shy child, I did not ask for more work; I did my own thing instead. Knowing I was not a disruptive child, my parents took me out of school and transferred me to a fee-paying public school. By the end of my first year I had completed two years of education, moved up a year and went from being one of the eldest boys in the class to being the youngest, almost overnight. Once more I was placed in a group of people who were older and 'more mature' than me, and the friends I had gathered in the year below were... well, a year below. I loved the lessons and being given tougher challenges. It was not that I was stupid; quite simply, I was bored.

Having passed the eleven-plus exam, aged only ten, I was set to enter King Edward's, one of the 'big boys' schools' in Bath, where I would do my O levels. However, before admittance my father changed jobs and the family moved to Chester. The King's School in Chester was similar to King Edward's and I was registered there as a pupil after an interview with the headmaster.

Five years drifted by, some friends were made and nine O levels were passed, some when I was only fourteen. Two were also failed, but we don't mention those – I blame the teacher, personally! My chemistry teacher, Mr Jones, was wonderful and I passed with my only A grade. Having also passed Maths and Biology, I decided to study these three courses for my A levels, taken at St Albans School, following another job move by my father. It was here that the problems that started in Chester were compounded: no matter how much I knew – which is more than anyone would give me credit for – I could not write scientific essays. This is a considerable disadvantage when one is taking science subjects for one's A Levels! Nevertheless, I entered the examination room full of self-confidence and left certain I had known the answers to the questions set for the exam. Even knowing my exam results, I still believe that. Today, you can ask me any question relating to the A level syllabus and I will probably know the answer. Unfortunately, my teachers were not aware of that. More annoying was that the answers were there... if you looked for them. Unfortunately, I was not able to set out the information in the way that the examiners wanted to read it. My essays were English essays in which facts could be found on the subject and my reflections on the question given. The trouble was that these answers were interlaced with a great amount of poetic, English Literature-type words; I wrote stories that encompassed the answer, but the teachers did not want stories. It wasn't that I did not know the information; I just couldn't write it down in a suitable style.

When the exam results were issued, I travelled to school to pick them up along with a friend, Sam Selvadurai, who lived nearby. With trepidation we entered the secretary's office, in alphabetical order. As he was first, I patiently waited for Sam outside and congratulated him when he came out wearing a big beaming smile. He had got the results he required and would go to the university of his choice. Then it was my turn.

I came out very distressed after getting my results. They were so bad that even my second choice university would turn me down. Sam and I slowly wandered off to the local pub. Although I do not drink, the pub's melancholy atmosphere somehow cheered me up and some colour had returned to my shocked complexion. By the time I had arrived home, though, the colour had totally drained away from my face. Not being one to panic, I carefully considered my options and, before long, started to phone round every university to see if they had a place. I looked north, south, east and west, large and small – I even tried Oxford and Cambridge, not wanting to leave any stone unturned. Unfortunately, everyone rejected me so I had to resort to my last option. I had kept one in the bag, seeing as I never wanted to go there: London.

I knew I would have hated being in that large conurbation and never wanted to go there, but all else had failed. Not wanting to attend a polytechnic, this may have been my only chance of going to university... well, that year at any rate. Rejecting many of the smaller colleges within London University, I concentrated on the five largest, positioned at the five main compass points. The Royal Holloway and Bedford College to the south: 'Sorry, already too many students.' The same went for Imperial College to the west. The City of London College to the north practically laughed at my results. Two left and I was getting frantic. King's College in and around the Aldwych at the centre of London was first on the list. 'Sorry,' they said. Once again, my exam results were not quite good enough. Although I passed all three A levels I only had five points out of a maximum of fifteen (excepting those boffins taking four A levels!).

Then a glimmer of light filtered down to brighten my sorry outlook. I was told that Queen Mary and Westfield College, towards the east of London, usually accepted lower grades than King's, so why not give them a try? I telephoned to ask and they sounded promising. They had plenty of space and they wanted more students. I went for an interview and was told I was in if I wanted, almost before I sat down. Why not? I thought. But East London?

I could hardly imagine living in the dark, dirty, squalid East End of our glorious capital. There is no way that this would have been my choice, but did I even have the choice or was the decision made for me – was I not meant to go there? Being a fatalist, I believe everything happens for a reason – I probably would have hated going to my first choice university. It may not be too far-fetched to believe that I went to East London for a reason: I would start a learning process that would take me north and send me south, before sticking me in the South-east, continuing down the path that I travelled, reaching my ultimate destination back in East London. Maybe I had to travel this path before I could continue with my life. Thankfully, we can be content with not having the ability to work out these sorts of facts.

While studying for my degree I joined various clubs, but although I had been interested in horse riding for several years, it took me until my second term to join. By then I was able to pluck up the courage to enrol in the Riding Club and meet up with the band of women, being the only man to enter this particular society. After all, when I started university the opposite sex was alien to me, and the prospect was quite daunting for a fresh-faced teenager having recently left all-boy education. Within a few weeks, when the only true friends I had were women, I realised what had been missing from my life throughout my single-sex education, and I joined the band.

Once I had courageously joined all these women, I used to go down to the stables on a Wednesday afternoon, the set sports period for just about everywhere. Although I got a car in my third year, this second year entailed my taking a tube from Stepney Green to Whitechapel, then the East London Line to New Cross, followed by a train journey to Lee, Hither Green or Grove Park before the ride on my first horse – Shanks's pony! This journey was chaotic. Once we were even dropped off at Lewisham due to engineering works on the railway and had to take a bus. Although I resented this long delay to my short ride, it all helped me fathom the surrounding road network and would come in useful in years to come.

On arrival at Willowtree Riding Establishment in Lee, everyone went off to get his or her horse from its box, ready and willing to be ridden. When I started riding, my horse was ready for me as well. Soon, though, they would leave my horse for me to tack up. It was bad luck if we arrived late, since everyone else would be riding while my horse would still be without a saddle! I didn't realise it at the time, but this too would prove to be very useful as my life continued. Usually, though, once I had got my horse ready we all rode for about an hour. Sometimes we went through some stable management, starting with picking out hooves and cleaning horses to eventually taking the British Horse Society Progressive Riding Test. Once the ride was over and we had put our horses away and I had untacked mine, we returned to East London and I went back to my digs in East Ham.

Although I enjoyed the riding, it did not take me long before I realised that this was not much fun and I was not really doing anything. I could see that life did not solely revolve around us having our ride; for the girls at the yard, the day did not end when we went home. Never being one to sit on my laurels and wanting to learn more about horses, I made an effort to arrive at the stables before we were due to ride. I also stayed on later; often not leaving until 5.30 when the day shift ended and the late night workers came in to take over. While not riding I helped around the yard, watching and listening to what was going on and asking questions.

During those couple of hours that I spent at the yard before going home, I learnt more about how to groom horses and was taught how to feed them, tack them up and other general rudiments of their care. I was taught quite a lot about horses and began to understand them, and they started to treat me as though I were another horse; basically, they began to trust me.

I loved this time at the yard and it wasn't long before it became a habit to hang around there. In my third year I got my car and I would often remain there until they locked up some time after nine o'clock in the evening. When the university holidays began there were no rides on Wednesday afternoons. Wanting to keep riding, I started to ride on Wednesday evenings. I arrived in the morning, staying all day and making a day of it. I began to learn about other aspects of looking after horses including how to muck them out. Over the two months of my holidays I picked up many facts, allowing me to understand features as diverse as ailments of the horse and instructing people how to ride, though it would be several months before I would teach anyone.

The manager at Willowtree, Jan Massey, normally looked after the Wednesday evening riders. She worked hard during the day, teaching and driving the Land Rover around: pulling a trailer loaded with horse manure to hungry farmers. By the evening she was rarely in the mood to stay and oversee the evening riders, being eager to go home. I had been riding on a Wednesday evening for a couple of months, though, and often helped manage the horses and tidy up. She took a chance and suggested that I might like to work there in the evening and have my ride free of charge. Sensibly, I snapped up this chance of advancement and used what I had been learning over the previous few months to look after the horses.

During the evening, I had to tack up any extra horses that were needed to cope with any unexpected developments and look after any ill horses that occasionally came in lame from the ride or, rarely, came down with a case of colic (thankfully nothing worse ever happened). After the rides, I had to make sure the horses had enough water and that their haynets were up, those needing an evening feed had been fed and rugs were being worn by those that required them. There was also a lot of PR involved at the yard having to deal with the riders, especially if they had been changed from their booked horse. This was an unpleasant problem when several people had booked for the same horse and some of them had to be changed. It shouldn't happen, I know, but it did. It was also up to me to make sure the tack room was tidy and that all the doors were shut and the lights were off before the yard could be locked. Jan always intended to come round to check the yard and lock it up herself. I gave her no cause for concern and she soon began to have greater trust in me, without needing to continuously check.

When I started back at university, I continued to work down at Willowtree on Wednesday evenings and, before I knew it, creeping up on me so quietly I did not hear it, I was spending all my days off at the yard as well – a pleasant break from lectures. Not surprisingly, the studies for my degree slackened. I was not disheartened, though, since I was still learning. It was just that it was about horses and riding rather than my degree work. I soon won the trust of the horses and, more usefully, of the management. Before I knew it, I was working there twice a week. I started by working on a Monday evening, and even tried Tuesdays a few times, before finally settling down to working on a Thursday evening, as well as the Wednesday. Unfortunately, due to this extra-curricular activity, the amount of work done for my degree hit rock bottom; but that did not seem to matter to me. As my studies progressed, my days off spent down the yard increased until I was spending almost half the week down there, including weekends, usually working most of the hours that I could. I became invaluable, helping to look after the horses and cope with all the children who rode there – my help on 'Hire a Pony Day' was indispensable.

I learnt the system and was soon able to cope with virtually any eventuality. I made several friends among the staff as well as with some of the riders. Of course, working there I would inevitably make friends with some of the customers. One of them, Alison Berry, who rode on a Wednesday evening, would later on become my girlfriend, so close were the relationships that developed. Naturally I saw more of the horses as well, and even began to look after one of them in particular. To this day, if you ask people whom Shannon (a flea-bitten grey Anglo-Arab) belonged to; they would invariably say my name. I was also closer to the action there and was able to listen – 'impartially' – to all the gossip. It was in this manner that I happened to hear about a member of staff who was leaving.

Although I had not yet finished my degree, by late May 1992, in a sense knowing the answer, I asked Jan if I could have a job. I started work almost before I was able to finish the sentence. This proved a troubling time for me, since I wanted to earn a living yet did not wish to let my father down by not completing my degree. Besides, having spent three years of my life studying, it was silly not to complete the work. Jan was very understanding and considerate and let me have the days off when I took my exams, though I worked around them. It may not be the best way to take your final exams at university, but I was not going to complain; I passed my degree in Zoology, to honours level, and that is all that matters.

My existence down at Willowtree yard gradually turned into a way of life, and I made several very close friends – friends I have even now. Not bad for 'passing acquaintances'. This simple way of life continued for two years, at which point I fell in love and bought a car. Having written off my first car in April 1993, I endured that summer without transport. I spent the weekends at my parents' home in St Albans, but during the week I passed the night in the horsebox or one of the caravans at work. Spending so much time at the yard and not having to dash off to drive home through London, I was able to spend more time after the ride with Alison. Usually her best friend, Debi White, stayed with us before Alison gave her a lift home. Occasionally, a fellow rider and friend, Hilary Kouriakous, joined us for fish and chips. It was through this that Alison and I really got to know each other and often stayed chatting until well after midnight, long after the others had returned home. One evening, however, she drove me back to her house to meet her two dogs, Kaz and Bruno. After taking them for a walk, Alison drove me back to the yard, accompanied by Bruno, who did not want to say goodbye. Once we had arrived at the yard I turned to look at Alison and bid her goodnight. She looked back and the noise intruding from outside seemed to lessen. Alison smiled seductively and an atmosphere of serenity enveloped us. It was obvious something was going to happen. Suddenly, Bruno leant forward and slobbered all over me, his warm, wet tongue excavating every crevice of my face.

'I knew something was going to happen,' I said, as much to him as to Alison, 'but I wasn't expecting that!'

Towards the end of the summer I moved in with Alison for four delirious months and by the start of the cooler weather in November I had bought a new car, but Alison and I had split up. Now homeless, I moved back to stay with my parents, conveniently coinciding with them moving house. Thankfully, though, by the middle of January, having coped for two months commuting from Hertfordshire to South-east London, I moved into a friend's flat in Forest Hill, away from my parents. Considering that I knew how to look after myself, it was wonderful finally getting the opportunity to prove it.

While there I also rescued two cats. It was lucky I was used to animals. One, Nimuë, had been given to me by a friend, Niki Kimm, another rider I had met on my Wednesday late nights, since her cat had produced a litter of unwanted kittens. Like all his siblings, mine was comparatively feral. The other, Bluey, a three-year-old queen, was domesticated, though she had spent most of her life outside. Julie Herbert, a colleague and her previous owner, gave her to me when she found out that Bluey did not get on with her new dog or the two 'feral' kittens that she had been given. This was fine by me, but I was out all day and lived in a fifth floor flat with no access to the outdoors. One was a handful... but two!

I grew up a lot in that period and my whole being changed. By the end of 1994 I felt I had become a different, more learned person, more at ease with myself; I was thoroughly enjoying life. All my friends were in South London and I did not know anybody in Stevenage, where my parents had moved at the end of November 1993, coinciding, almost to the day, with the end of my time with Alison. By that stage my life was in London and there was no way I would make a backward step by going to live with my parents again... or so I thought. That is what I believed, and I saw no reason why it should differ from how my life would pan out. I was going to move or change jobs; I knew that. Through the small and not very well developed psychic ability that I am convinced I possess, I had informed my mother that '...the winter of 1994 would be my last'.

No one understood the real meaning of this statement, as is true for most of my cryptic premonitions. I could not imagine leaving the yard and it was highly unlikely I would get another job, seeing as I was not looking. I was quite happy stuck in my little rut and did not want to go anywhere else. Even so, when I first mentioned this truth, we all imagined it meant that 1994 would be my last winter living on the cheap, working at the yard for little money. Certainly my 'vision' could have been interpreted in that way. Reality very rarely complies with one's expectations, and whatever anybody believed 'before' never quite follows. It was halfway through my twenty-fourth year, 9 December 1994 – a date I shall never forget. Mother saw a horrific alternative meaning to my prophecy as she began to understand what had happened on that eventful day. Taking it at face value, she honestly thought that my time had come. Later, when she found out that I had recently taken out a medical insurance policy, she erroneously convinced herself that I had run out in front of the car on purpose in order to claim the money and it had all gone terribly wrong. Obviously she was heavily traumatised and in a tremendous state of shock. She has since calmed down, realising her ineptitude in taking me for an idiot in wanting to do myself a serious injury for such a small amount of money. If money had been that important I would have studied law or accountancy at university.

As it was, I studied what interested me though I knew any resultant job would bring me little money. Having passed my degree, I was working with animals, finally doing something I really enjoyed. No, the money was not very good, but I was happy and I intended for this simple life to continue for as long as possible. So what went wrong? Did I run out in front of the car? Did I trip, or was I pushed? Maybe I did not see it coming. However it happened: there I lay, in the middle of the road, a crumpled, bloody mess, clearly unable to go to work that day.

Cars around me ground to a halt, annoying all the high-flying executives as they were suddenly confronted with this delay to their smooth drive to work. Through all the confusion that arose from the minor thump I had with the car before being thrown headfirst into the side of a bus, a semblance of order started to evolve.

Seemingly out of nowhere, Louise Dunn, a district nurse, arrived. She would later be joined by Giovanna Richards, a police constable, and these two wonderful people would stay with me until the arrival of the paramedics, who were called as the bus driver radioed his control.

'I only happened to be a few yards down the road sitting in my panda car wondering what the queue of traffic was about. It wasn't until a woman banged on my window and told me there had been an accident that I realised the traffic jam had a source!

'I put the blue lights on and parked my car to protect you from oncoming traffic. Then I shooed away all the "rubber-neckers" who were crowding around you, and basically assessed the situation. I checked your airway, breathing and circulation [ABC], and bandaged your head. I then made an assessment of your injuries and vital signs ready for the ambulance crew.

'I remember helping to load you onto the helicopter.

'Considering your condition as I found you in the road, it is amazing, or perhaps miraculous, how you have recovered.

'At the scene – and can I be brutally truthful – I informed the inspector that it would probably be a FATE-ACC [fatal accident]. Thank God it wasn't.'

Giovanna Richards, PC178, Sydenham Police Station

After being called, the ambulance only had to travel less than two miles, arriving at my side at 8.18 in order to check on my condition and to ferry me to hospital. Joining Louise and Giovanna, it gave me as much help as should be considered necessary for a simple road traffic accident. That said, my 'simple' accident had far-reaching ramifications. I may have had no complex injuries, but the condition the paramedics found me in was far from simple. If nothing else, my accident took place in the middle of the morning rush hour. The roads to the local hospitals would have been blocked with businessmen trying to get to work as fast as possible, cutting each other up and shouting abuse at one another.

Carrying out the correct procedures to the best of their abilities, the paramedics discovered that I was critically injured and my condition was near fatal. How would I have coped with an ambulance journey through the traffic, roadworks and potholes, the width restrictions, speed bumps and other hazards on the road? Would they even get me to hospital in time? It was deemed that the chances of success were slim, and an ambulance journey through London would have terminated my visit to this planet. Because of the possible severity of my head injury, it was decided to activate the service's helicopter. HEMS was called from the London Ambulance Service Control Centre in Waterloo.

'Just as anyone of a certain age can remember where they were and what they were doing when they heard of John F Kennedy's assassination, so I can remember precisely. It will live with me for ever.

'It was a Friday, 9 December 1994, at 11.55 a.m. I had just pulled into the car park opposite the library of Loughborough University to collect Simon and Claire at the end of the autumn term. My car phone rang. Rosemary's voice, quite calm, told me of Philip's accident and that he had been taken to the Royal London Hospital; my first thought – was he dead? – No, he was alive. Thank God, I thought.

'Simon and Claire came bouncing out of the hall with the first of their luggage; immediately, Simon sensed I was not my normal self. After telling them the news as I knew it, we had a very quiet and long journey home.'

Nigel Watling, my father

HEMS, the Helicopter Emergency Medical Service, is a unique operation in London, based at the Royal London Hospital. It often has the nickname of 'air ambulance', but it is more than just an ambulance. What sets it apart from these 'knights of the road' is the fact that there is a doctor on board. Paramedics in this country are very well trained, they are wonderful people, and one may wonder why it is so important to have a doctor there. In a sense, whereas paramedics might be thought of as 'knights', doctors are 'king'. They are allowed to do everything by law and prescribe every drug available. There are many procedures and drugs paramedics are simply not allowed to use. As the HEMS doctor, Darren Walker, said in the *East London Advertiser* on 13 March 1997, 'We are like an arm of A&E [Accident and Emergency] which can reach out to the scene of an accident.'

The fact that there is a helicopter is also vital. It is able to go anywhere, with an effective radius of fifty miles in twenty minutes, land close by and assist very quickly. Not only does the doctor arrive to attend the patient within the important 'golden hour' – since one's chances of surviving skyrocket if one receives the proper medical attention in that first vital hour – but the patient will also be transferred to the most appropriate hospital for his or her injury very fast. The flight from the Royal London Hospital to where I was lying unconscious on the South Circular Road – a distance of 4½ miles – took six minutes.

On arrival, Dr Phil Hajimichael, with help from the helicopter paramedic, Senior Registrar Gareth Hughes, stayed with and looked after me for over twenty minutes before he was satisfied that I was stable enough to be transferred to hospital. HEMS then flew me to the Royal London Hospital in Whitechapel, which oddly enough is only a mile of two away from Queen Mary and Westfield College. Unlike a similar journey by ambulance, the helicopter flight was smooth, bump-free and fast. Within half an hour I was safely taken back with them to hospital, having received medical attention for most of that time. In my view, the flight in the helicopter – indeed its existence – was literally a lifesaver: I am living testimony.

Every one has the right to use the helicopter in an emergency providing the ambulance paramedics have agreed that their condition is serious enough. The helicopter, sponsored by the *Daily Express* (since spring 1997, Virgin have been sponsors), is funded by Express Newspapers – now funded by Virgin (HEMS) – and The Royal London Hospital Trust, covering its costs: fuel, pilots and everything else needed to keep it airborne. The patient's local health authority picks up the cost of any spell in the intensive care unit, while any other costs are met by the Department of Health; there is no charge to the patient. Even so, it is an expensive service. Is it worth it? Put simply, have I justified my life having been saved? What, indeed, does anyone have to do to justify his or her existence? Being born and wanting to live – that, surely, is as much justification anyone has for existing. Everyone deserves the chance to live for as long as they can, and in our country this is expected, whether you want to live or not – and I did.

After being seen by the doctor for half an hour, I went through the casualty department and ended up in the Trauma Unit in a death-like state. I feel it fair to say that the only reason why I did not die was because I was airlifted by HEMS. As it was, I was in a bad way. The collision with the car and the filling I made for the sandwich between it and the bus should have killed me. Certainly, the consultant I had in Royal Ward told my parents that I would never live an independent life; I would never ride a horse or drive a car again. He doubted I would even be able to walk. And yet, here I am now, driving a car, riding horses and walking around quite happily, showing few signs of my brush with death.

Life Before Death

It was a typical winter's day, though the season itself was unusual. The winter of 1994 had appeared, as winters should: a continuation of the somewhat unexceptional weather Britain had been granted. The days were cold and you wrapped up warm, in coats, scarves, gloves and hats, cursing every time you had to go outside. Sensible people stayed indoors and those who worked inside rejoiced at their good fortune. Thankfully, it was not that cold, which was lucky, since some of us, in the desolate shroud that most winters cast over this fair land of ours, have to work outside.

Even though most of the customers at Willowtree Yard are 'warm-weather riders', some people are daft enough to ride in any weather, braving rain, snow and thunderstorms for the simple pleasures associated with sitting on a horse. For many, the only day they ever took off was Bonfire Night, in case the bangs of the fireworks would frighten the horses. From our point of view, it was beneficial to have these 'winter riders' since, we had to look after the horses anyway and these kind people indirectly paid our wages.

Winter had begun, yet autumn seemed to linger. It was not in any great hurry to leave us to the desolation of winter. Even by the middle of December, most days were calm and the wind, although cold, never blew very strong, hardly registering on our consciousness. Despite this good fortune, British weather always has the habit of catching you out, spinning you around and changing before you know what has happened. On some days the wind was very blustery, picking up leaves and blades of straw and hay, hurling them around your head until you did not know which way to turn. The dust which lingered everywhere blew over the yard in clouds that would sting our eyes, making us all walk around with heads bowed not looking where we were going. Although this winter was usually relatively mild, there were days when an icy wind could blow freezing you to the marrow and making your skin cold, regardless of the amount of layers of clothing worn. Even thermal underwear was of little use, there was no sanctuary for us and we had to bury ourselves in our work, since that would keep us warm, and I suppose that was the point. Certainly it was preferable to sitting in the old caravan of the time where the gas stove had long since given in to the cold and retired, and the only source of heat – an infrared lamp – was solely for the elderly cat. It was a room that made us thankful to be outside moving around.

The trouble with outside was that everything was cold to the touch and gloves were too bulky to use for many tasks; the buckles of a bridle, for example, are far too fiddly to adjust while wearing gloves. About the only way to keep frozen fingers warm was to place them within the trapped heat in the space created where the mane curls over the side of a horse's neck. There was no escaping the cold weather; we simply had to endure it until the day ended and we could go home.

The worst job was giving the horses water. They need fresh water at least three times a day, repeated if the bucket is kicked over or messed up. The water was really cold, yet there was no way of avoiding its use. Every morning the tank used for storing the drinking water had an inch of ice over the top of it that had to be broken with one's boot, though it was often too thick for that, the available axe proving more useful. Long boots were a necessity since we were always ending up with our feet in puddles of water, more so when the mud grew thicker and wetter as the days wore on. Often a boot would become stuck in the mud, your foot leaving its shrouded confines as you continue walking exposing it to the cold air and the mud.

The filled hay nets often had to be soaked in the water tank to make the hay wet and prevent susceptible horses from coughing due to the dust present in hay. Quite simply, the dust swelled in water and became too big to get caught in the trachea, being swallowed instead. If left to soak overnight these hay nets had to be 'snapped' out of the water tank, and even when only sprinkled with water they used to freeze before we hung them up in the boxes for the horses to eat!

We were fortunate, since it was unseasonably dry; the freezing weather was not often accompanied by rain, which we knew could come down grating our skin like shards of glass. Even so, there were occasions when it did rain, sometimes bucketing down until everything was sodden, dampening one's spirits no matter how fiery they were. When it did rain it felt as though it would never stop, simply becoming worse until we were past caring, believing there was no let-up to these vile conditions.

As the winter wore on the weather became so bad that at its height it seemed as though summer would never come round again. No doubt it would, but before it could come and rescue us we still had to contend with this unusual winter: even though it was bitterly cold it did not snow. This was a shame, as we had the time to partake in wintry delights such as throwing snowballs at each other and building snowmen. The snow only hit us hard in early 1995 when school children had returned to their academic endeavours. When it did come it was relentless so that by March it would blow like a blizzard. These were weather conditions that suited me very well.

Life at work was as typical as the weather. Every day seemingly like the one before. We left home and arrived at work when it was still dark; we had fed and watered the horses and often mucked out a few stalls before daylight was finally coaxed out to reveal the harsh environment. We left in the afternoon after darkness had closed in around us, often making us wonder whether we had seen daylight at all. The conditions we had to work under were persistent and unavoidable, with the ability to quash the most cheerful spirit, depress the hardiest soul.

On the other hand, the horses managed very well. These most depressing of human days did not seem to affect them, and they carried on in their normal way as if the weather was immaterial. As long as they were fed, and the energetic ones had some exercise, they coped very well. Most of the horses were quieter at this time of year, though, their behaviour somehow mirroring our own perspective. Even so, some liked to mess about. My section of eleven horses and ponies was a mixture. Half of them were big, three of them very big. 'My' Anglo-Arab, Shannon, was a lovely horse to know and was always there for me if I felt a little down. He was quiet and, like the other five horses, reasonably well behaved; as for the other six… well, someone has to look after the ponies! Being the only man down there I was given all the 'nasty' jobs, and I loved my little ponies anyway. Most of the year it was a joy to look after them – even during the winter, most of them were very amenable. Yet they were not always a delight, and two of them were little terrors. Captain and Chelsea are two miniature Shetland Ponies, and I loved them as though they were my own. If you were not able to guess, the smaller the horse, the more of a handful they are!

Ponies – sturdy, intelligent horses less than 14.2 hands (4'10") high that are highly energetic and sometimes a little stubborn – are an extreme case, and even big ponies tend to be more infuriating than small horses. Small ponies are the most trouble-some, and the colder weather did not dampen their mischievous spirits. In the winter, Captain has far more energy than in the summer, and spends most of his hours out cantering around and picking on the larger ponies, even though he is a tiny 27" tall himself! Even compared to the three other miniature Shetlands that Willowtree has he is small. However sweet he is, these actions combine a mixture of courage, insolence and utter stupidity! What was amazing was that he got away with it. Most of the larger ponies, although standing up for themselves, allowed him his token amount of fun.

Although Chelsea is quieter in what she does, she is far more annoying. She has the habit of finding the thickest, wettest, muddiest area of ground available and rolling on it. Although starting the season as a skewbald, with a lovely coat of brown and grey patches, she rapidly turns black and the mud, when dry, refuses to be removed from her thick winter coat – not that you should brush it off when it is wet. Many futile hours would be spent trying to clean her, although you knew that you would be unable to until the spring, when she could have a bath. When not rolling in the mud she is eating it. In fact she eats roots, somehow finding them in the ground, and digging through the earth with her hooves until they are brought to the surface. Then she happily pulls them out and chews them, her muzzle turning ever blacker as the winter draws on. Some say she may have even done this just to annoy me!

These ponies were as temperamental as ever and I was becoming slower, neither wanting nor able to move fast enough as the landscape froze. Human hands and fingers do not move as quickly when the weather turns colder and the odd nip becomes more frequent. The sooner the day was over the better as far as we were concerned. That does not mean to say we did not work hard. If you look after animals they must always come first. It was an understanding we all had, having pets of our own. Four of the staff even had their own horses in the yard. We spent most of the day caring for the horses. Since we were slower than in the summer jobs like tack cleaning were not done as often, since there were just not enough hours in the day. We expended all our energy on the horses making sure they were fed every day. They also had to be mucked out and cleaned – apart from those that were regular partakers in mud baths!

Like everyone else, we needed help keeping our minds off the weather, especially since we were a lot closer to it than office workers. We spent a lot of our spare time moaning about other people. It was fun without being terribly demanding on our intellect and caused no real harm. We only commented jocularly and we meant little of what we said. It was simply used as a release for each of our frozen minds, as though these rushes of emotion could defrost some small part and let out the person underneath, craving to be allowed into our frozen world.

Friday was a quiet day since the horses had a day off and we did not have to tack them up, teach or lead on any lessons, or give them a short feed, though they all had hay. This short feed contained chaff (chopped hay) and sugar beet with differing amounts of bran, barley, flaked maize and oats depending on the horse, its age and its temperament. Some were even given a brand-name mix. This feed was usually only given to horses in work, although some of our older horses did receive a short feed on a Friday. There was little else that had to be done, and we had the opportunity to do other tasks, whether clipping horses during the summer or organising and cleaning the tack. Training was also given to the YTS (Youth Training Scheme) students; we even found time for a bacon sandwich each on Friday morning, its ingestion surrounded by touches of humour.

Most of our lunchtime was spent doing crossword puzzles and reading funny articles in teenage magazines. For teenagers these articles are quite serious, but a little maturity sheds light on the humour that is inherent in most of them. This humour became more apparent as the weather turned colder and we became even sillier. We spent many pleasurable moments laughing and joking, in between mouthfuls of our sandwiches. When not picking on other people the laughter arose from picking on one another, though none of it was meant to harm. The 'cruel' words thrown were merely aimed at hitting the funny side. Naturally, nerves were always brought to the surface where they often became slightly frayed. I and one of the YTS girls, Catherine Fewell, were always playing at verbal fencing, whereas Julie Herbert and I would have philosophical discussions and try to put the world to rights. We all treated each other slightly differently.

As these tedious days dragged into ever more tiresome weeks and the days became progressively shorter, we became more and more depressed, our daylight hours together rapidly diminishing. We started to open up and became more aware of each other's problems. We were all in the same boat, instinctively knowing what horrors the others were going through, and we began to appreciate each other's company more, pulling together to make the job work. We had to get on together or our jobs became that much harder and it might have left us facing longer hours in the cold weather. The camaraderie that was apparent in the winter seemed to calm us down; we seemed to be better behaved and were more willing to help each other get by each miserable day. We became friendlier and were more approachable to the few members of the public crazy enough to venture down to the yard on those dark, grey days. The mental barrier we all erect to protect our independence showed a few chinks in its armour.

Even so, our good spirits could not last for ever and we all had days when life used to get to us, trying to drag us down to the melancholic sea that surrounded our islands of cheerfulness. I remained mainly unaffected. Nothing seemed able to get to me and rob me of my soul, since I was usually the same regardless of the time or the season. Little was able to sway me from the path of happiness that I chose to follow as I rushed towards the end of my day.

Life at the yard with the work and the people, as well as my spare time spent with my friends, went on as normal. When at home I spent most of the evenings awake, never being able to go to sleep early. When I did finally drag myself off to bed I slept very well and had to be woken by a very loud alarm, usually set for around 6.30. It took me a good fifteen minutes to force myself to get out of bed, much preferring its warmth and comfort. I used to leave my flat around an hour later having had breakfast and rescuing Bluey and Nimuë from their night's fast. By eight o'clock my early morning panic was over and I drifted into work. I worked hard and kept busy until 8.30 when I officially started work. In fact, we all worked hard, it being the only way that we could complete the number of tasks that needed to be done; in the winter it kept us warm as well. What made life worse was that the hardest part of the day came in the morning: most of our work had been completed by noon. Our hard day's work continued until 5.30 in the afternoon and we usually had close to an hour off for lunch – after the horses had been presented with their food, naturally. That was the manner with which we carried out our lives, and it was perfectly acceptable, except on those days when we were not able to break for an hour at lunchtime.

To make our pathetic lives worse, most evenings we were unable to leave until nearer six o'clock. We were kind enough to leave our horses in a fit state for the late-night staff who had to cope with the evening customers and make sure that we had tacked up all the horses for the rides. This was easy for me since I was the evening staff on Wednesdays and Thursdays, not leaving until nearer ten o'clock. The only problem arose on the Wednesday evening, where the lack of help normally provided before 5.30 only added to my frustrations. Unlike my usual calm persona, I used to grow very annoyed. As everyone, including me, was too busy leading on the children's rides, they rarely had time to perform the preparatory work for my late night. Most of the work was left to me when I came in from leading and everyone else had gone home. I would get very angry and scream and shout, often kicking and punching walls and other inanimate objects for the purpose of giving me pain. Somehow physical pain would take away the mental torment I was going through to allow me to continue with my work unhindered.

This 'anger' was always aimed at me and in no way would I harm anyone else – or badly injure myself: I'm not *that* stupid! Even so, a young teenager, Vicki Blake, who later became a very good friend, used to come down in her free time and help me every Wednesday evening. She worried about me all night and the effect that my 'raving' might have on everyone, though she was more concerned about the effect it had on me than about any danger that a horse or she or anyone else was in. In truth, none of us were in any danger. Besides, if she was at all worried, she would not have come down to help me. I simply used Wednesday evenings as a vent to purge my own frustrations, allowing me to cope with the rest of the week calmly.

'I first became friends with Philip when we used to work on a Wednesday late night at the stables. Through our shared love of horses we became good friends and often spent many evenings chatting away the time about the virtues of the horse. Even when I had left the stables we still kept in contact, and Philip used to visit me at home; sometimes we'd even go hacking together. At the time of the accident I was just beginning my GCSE course so I seemed to see less of Philip, what with the amount of work I had. Philip was still at the stables, driving his battered car there or sleeping overnight in the horsebox. It seemed then that nothing would change.

'One of my close friends, Leigh, from school and the stables, told me one morning going to school that Philip had been hit by a car and then airlifted to hospital. Obviously this meant it was very serious indeed. At the time I was too shocked to take it in and the tears didn't begin until I got to school and finally realised what had happened. Our head-mistress was very supportive of both Leigh and me. The news, as with me, was received with shock when I returned home that evening. All my family was used to seeing Philip around, and now we knew he was in intensive care. I don't remember much about the first few days, but we weren't allowed to visit him at the time as his condition was very critical; he could die.'

Vicki Blake, friend

In spite of these long days, often exceeding twelve hours, I was still able to cook myself a meal once I was home, and wound the evening down eating it in front of the television. Of course, before this I had to turn my attention to my own animals, feeding my cats. It was lucky for them that they ate any available food – Nimuë even loved Sugar Puffs! This was a pleasant, relaxing end to the day, and usually left me happily exhausted so that I finally crashed out in a relaxing, warm, comfortable bed. The next morning I repeated the day, continuing until the weekend.

Although there was a separate weekend staff, so that we did not have to work then, I often went down to the yard anyway. It was enjoyable going down at the weekend; in some ways it was a holiday, being down there and not working. I simply went down to chat to the staff and to see friends that I was not able to see during the week. I also went down to see Shannon and to look after him, never having quality time during the week, trying to fit too many hours into too short a day. On the odd occasion I was even roped in to act as the senior weekend member of staff. Mind you, considering the fact that I had nothing better to do and normally spent my weekends down at the yard anyway, it was marvellous knowing I would get paid. After all, it was a very hard life, and did not command much pay. It was a livelihood, not a career, and we all undertook the work because we loved it and the horses. There was no other reason for being there.

My lifestyle was to change, however, on Monday, 31 October 1994. I had gone up to Barnet to see a friend of mine, Rebecca Teacher, and her family on the Sunday as I used to do every month for a Mensa get-together. As I enjoyed the company and relaxed atmosphere there, though mainly out of habit, I did not leave until the early hours of Monday morning, Becky and I spending many hours chatting, unaware of the time. Quite often we were up so late that I stayed the night, which, in hindsight, is what I should have done on that fateful night. I wanted to get to work in South-east London on that very same morning, however. I left in haste, through the miserable, rainy early morning, back to my flat, where I was going to change and proceed to work. I was not rushing – that would be dangerous and I wanted to get home safely that night. I almost made it, as well.

About two miles from home, my car aquaplaned on a patch of water and crashed into a street sign. As the car ricocheted off the street sign I remember hearing the words *'Not on the roof!'* scream in my mind, almost as though any accident doing less damage would salvage my car.

It was to no avail … the car not only turned onto its roof, but also went spinning 180° into the road, almost as though it was trying to screw itself into the ground and hide its embarrassment from the disorder evolving around it.

The next few moments that passed gave my shaken head time to settle and allowed me the opportunity to admire the new landscape that my car had just created, altering the quiet urban neighbourhood and causing heads to materialise at windows to see what had happened.

The windscreen of my car had popped out due to the impact and for several weeks afterwards lay half smashed on the side of the pavement. The engine (I later discovered) was cracked in four places while the right-hand wing had wrapped itself around the offside front wheel as though it was, unnecessarily, trying to prevent the car from leaving the scene of its own destruction. The death of my car was harrowing, but I wouldn't have minded so much if I hadn't spent the previous weekend repairing a dent in the door!

Turning over onto its roof caused a large dent to appear in the roof of my car. This dent narrowly missed my head, though how I will never know. A V-shaped dent in the front of the car matched the part of the street sign with which it had impacted. Flakes of paint lay everywhere, both from my car and the sign, and two plants I had in the car with me lay in mangled messes on the road. Although it seemed matters couldn't get much worse, it was also raining.

'Mind your head!' I heard, and looked to see a young man wielding a long pole in the direction of one of the car's back seat windows.

There was no doubt as to his intention and my first thought was instinctively for the safety of my car. 'No! No!' I shouted. 'Not the window!' He paused.

A smashed rear window was nothing compared to the destruction that had been wrought to the car already, but not surprisingly, I was not thinking straight. I undid my seat belt and fell onto the roof of my car. Thank God for seat belts, I now say to myself, reflecting back on the stark image as it lies, still clear in my memory.

I tried my door and window, but neither would budge. The metal had twisted and buckled and was holding firm. Not thinking of climbing through the hole where the windscreen had been, I tried the passenger window, finding that it could be wound down. By some miracle, I crawled out completely unscathed.

By comparison to my wreck of a car, the street sign looked much better. It was still standing, though it had a large dent matching the shape of my car, but little else. It stood on a traffic island, the kerb of which somewhat hampered my progress 'across' the road. In front of the street sign had sat a traffic island bollard. Placed in this precarious position, it had become trapped between the street sign and my fast approaching car, vaporising in the rapidly diminishing gap as my car headed for its own annihilation. I cannot have done much damage, though, the council took over a year to change the beautiful architecture I had created.

This 'traffic hazard' blocking my way also doubled as a zebra crossing, and the orange light attached to the beacon, sprouting off the side of the street sign, fell off and rolled down the road. Later, a police constable, having disappeared a few moments before, strolled up the road softly whistling to himself. 'Is this yours?' he said, as he presented me with a large orange dome.

Despite my lucid and clear-headed state, the arrival of the police prompted the appearance of a breathalyser, though they did not seem to think that I was drunk or had driven into the street sign deliberately. I had little worries there, since I do not drink and was not surprised to find the test was negative. In spite of this, I spent what now seems like an eternity answering their questions and helping them in their enquiries, since they had to be satisfied with what had happened.

An ambulance was called, as a matter of course, but as I had no injuries other than being slightly shocked, I said it was not necessary. Unusually, I did not even suffer from whiplash. A tow truck was also called and it soon arrived. My car was loaded on to the back of the truck and taken back to the repairer's depot, while the police drove me home, leaving the night to continue quietly and the urban destruction to be cleared by the local council later in the morning. For me, though, the morning meant going off to work; so, after a couple of hours rest at home, I walked back to work, past the scene of the accident.

It was a strange feeling arriving at work and having to explain my quiet entrance to my colleagues. Several other people came in that day, all of them surprised to see me, as my car was not there. Naturally everybody asked where it was. In between telling them, I got some of my work done, but for me the day passed very gently and quietly and finished early since my employer, Arthur Massey (Mr M), drove me down to the depot where my car had been towed so that I could take all my possessions away. Sitting in the car, I could not understand how the large dent in the roof had missed my head. Whichever way I sat, I banged my head; there was just no way of avoiding it. Funnily enough, it was on this day that I received my only injury. While bending down to pick up a bag, I banged my head on the edge of the open door, receiving a small bump just over my left eyebrow. It soon disappeared.

The man who towed my car back the previous night must have felt sorry for me. After a brief discussion he said he would tow my car back to the riding yard where I worked, free of charge. This was an unexpected show of kindness and saved me a lot of money – money that I did not have. It also left the car in a useful place for me, and I must thank Mr M for letting me leave my car there. After all, we were running a riding school and equestrian yard, not a breaker's yard!

Having the car there was useful, though, as I had bought most of its components, either doing it up or replacing parts that had worn down or were broken. I had decided to strip it clean and remove any parts that I thought might be useful. There was always a chance that I might be able to use some of them again; failing that, I could try and sell them. If nothing else, I had just bought four new tyres and was able to salvage three, the other being wrapped in the metal of my off-side front wing. I knew very little about cars other than that which I had picked up already repairing parts that I could not pay to have serviced, yet I considered it a very good way of learning. It was depressing work, though, as it was the carcass of my own car; but somehow it was strangely enjoyable as well. It was while doing the work that I realised, especially with the hindsight I have now, that this violent end to my car could also have been the end of me!

In spite of these morbid thoughts I spent a happy six weeks covered in grease, getting annoyed with my car and becoming frustrated when old, worn and rusted nuts and bolts had become too seized up to undo. To a large extent my fury from my Wednesday evenings was transferred to these poor nuts, but when I had vented my anger, they were in due course unscrewed.

After my accident, I went back to work, apparently as though nothing had happened. I had animals to look after, and not having a car was no excuse, although it did mean that I was without transport and had to walk into work. There is nothing like a 4½ mile jaunt to wake you up in the morning! That did not matter to me as I love walking – I always have. It was a favourite hobby of mine to watch the buses pass me in the morning then look at the annoyed bus drivers as I walked passed them a few moments later. Most of the buses I saw in the morning turned off before my stop anyway. A bus with the correct number would usually pass me early in the morning, but it went in the opposite direction. I would be long past the halfway point before my bus overtook me, making it a costly waste of time waiting for it. Needless to say, I never did.

Getting to work in the morning was great fun; I was wide awake and full of energy and could even be heard singing on my way in sometimes, so ecstatic was I at the beautiful autumnal interlude we were experiencing that year. My car may have been destroyed, but there were more important things in life. Getting back in the afternoon proved more difficult, as I'd be both tired and physically exhausted, though I did manage to con a lift on the odd occasion. Several of the mums whose children we looked after during the day were very kind. Some were people I met on my late nights who happened to travel home in the same direction. Others were just plain friendly.

Some of these lifts proved very helpful, and I tended to rely on them, working both Wednesday and Thursday evenings and finishing by 9.15 at the earliest and usually later. There was a family who rode on Thursday evenings whom I had been acquainted with for a long while: Pat Price (Mrs P) was one of those people you could not avoid knowing if you worked down at Willowtree, and our paths had crossed on the odd occasion. Seeing her every week bred familiarity, and she and I, along with her two daughters, Fiona and Melissa, who also rode, had become good friends. To be sociable, they, with some other Thursday night riders, used to go to the pub at the end of the ride. Until that fateful Halloween it had also been a treat for me. Although I do not normally frequent pubs, the company made it well worth the effort. Among the many people I saw there was Karen Lawley, who was to become very important to me in the future, an aspect I was unaware of at the time.

Within a couple of weeks of my accident, my bicycle was reunited with me from my parents' house and I started to use it to ride to and from work. It was certainly much faster, though riding back at eleven at night after visiting the pub, and usually before supper, did not exactly enthral me! I was stuck with the prospect of not having this weekly token amount of fun. However, since I had become very good friends with Mrs P and her daughters, she insisted that I still went to the pub with them to revel in the warmth, comfort and company there; she would then kindly drive me back home. The drawback with this, of course, was that it meant I would have to walk in on the Friday, my bicycle still being at work from the Thursday. It wasn't really difficult; in fact it was quite enjoyable.

We persevered in this way for several weeks, time not seeming to pass. The company was so pleasant and the evenings so agreeable that I became unaware of each passing moment. It is true that we didn't do much, save chat, drink and play the odd game of pool, while Melissa and I ate several packets of crisps, always having a go at each other over the amount the other ate; but that was not the point – it was relaxing. It was all I was capable of doing after a long, hard day. At the end of our relaxing Thursday, Mrs P drove me home, where I still found sufficient energy to cook and eat a fast meal as well as look after Bluey and Nimuë.

Because I did not have my normal transportation the following morning, I tried to leave a little bit earlier since I was walking into work. It used to take me around three-quarters of an hour to walk to work rather than fifteen minutes on my bicycle, but if I was late it did not matter; it was Friday after all. Even so, Fridays were busy; as the horses grew older they all started to have a short feed on the Friday morning, rather than just our four or five regulars. That being so, Friday mornings were normally as busy as those during the rest of the week, the only difference being that we were in no rush to finish, as it was the horses' day off. Since there was no teaching for us to worry about, there was no hurry to be ready for an early morning lesson. Being much quieter, it also meant there was more opportunity for me to strip my car clean; but eventually Mr M started to wonder how much longer I would take.

All good things must come to an end, and after hearing his concerns I finished with it. There were some parts I might have been able to take off, but I was not sure quite how to remove them – and after all why should I even bother? It would have taken too long anyway. All I needed to do was organise a scrap merchant. I half remember looking for one in the local paper during the weekend of 3 and 4 December. I was not on the telephone at my flat, and I was too busy at work to pop up the road and make a phone call. I therefore never got round to telephoning for someone to take my car away for scrapping, which proved most fortunate. I didn't know it, but my car had one last job to perform before being scrapped – helping in my identification. Although being unlucky in having the accident in the first place, it was strange how I was blessed with an inordinate amount of good fortune at the same time.

Angels of Mercy

Friday, 9 December was sunny, calm, cold and rain-free, much the same as every day had been since the events of Halloween a few weeks before. In fact, we had experienced several months when the weather had not varied a great deal. It was turning out to be a very mild winter. That Friday no doubt started the same as every other day that week. There was no reason why it should not have done. However, there might always be the chance that some unforeseen event happened on the Thursday evening to change the course of my life irrevocably – an event that may have upset the balance, invoking an alteration to my lifestyle.

Unfortunately, I do not have the ability to remember and so do not know of such a phenomenon. This event is so unlikely that it makes that particular Friday perfectly normal, meaning I left on time and proceeded to walk to work, travelling through the back streets of Catford towards the South Circular Road. It may not have been the most pleasant route to walk, but it was fast and direct, avoiding the railway lines, Hither Green sidings and the local cemetery.

I caught a bus though. Don't ask me why; I never ride on buses around London. Waiting behind a queue of cars annoys me; I would rather keep moving, even if it takes me longer. As far as I know there was no real reason for me being on the bus, I was not even late for work. It had just gone eight in the morning, and on a Friday as well. I had no reason to hurry to work. Yet I was on a bus. Why, remains one of those mysteries that will probably never find an answer.

The bus stop nearest work is up the hill along St Mildred's Road, Lee, opposite Rayford Avenue – a road that opens out into Ronver Road, leading to Willowtree. The bus pulled over and I jumped off and ran across the road – at least that is what the eyewitnesses say. Sounds like a load of rubbish to me, but I cannot remember any of the events that occurred on that fateful morning. It is frightening to think that I am the only person who can know what happened on the day of my accident, when I cannot now remember the circumstances. Various eyewitnesses all say the same: I just ran out into the road without looking. I do *not* do this.

I have spoken to some of the people who witnessed the accident and have read the police accident report. Using a bit of common sense and knowing the kind of person I am, I think I 'know' what happened and it shows that evidence can easily be misinterpreted. Eyewitnesses can only say what they saw and cannot get inside the mind of the person they witnessed. In no way am I saying that their statements are false, but saying I ran out into the road without looking is ludicrous. I walk fast; I take fast, fleeting looks. My interpretation would be that they did not see me look and only thought I ran. However, like the Big Bang, nobody knows what really happened and, to be honest, it doesn't matter that much anyway.

However it happened; we all agree on the same point. As I crossed the road I had a slight bump with an eastbound car. Thankfully the car was going relatively slowly, only twenty to thirty miles per hour. The A205, South Circular Road, is South London's major artery, spreading right the way across the south of the city from Kew Bridge in the west all the way to the Woolwich free ferry in the east. Of course, being a major route means everybody uses it, and nobody can go fast along the South Circular Road in rush hour, whether they want to or not. Curiously, so many cars were on the road as their drivers 'rushed' to work that my life was spared.

This slight bump, which judging by the damage to the car was all it was, may only have been small, but it did cause my knee to swell up, dislocate my right shoulder and cause a large abrasion to appear on my upper lateral right humerus. As the car (no doubt) braked and I bounced off the bonnet, I was flung into the air and twisted around, banging my right temple against the side of the bus as it pulled away, the fold of metal where the top and bottom halves of the bus meet embossing the side of my head.

As accidents go this had been a bad one. It was to totally change my life and would make me reassess the values that had been foundation stones of the person I had been before, a person I would never be again. Changes occurred that could have turned out to be disastrous, maybe ending with me being 'chained' to a wheelchair for the rest of my life, or even worse. Thankfully, this is not the case, though never must I forget that I had a life to go back to in the first place.

In spite of its grave outcome, this had just been a simple accident, a small prang that should have been forgotten by the next day. It was not for me to forget, though, but the start of a process I somehow had to undergo to better myself; a voyage of self-discovery I maybe had to travel before I would be able to continue with my life. After all, it was up to me to learn from my accident; there was no other way to treat it. No blame could be laid, and there would be no recriminations. Neither the car driver nor I had any reason not to be where we were. We were both carrying out our normal lives to the best of our abilities. Neither of us was in the wrong place.

Time, a factor I never quite did get the hang of, was the linchpin. We were both where we should have been, just at the wrong time. It is a very simplistic view yet it has a ring of truth. Of the many thousands of eventualities that could have happened to prevent us from meeting each other at that exact same spot at that exact same time, none of them came about. Was it pure chance that I came to be in front of that car at that instant, or was the event preordained? Was I supposed to greet the bus that morning with my head? Was I going to live or die? It does not bear thinking about, though it did evolve to offer me a reason for my continuing life, a shred of hope for the purpose of my enduring existence.

No matter how bad the accident was it could have been far worse; all said and done, there did not appear to be that much wrong with me. My bones did not break yet the car had a dent in the wing. Even so, as my head melded, momentarily, with the side of the bus there was a loud noise. My head must be harder than I thought, though maybe there was a hollow ring...

To some extent the traffic had ground to a halt. The car that hit me, the bus and my prone body were causing a fairly effective roadblock. Amid all this confusion, Louise Dunn heard the noise my head made as it hit the bus. A district nurse, she pulled to the side of the road on the opposite carriageway and rushed over to offer her assistance. To her surprise I had landed in the recovery position. Unfortunately, this meant that she was not able to examine me thoroughly, but she was able to check my airway, making sure that it was clear and that there was no blockage, as well as my breathing and my circulation. Happily, she was able to ascertain that I was lucky in that I was still breathing, my heart was still beating, life was still flowing around my broken body. My breaths were shallow (they were not deep enough, and possibly too fast), but she did not dare move me, not knowing whether my neck or back were broken, and she prayed that I kept breathing. If I showed any indication of getting worse she would have had to move me so as to be able to start mouth-to-mouth resuscitation or CPR (cardio-pulmonary resuscitation), neither of which she wanted to start without the proper equipment and services, as she might injure me irreparably. She kept me comfortable and warm, but there was little else she could effectively do. Luckily, I never stopped breathing; my heart never stopped beating.

The driver of the car that hit me pulled over a few yards further ahead and was by the roadside suffering from shock, being comforted by a passer-by. The bus driver, Gary Plowman, also suffering from shock, was doing what he could; the minds of his passengers had started to mingle, trying to ascertain the situation, their bodies not really able to move around and find out exactly what was happening, too stunned by the incident. Mr Plowman radioed his headquarters, informing them of the minor delay to his route. London Buses Control then relayed this information to the police and the London Ambulance Service at 8.10.

When the LAS received the 999 call, stating '...Adult male, hit by car, unconscious on the floor. Query serious,' they passed on the information to New Scotland Yard, and also to Lee Ambulance Station, where it was received by ambulance November 401 at 8.13. The ambulance was driven by Bill Brooks QAP (Qualified Ambulance Paramedic) and attended by Glynn Harris QAP and Richard Ranshaw, the Station Rep, who volunteered to assist hearing the nature of the call. They immediately left the station and headed for the location given: '...junction of Brownhill Road and St Mildred's Road, SE6'. Seeing nothing on arrival five minutes later except for the traffic at a standstill on St Mildred's Road, they continued up St Mildred's Road until the incident was found at the junction of Rayford Avenue, SE12. There I lay on the road, surrounded by a crowd of onlookers.

Before the arrival of the ambulance, however, PC Giovanna Richards turned into the road going about her normal beat moments before receiving the call about my accident on her radio. She had previously been a nurse and had had some training as a paramedic; she rushed over with the small first aid kit she carried with her in the car to see how I was and to check my vital signs – in the circumstances healthy enough, thanks to Louise – and to start the initial police work.

A second constable, PC Roger Cook, arrived shortly after the ambulance and proceeded to take down people's statements. The police were able to find out who I was from my drivers licence and phoned Mum and Dad at home in Stevenage, Hertfordshire. Unfortunately they had both left for work. Why was I in South London? Where did I come from? Luckily, Claire Barnsley, a friend of mine from Willowtree, was walking past on her way to school.

'I can remember the accident happening one morning on my way to school with two friends, about 8.30 in the morning. For some reason we decided to walk down to the next bus stop, where we noticed an accident. I can remember everyone standing round a man lying on the ground, a couple of metres in front of a bus. The driver of the car was standing to one side, shaking and crying. Although not a nosy person, I decided to have a look. Some silly bugger's walked out into the road and a car's hit him, I thought. That was until I noticed that it was Philip.

'I couldn't believe it; I mean, he's done some silly things in the past but this time he had gone too far.

'It took a little while to sink in, but before I knew it I was also shaking and crying.

'Afterwards, I was waiting to hear how he was – it seemed to be one of the longest times of my life.

'Then one day I heard that he was OK. It turns out that after some patient rehabilitation he is walking and talking again.

'He has made a miraculous recovery in such a short space or time.'

Claire Barnsley, friend

Once more the inordinate amount of bad luck that was plaguing me had been miraculously turned to my advantage. Out of morbid curiosity (a sign of good health?), she looked to see if there was any blood and gore. On the shocking revelation as she realised who it was, her perturbations caused the police to ask if she knew my name. She said she did, but unfortunately was not able to tell them where I lived, as she did not know. However, she was able to tell the police where my car was and from the number plate they were able to trace Mum at work through her insurance company.

'It was not the kind of day you will ever forget. John [Sarah's boss] had gone to a meeting with the Managing Director and told me to wait by the telephone and fetch him if his insurers phoned.

'It was about 9.15 when the phone rang. It was a police lady asking if she could speak to John. I asked what it was about, but she would not tell me.

'Several minutes passed and I told her that I would not be able to go and get John as he was in an important meeting.

'She then told me what it was all about, and I went very silent for a moment. "Ah!" I said. "Hold on a moment," and I dashed off.

'Bursting, apologetically, into the MD's office (somewhere I had never been allowed into before), I informed them of the accident, and John rushed off to talk to the police lady.

'The next hour passed very quietly.

' "You look like death," I was told on a number of occasions. "What's wrong?"

'Of course, Rosemary had not yet been told and I could not say anything to anyone.'

Sarah Mawdsley, Personal Assistant,
UPM – Kymmene Limited

'My first involvement, I guess, was when it was reasonably early in the morning and I had a phone call from our insurance brokers. They asked me if I knew whether a Rosemary Watling worked at Lamco. After saying, yes, he mentioned that her son had been involved in an accident and the police had called him because they had found some document to trace you to our company's insurance company. I confirmed that your mother worked here and he told me that he would go back to the police and confirm that this is the contact point. While waiting for the police to call me, I went up to see our managing director and I didn't mention the problem. Of course, a call did come back from the police and my secretary, Sarah Mawdsley, came up and said there was a phone call and she said, "I think you better take it now immediately, it is the police."

'I spoke to the police and, again, they didn't know very much, they just knew there was an accident and her son had been taken to hospital by helicopter.

'Overhearing the conversation, the MD volunteered to get Rosemary and brought her into his office. I just said to her what I knew so far, and mentioned that we had a phone number to ring. In fact, initially of course, I am not even sure we knew which son it was, though the police had told us where the accident happened, so that made it very clear to Rosemary that it was you. Rosemary then asked me to ring the hospital, which I did. It probably took two or three minutes but it certainly seemed like a long time.

'At this stage Rosemary was just sitting there waiting. The ward sister spoke to Rosemary and gave her some preliminary information to say that you were now stable in the Trauma Unit. She then immediately arranged to get a taxi to go over to the Royal London Hospital.'

John Cronly, Finance Director,
UPM – Kymmene Limited

One of the paramedics checked my 'ABC' (these vital statistics were relatively healthy, considering, due to the wonderful help from Louise and Giovanna) while another fitted the appropriate size stiffneck cervical collar. An oropharyngeal airway was inserted and oxygen therapy started, and I was attached to a cardiac monitor. A quick visual check showed no major haemorrhage, so a more thorough secondary survey was started whereby I was checked to see whether there were any obvious wounds or deformities, and my skin condition (colour, texture and moisture) was assessed. This also included a head-to-toe survey of my condition checking my scalp, nose and ears for any deformity or bleeding/CSF (cerebrospinal fluid) discharge. My eyes were checked for injury, pupil equality and movement, and my neck checked for any deviation of the trachea, wounds or distension. My chest, abdomen, pelvis, back and limbs were each checked for any bruising or fracture. The observations found were: a systolic blood pressure of 110 (a little low), a pulse of 96 (a little fast) and a respiration of 12 (normal, but fast for me and probably shallow). My pupils were also fixed and dilated to the left (indication of an internal cerebral bleed); I had brief shaking spells (possible epileptic fits), abnormal reaction to stimuli (e.g. pain), a fractured right humerus (dislocated shoulder), and the possibility of internal injuries. From the Glasgow Coma Score, a scale ranging from three (dead) to fifteen (normal) which is used to determine the level of consciousness, it was ascertained that I had: verbal, 1 (out of 5); eyes, 1 (out of 4); motor, 3 (out of 6). A total score below five (out of fifteen) is very bad and the chances of recovering without a degree of irreparable brain damage are slim. I had a GCS of five. Looking on the bright side I was haemodynamically stable – essentially, I wasn't bleeding!

Even though the ambulance was there, waiting to take me to hospital, it was decided that due to the possible severity of my head injury I was not stable enough to be rushed to hospital in the back of a moving vehicle (London rush hour permitting). However, there was an alternative.

The Helicopter Emergency Medical Service, based at the Royal London Hospital, has been operational since May 1989. HEMS is specifically designed to cope with situations like mine – there being an average of five major incidents a day in London alone. It is the only helicopter of its type in London and is only called out to very bad cases; it would be too inefficient to use it for any trivial undertakings. A HEMS paramedic screens all emergency calls to the London Ambulance Headquarters in Waterloo. He checks to see if any calls are serious enough to warrant the call-out of HEMS.

As this is done, the paramedics assess the patient's injuries against a short list of 'Guidelines for requesting HEMS' while dealing with them. Several points are taken into consideration, including the extent of multiple areas of the injury, whether the respiration rate is very fast or very slow, the pulse is fast or the systolic blood pressure low, and if there are extensive burns, paralysed limbs or long bones broken. It is also ascertained whether the accident was caused by various events, including a fall of more than twenty feet, a blast or cave-in, or a pedestrian hit at more than twenty miles an hour. The activation of the helicopter depends a great deal on the judgement of the paramedics.

Once I'd qualified, the call was made direct to the HEMS office in Whitechapel at 8.27. Meanwhile my limbs were splinted and a 14 g cannula inserted into my right arm to start a saline drip and to administer intravenous Diazemuls if I fitted again. I was then packaged ready for transport by HEMS, and another cannula inserted in my left arm as a precaution against me having internal bleeding, while another saline drip was also started on a TKVO (To Keep Vein Open) rate. I was then positioned onto the orthopaedic scoop stretcher, my head restrained in a neutral position and taped down, placed onto the ambulance trolley bed and positioned inside the ambulance. Meanwhile, the helicopter was making its way to my position, taking six minutes to cover the 4½ miles and landing in a nearby playground.

A Royal London doctor, Phil Hajimichael, was then able to attend me. Better qualified than a paramedic, a doctor is legally allowed to do many procedures which paramedics, even though they may know how, cannot perform. There are various drugs – especially hard drugs like morphine – that only a doctor is allowed to prescribe. Having a doctor there was very important, bearing in mind my condition, and he remained with me for over twenty minutes, getting me in as good a condition as he could before I was airlifted back to hospital.

My fluctuating vital signs were measured again and it was shown that my blood pressure was now reading a more respectable 128/67, while my pulse rate had returned to a practically normal 71 beats per minute. My breathing rate, though, had increased to an alarming twenty breaths per minute. By now my breaths were very shallow indeed! My GCS was taken again, but now it was measured as being six. Even at this early point my body had recovered incredibly well, but I was not out of the woods yet.

In the back of the ambulance, Dr Hajimichael anaesthetised and intubated me for the journey, using a size nine endotracheal tube (ETT 9.0). He then administered Mannitol, a diuretic used to prevent brain swelling in head injury patients, and connected me to the ventilator and all the monitoring equipment carried in the helicopter. The ventilator could be adjusted so that breaths could be faster, slower, bigger or smaller than normal. This was very important, preventing the build-up of carbon dioxide in the bloodstream of head injury patients. On arriving in casualty several minutes later, ventilation on Mannitol was kept up – in fact it continued for several weeks afterwards. I was also hooked up to two peripheral lines (one into each arm) so that IV (intravenous) drugs could be administered.

When Dr Hajimichael considered that I was stable enough to be transported, the ambulance drove the less than 200 yards to the helicopter where I was transferred. Once airborne, Louise Dunn and PC Richards were able to return to their normal lives and I was able to put that disastrous scene behind me and 'wave goodbye' to the crowd of onlookers, as they stood around watching the changing situation and taking photographs.

> 'First thing in the morning, we would only have been on the helipad for twenty minutes before being tasked at 8.27. Six minutes later we were landing on a small playground below the level of the road. It was surrounded by a little wrought iron fence. I remember the fence because Phil Hajimichael ran up the slope and climbed over the fence under the rotor blades, which were still running. We thought he was going to get a rather short haircut! We had seen from the air that you were already in the ambulance with the doors closed. Both Phil and Gareth dived inside. We didn't see them for another twenty minutes. When they emerged they had intubated you and all we had to do was load you onboard and fly you back to the hospital, landing at 9.02. It all went very smoothly really.'
>
> David Gurney BSc, HEMS co-pilot

The quicker return journey to the Royal London Hospital was carefree as they have their operation very well organised, running like clockwork. Once the helicopter had landed, the pilot and co-pilot, Captain Ian Field and David Gurney, were left to finish dealing with the helicopter, help coming as the ground crew hurried forward to assist, while Dr Hajimichael and Gareth Hughes were concerned with me.

Once the doors were opened, I was swung out on the

stretcher, lifted down onto a hospital trolley and wheeled off the helipad (situated on the roof of the Royal London Hospital) to casualty, finally being admitted at 9.07. An anaesthetist, a general surgeon and a neurosurgeon had all been paged just before nine in the morning and were all ready to greet me when I arrived. These doctors, led by Alastair Wilson, Clinical Director (A&E), were able to patch me up well enough to go to the Trauma Unit – basically to get me off the critical list and onto the 'not doing particularly brilliantly, but is not going to die immediately' list.

I talked to Phil Hajimichael two years later and asked him about his reflections on the accident. He told me that he did not really have any; there was nothing to make that particular day especially memorable. I suggested it had probably been 'run-of-the-mill'.

'No, it wasn't that,' he said. 'It is just that we are all so used to doing things like that, we just do it. We don't have time to stop and think about what we are doing, we just get on with it. Emotions don't play a part, we are too busy.'

First action on the list once I had arrived in casualty was to reduce the dislocation to my right shoulder. The abrasion just below this shoulder was left open, though Betadine was applied once in the Trauma Unit. My other injury, a minor abrasion on my right patella with ligamentous damage to my right knee, settled spontaneously over the following few days. Shortly afterwards, the three standard X-rays were taken: cervical spine (the neck), chest and pelvis; they showed no abnormalities.

A triple lumen central line was inserted, right subclavian (just below my right collarbone) for ten days, and an arterial line started in my left wrist. After four days this was removed and another started in my right arm for another six days. The small indentation superlateral to my right eyebrow where my right temple had smashed into the bus, about one inch long, was steristripped. These steristrips, a type of sticky tape used instead of stitches, would finally be removed on the 16 December, leaving the site clean and dry, though the wound was covered by loose scalp; this head laceration did not require any other intervention.

A surgical SHO (Senior House Officer) performed a 'diagnostic peritoneal lavage' (DPL) whereby saline (1000 mls) was infused; 900 mls, virtually crystal clear, was returned – 4 mls of peritoneal fluid was also aspirated. These two samples were analysed to determine my blood cell count. It was found my white blood cell (WBC) count was 10/mm^3 and my red blood cell (RBC) count was 600/mm^3. If the WBC count had been greater than 500/mm^3 or my RBC count had been greater than 100,000/mm^3 then the DPL analysis would have been positive. Hence it was negative and I was not bleeding internally. This procedure is only performed in the A&E department and also involves an incision next to ones navel and the insertion of an endoscope to visually confirm the lavage. After the incision was closed, it left an approximately 2" long DPL wound which was subsequently sutured and dressed with a dry dressing. These sutures would also be removed on the 16th, leaving the site well healed with no evidence of infection.

Thankfully, I was not bleeding from my nose, my mouth or my ears either; this was indeed good fortune, since any one of these could indicate a much more serious condition. Had I been bleeding internally, the surgeons would have had to perform an operation to stop the bleeding. Although it is probably true to say that my body would have recovered from the shock of an operation concurrent with the shock from my accident, it would not have been very pleasant. Mind you, I would have had a scar that could be attributed to my accident. As it turns out, other than a small scar on my left elbow and small, white 'dots' on my wrists, arm and chest, it is very difficult finding any scars due to any of my three car smashes. I seemed to have emerged from another car accident relatively unscathed.

'I recall being told outside the Trauma Unit to be prepared for a shock, as Philip was wired up to an amazing amount of machinery.

'I was nervous but calm as we entered the small, four-bed Trauma Unit.

'My first reaction on seeing Philip was, "There is no blood, no head damage... He looked peaceful." As I took it all in, my firm conviction was that he would be OK, he would not die. This came from a deep, innermost feeling that is impossible to rationalise. I was quite calm.'

Nigel Watling, my father

By 9.55 on the 9th, my blood pressure was measured at 137/82 while my heart rate was a little fast at 88 beats per minute. As my respiration was being controlled by the ventilator, my blood-oxygen saturation was finally up to 100 per cent, rather than the 90 per cent it had been when I was attempting to breathe on my own. My pupils were measured at being 4 mm on the left, but only 3 mm on the right; they were non-reactive. A neurosurgical registrar took me to have a 'CT' (Computerised Tomography) scan at 9.44 in the evening, long after my move from casualty, but they could not take me for the scan until I was stable. This 'cat scan' showed that there were some intracapsular, though mainly intraventricular, haemorrhages on the left-hand side of my brain, diffuse axonal activity and some evidence of cerebral oedema.

Rather than only a few areas being badly damaged it seemed as though my whole brain had suffered minor damage. It appears that this is the way with most head injuries. With me, most of the damage had been to a small area to the left-hand side of my brain. Even so, problems remained with my balance, walking, speech and motor skills to my right side. Other areas – some to the right, some to the back, affecting vision – had been damaged to a lesser extent. These injuries were bad, yet I found it hard to explain to friends exactly what was wrong with me. It was nothing as simple as a broken leg, for example. It could only be described with the blanket term – 'head injury' – but what does it mean?

Once I had regained consciousness fully, I was not able to walk or talk and my balance still worried me a year later. These few physical matters aside, there was nothing that was really wrong with me. Why was that? Put simply, why am I still alive? Was it pure chance? Having potentially died in my previous two car crashes as well as the most recent collision – not to mention the several times I relapsed while in the Trauma Unit – this seems unlikely. Why am I still here, then?

It is almost enough to make one feel quite saintly, believing they are here for a purpose and some higher power will not let them leave this world until they have fulfilled their destiny. I was certainly not destined to die; I was not confronted with a tunnel, swirling with luminous mist, or beckoned by distant ancestors tempting me with the promise of everlasting peace and happiness.

I did not even see a bright light. Perhaps I am intensely evil, and God did not want me in Heaven! Personally I do not think my time had come. Why give me a choice between life and death if I was going to live? Maybe there is a reason for my continuing life? Then again, maybe I am invincible, a human Superman? More likely I am just very lucky.

This is the problem with surviving near-fatal accidents. It makes the survivor feel that they are unstoppable, that nothing can touch them. It seems as though whatever life throws at these survivors, it just bounces off, leaving them unharmed underneath. Coupled with the lack of fear that these accidents can bring, this creates a very deadly combination. Heaven help anyone who pulls a gun on me since bullets cannot harm me!

This leads neatly on to my theory of a test for the existence of God. Assuming there is a God and I have a reason to live, if I point a gun at my head and pull the trigger, the gun should jam. Fear or no fear, invincibility aside, my head injury did not leave me with the stupidity to put this test into practice. I do not fear death; I just like life too much.

Whatever can be said about this kind of accident, and whatever your views on the outcome, there is one fact that remains unaltered. Most of my friends have not noticed too much of a change. Even so, I defy anyone to go through this kind of accident and not change. I have changed, and am still discovering the permutations of these changes. Most of them altered the way I had been for years, forcing me to learn a new style of living.

Many of these aspects of life can be learnt very quickly. Making one's bed in the morning, brushing one's teeth twice a day instead of once, or doing up the button on a shirt breast pocket, are all easy changes to make. Some changes, however, go against what has been learnt throughout a person's life, causing a radical reassessment of opinions and feelings.

Of course, mistakes happen. Often I have done or said something, only to regret it later on understanding the meaning. I would realise later on that I mostly did not really mean what I did or said either. I had a very good friend whom I love very much, yet I had the foolishness to drive her away by what I said to her. I now have regrets, realising I did not mean what I said, though I came to this conclusion too late; I had said it – sometimes words cannot be unsaid.

I was able to learn though, as a child does. Much of who I am and what I can now do had to be learnt from scratch. Since the area of my brain governing the ability to talk had been destroyed, another area had to learn anew how to talk. All very well, yet I could remember how to talk, it was just that I was not able to. Although having to relearn meant that many activities like talking would not be as good as when I first learnt, I had a second chance, to get things right that I got wrong the first time around through picking up several bad habits. In many ways I am a better person for it.

Just before I left casualty, a Camino ICP monitor was inserted; this Intracranial Pressure ventricular bolt was planned to be inserted for three days, and needed to be managed. Having survived the worst and now needing constant nursing, I was transferred to the Trauma Unit. I stayed there for nineteen days and the ventilation and sedation were continued.

'I sat on the edge of my seat during the taxi ride to the Royal London Hospital. The journey seemed for ever but was only twenty minutes in the lunchtime rush hour.

'On arrival, Jo [Fresson] talked me through your present condition explaining the many pieces of equipment I would see surrounding you and the number of tubes and wires attached to you. None of these would cause me concern. Eventually Jo took me into the Trauma Unit to see you in the bed by the window. You appeared perfectly normal - just asleep. I noticed a livid bruise on your upper right arm and an indentation extending from your right eye straight back to above your ear.

'I took your hand in mine and felt certain you would pull through - a mother's intuition?

'Jo was monitoring your every move. She stopped to offer me a bed for the night and seemed most surprised, almost worried, when I turned her down.

' "No," I said, "I'll go home, Simon is back from Loughborough today."

'I knew you were in good hands - far better than mine.

'It was three weeks later, when I saw Carrie Ross, that Jo's reaction was explained to me. Hospital accommodation for relatives was only offered if the chances of survival were on the low side. Perhaps I was better off not knowing that; any-way, the medics had not accounted for your great tenacity, determination and strength to survive.'

Rosemary Watling, my mother

By the 11 December it was decided that the ICP bolt could come out and I was allowed to wake up on my own. It was even scheduled for me to be extubated on this day. The surgeons 'would be happy for their patient to be woken up'. My waking up was slow, though, and it took a further day before I started to rouse myself from my unconscious state. Mind you, I liked my sleep and, though conscious, I was very dozy; I slept a lot.

I was still having unconscious spasms – extensor in my legs, flexor in my arms. This abnormality, where one's legs stretched out and would not bend, and (usually one) arm was held close to one's chest, refusing to straighten, was typical with extensive brain injury. Over time the biceps muscle becomes locked in this position and it grows increasingly difficult to straighten this bent arm. The longer it is left, the tighter the muscle develops until, eventually, it becomes too difficult to straighten the arm since the resultant 'stretch' on the muscle causes a tremendous amount of pain. It is only by progressing through the pain that the arm can be used properly again.

'On 11 December 1994, I was sitting soporific in front of Sun-day television when the telephone rang. After exchanging greetings, Nigel bravely uttered, "We have some very bad news. Philip has been knocked down and is on a ventilator."

'What do you say? What do you feel? "He must be all right," I thought, Philip is such a positive, enthusiastic young man.

'We talked briefly of support, faith, prayers; I cried, I panicked, I thought positive thoughts, I prayed.'

Cynthia Matthews, family friend

A day later my pupils were measured again at 4 mm each. They were reactive and I was attempting to open my eyes, though it was several days before I could see anything and a few weeks before I would remember what it was that I saw. There was flexion in my left limbs and abnormal flexion to the right side. By the second week, there were small, spontaneous movements in my left leg and left arm. Movement was possible to the right, but it brought pain. I spent the subsequent few weeks half awake and half asleep, remaining semi-conscious.

Even though I was critically injured in hospital I was not allowed to rest. I had physiotherapy every day, including weekends (the therapists' days off), overseen by Ros Wade, assisted by Jackie Newitt. It had all started one day after my arrival with an assessment, though the physiotherapists did in fact treat my chest, as I was on a ventilator. Once I had had the assessment, treatment was started immediately. It was tough in the first couple of days since I spent most of the time unconscious. Thankfully I was never in a coma, though I would spend several weeks drifting in and out of consciousness and I have only hazy half memories left from that time, though most of it cannot be remembered at all.

When I was awake, the therapists were starting to sit me over the edge of the bed – not easy when you have no head control and no sitting balance! Consequently, I was given support for my head while the physios tried to develop a normal posture. It was good that they did this. In subsequent hospitals, none of the physiotherapists could understand why my balance was so bad when walking yet it was so good when sitting.

> 'Your whole rehabilitation from day one was designed to teach you how to feel normal postures and positions and then learn to move again normally. Your left side improved quickly - the right took a lot longer.'
>
> Ros Wade, Senior Physiotherapist

Though my chest was treated by the physiotherapists, it developed several infections that prevented the scheduled extubation. Even on the 16th it was noted, 'Still chest preventing extubation.' However, this was only one day before my brother's first visit, when my conscious state was seen to improve. Although I had survived the accident, there was no way of telling how well I would recover and whether I would end up as a vegetable or not. My mother believed I would be OK, but she had no evidence to back her up; none, that is, until Simon's visit.

As he was in his last year at university, my brother Simon had not seen me since the previous summer. When we were younger, we were forever having little squabbles about silly, inconsequential matters but, as we grew and gained maturity with each passing year, we began to really get on and became very close.

My accident shook Simon and he was seen by a counsellor for a long time afterwards. It was unfortunate that he was in his last year at university, as a couple of potential job interviews taken during the holidays went slightly awry. As Simon approached the foot of the bed, Mother stood to one side and watched me for any sign of reaction. As he spoke, my left eyebrow shot up (my right still was not able to due to the muscle damage from the accident) and Mother smiled with relief. I obviously recognised this voice and knew it belonged to someone who meant a great deal to me, and was not simply one of the nurses I had heard a few times before.

The nurses and therapists also noticed my improvement, as I was beginning to open my eyes to stimulation. This was usually by the physiotherapists – or 'physioterrorists' as Harry Secombe once called them – tapping me or talking to me very loudly. However, they would regularly pinch me, prod me and tickle me as well, all in an effort to keep me awake. Something else they did when I was sitting was throw a balloon to me to see if I would catch it. I can half remember playing a game of this with Mother after Christmas. I found it difficult, though it was not until February that I noticed I was having a problem with my vision. Although I could not do much then – to be honest I was not expected to – I worked hard, my efforts aimed at getting better.

At long last, at 8.30 in the morning of 18 December I was extubated, and finally taken off the ventilator allowing me to breathe on my own. Unfortunately, I found breathing difficult. I was lazy and could not be bothered – it probably felt too much like hard work! I was re-intubated on the 20th using another ETT 9.0. There was 'no real change in neurological status', and I was 'just a little more fidgety'. Once again my pupils were measured and shown to be much more healthy, at seven to eight millimetres wide; they were equal and reactive, and my gag and cough reflexes were normal.

At 4 p.m. I was extubated again and a percutaneous tracheotomy performed to help make breathing easier and to be used as a bronchial toilet and suction to clear my chest of excess secretions. Unfortunately the tracheotomy tube inserted was too small – I produced lots of secretions. The very next day, a second tube was inserted below the previous site, leaving me with an unusual neck having two small 'trachy' scars. I think that more than any other, this time was very distressing for my parents, especially my mother, as it was her birthday. Almost as if I had had a premonition, I had already filled out a card for her and left it in my room; it was like a letter from the grave. To make matters worse I had written in the card the simple phrase, 'Be optimistic.' Why that was written no one can remember, but Mother 'knew' what it meant and reading the card made her very upset.

Throughout this tumultuous time all the physios would not leave me alone. They continued to treat my chest trying to clear it of excess secretions and were forever sitting me on the edge of the bed with support for my head. By 22 December they had me sitting on a chair supported by a lot of pillows. They even had me standing, though it took four people to support me! It was hard work, certainly, but it did me a tremendous amount of good. By the 27th I was managing to hold my head in place for thirty seconds.

There were several nurses who were on duty in the Trauma Unit when I was a patient there, most of whom I do not know and have never met though they doubtless can remember me. Some names – Steph, Fiona, Dermott – are known to me yet they mean very little. However, there were two staff nurses who do mean a lot to me, who I have met and do know. They were my nurses and I was their patient. For Sonja Downey, though, I was 'another patient'. She had worked in the Trauma Unit before and had already seen patients like me. Time changes attitudes, and a year later she would be the only nurse to come to my celebratory party. On the other hand, for Jo Fresson I was her first – the first patient she had looked after from the very beginning since becoming qualified to work in the Trauma Unit – though she had helped with other patients for some time. If what they say is true, I was special! Joking aside, my heart goes out to these nurses.

They did (and do) a wonderful job, and I could not have expected better care anywhere. In those days, I literally balanced on the line between life and death – I could have fallen either way.

When in the Trauma Unit I had a couple of epileptiform-type seizures, the appearance of which started my yearlong dependence on Phenytoin, starting on the 19th. This drug was given as a precaution against possible epilepsy. My dependence had nothing to do with the drug itself, but with the Driver and Vehicle Licensing Authority (DVLA). Quite rightly, the mere mention of the word 'epilepsy' and the DVLA takes ones driving licence away with the aim of preventing any harm being brought over someone else as a result of an epileptic having a fit while driving. My 'knowledge' that I was not epileptic was not good enough and I had to prove it before I would be allowed to drive. Although there is no cheap and precise proof for the lack of epilepsy, the DVLA have devised a system that has to suffice. Quite simply I had to last for a year on the drug before slowly coming off and then be shown not to have another episode. I applied for a replacement licence on 9 December 1995, was given it without any fuss, and have been driving ever since showing no sign of epilepsy.

These seizures and my chest infections made my progress on the Trauma Unit seem slow, especially just before Christmas, possibly mirroring my 'love' for these seasonal festivities. So slow that many times my parents were noted by the nurses as being very distressed in their extensive daily reports about me. The chest infections were so bad that at around six o'clock on Christmas Eve I was given a 'pint' of blood. 'A pint!' Tony Hancock once said. 'That's very nearly an armful!' Four hours later they filled up the other arm.

Christmas comes at the same time every year; there is no getting away from it. It is not my favourite time of year and I normally spend most of it trying to hide, attempting to ignore it, but it was going to be different in 1994. I had been invited to Mrs P's, to spend Christmas with her and the rest of the family. This was a makeshift excuse to have a party and had little to do with my family's normal interpretation of Christmas. I was really looking forward to it and to seeing Melissa away from the stables. Since it involved few family celebrations the probability was that I would have enjoyed myself as well. It was going to be my way of avoiding Christmas that year.

And avoid it I did, lying on my back, semi-conscious in hospital – but it was not quite what I had in mind. It may have been one of my least enjoyable Christmases, but on the basis I did not know Christmas had come, maybe it was a good one. Certainly my parents, who came in to see me on Christmas morning, did not enjoy it. It was surely very different when compared to the family 'celebrations' they were trying to have at home with the American relatives from Oregon.

Christmas or not, as I was in hospital my care had to be continued constantly. Poor Sonja had to stay in with me and spend Christmas Day at my bedside. Even so, it was a special day in hospital. Apparently she even opened some presents on my bed. Although I should be annoyed at this lack of professionalism I am happy for her. She tried to make this important day a little bit special. At least *she* could; I didn't even know what year it was, let alone that it was December. Besides, the heat in the hospital to keep the temperature constant was higher than a normal summer temperature – there was no way I could realise what season it was supposed to be. The police did not take Christmas off, either. Throughout my duration in the Trauma Unit, they had been calling every four hours to check on my condition and kept up this observation over the holiday period.

'Christmas Day was a memorable day. In spite of having a house full of people, our first priority was to visit Phil. The Trauma Unit was, as usual, quiet but there was an underlying feeling of it being a happy day - it was after all Christmas Day. Some of the nurses that visited the unit were dressed up in funny costumes - ballerina skirts with violets as posies pinned to their uniforms. Mince pies and chocolates were in great abundance. On duty that Christmas morning was Sonja, kind, understanding and always calm, reassuring and hopeful. Philip remained oblivious.

'By now the worst was over, Phil had had at least two crises and survived. From now on I *knew* he was to start the long road to recovery.'

Nigel Watling, my father

Though Christmas itself was fairly peaceful, it was not unknown for me to relapse on occasions. After my accident I apparently 'died' twice more during my initial recovery (would *I* remember?) Three times Death had me in his jaws, but I was pulled back – I was not going to die on these occasions. Although a lot of my recuperation can be put down to me, I owe my life to the wonderful team of doctors and nurses at the Royal London Hospital. Care in the four-bed Trauma Unit is one hundred per cent, round the clock maintenance. On her visit on 15 December, my aunt remembers:

'My initial visit to Phil in the Trauma Unit was brought on with a feeling of "I must go up and see for myself." Not wanting to phone his parents and add to the countless "intrusive" phone calls they no doubt were getting led to my arrival at the Royal London on the off chance of seeing Phil. Why did I buy those flowers? Well, they weren't allowed in and were handed to a bemused porter in the hospital. No appointment, no previous knowledge - and quite rightly the nurses sent me away - I could have been from the *Sun*! But walking down the steps, who did I see? Phil's mum, Rosie walking up them! I'm not sure whether a few tears were shed - Rosie was fairly stoical as usual. Anyway, we saw Phil - very restless - and it was so hard to carry on a conversation, although I really don't think Phil knew we were there at that stage.'

Carrie Ross, aunt,
hospital sister, Wessex Nuffield

When I was ready to leave the Trauma Unit I still had little control over my head. My left-hand side was becoming looser and movement was coming voluntarily, though the right-hand side still had increased tone and the right arm was limited by the dislocation of my shoulder. I was being stood by three or four therapists getting my legs used to taking my weight and trying to reduce the tone in my right leg. By Boxing Day I was able to open my eyes and focus on normal vocal stimuli. There was no doubt that I was getting better. My broken mind, though, was receiving images that were very muddled and confused and often bore no relation to what was going on around me. I was probably picking up impulses from the senses that I was still able to use, predominately smell and hearing. However, my interpretation of these impulses was unique and they have left me with images that I do not fully understand.

There is much of my life in the Royal London that I still do not remember and probably never will. Much of it was too traumatic and has been forgotten. The rest of it holds memories that lingered in my subconscious yet are too incomplete to put into words. These faint memories never really registered in my brain and their images are too murky for me to decipher. They may come back, flowing into my consciousness as my brain heals and I start to rationalise what happened to me and am able to cope with the situation. However, I believe that whatever part of my brain was used as storage for the events of my accident and the immediate aftermath has been destroyed in the same way as those parts of me that knew how to walk and talk: I will never remember. Whatever the outcome of any investigation into my memory, through hypnosis or any other activity, one event remains clear. When I started to come round at the Royal London, and for a short while afterwards, some memories were able to come across that void between the conscious knowledge of reality and the unconscious dreamlike state of the imagination.

Two dreams that came over with a crunch are so vivid they deserve to be remembered. The first one I remember, though, is more of a nightmare. It took place some time in the nineteenth century and involved two sailors who were best friends. They were aboard a submarine that was slowly letting in water, filling up and sinking. The only way they could survive was to wear the diving gear and have tubes pushed up their noses in order for them to breathe (a common practice, I believed, for the era of the dream). While one of them was getting ready, his friend was making excuses because he was scared. Not wanting to die, he would wear the suit as a last resort if all other avenues had been tried and exhausted. The first man tried everything possible to prevent the submarine from sinking, but failed. He was explaining this to his friend... when it ended – I probably woke up. I have no idea of the outcome, but luckily, the end can be inferred.

While in the Trauma Unit, and for a while afterwards, I had tubes put in every orifice – apart from my ears! Some of them tickled – naturally! – and I took offence at them being there. I was forever messing about with them, and even pulled out the urethralcatheter. I was told it would hurt, but I did not know to care. Anyhow, my nostrils suffered the worst; I would often tug the tube out of my nose. Once, a young nurse was putting it back in, and I guess I took offence because I bit her! In no way did I mean to do this; I didn't even know what I was doing and I am very sorry. If the meaning of the dream is to be taken literally, the diver assented to the tubes up his nose and lived, since I did. Later, I discovered that this NG (nasogastric) tube was used to help *feed* me, not help me breathe – not like me to refuse food!

My second memorable dream is a bit of a mystery, there not being enough of it to make any sense. The sense that is available is so vivid and so in keeping with the kind of person I am that it must hold a meaning somewhere, even if I have not been able to define it. The dream started off as a rough collection of snippets from a book about a bird of prey and a falconer. As the dream progressed it became clear that I was reading the book in a library at the top of an old, high, airy tower that appeared to be part of a castle. I can remember feeling safe, secure and very warm – perhaps not unlike being back in the womb. In the back of the book I recall a page to fill out, enabling the reader to order the rest of the books in the series. I was reading by candlelight, the wind was blowing quite hard, and the curtains at the holes in the walls where once were located windows were flapping, causing the flame of the candles to dance in the wind. In despair I ran molten wax off the candles down the intricate, lacy pattern of the curtains and stuck them to the wall. I would have been able to read on then, but for whatever reason the dream ended at about this point.

There were other dreams as my recovery continued and my memory became more lucid, including one where I dreamt that my shoelaces were tied around my wrists – very Morten Harket! I seemed to be trying for days to undo the knots, but could not manage it and had to ask for assistance from Mother. Later I was told that the nurses had bound my hands to prevent me pulling out any tubes. These restraints were only removed when my mother came in to see me, and only then so as not to distress *her*. Another dream involved the headquarters of the 'Tyrell Corporation' from *Blade Runner*, though the memories of exactly what happened were given up to the ether long before I could remember having the dream in the first place. Several involved me fighting fire, including one where I was asked to use a hose to dowse the flames of a Second World War fighter plane that I had just crashed. One of these dreams I know occurred just before (temporary) incontinence caused me to 'spring a leak'!

One of the last dreams I truly remember, before memories of reality swamped this imaginary world, involved my father and me. We lived in an old house, somewhere in Wales. We had no money and survived off charity and the coupons we salvaged from used magazines and from food cartons – perhaps this had something to do with my penny-pinching existence when I worked at Willow-tree? I also had many patchy dreams concerning the horses I loved, about how they were coping without me and whether I would see them again. Yet, why was I there? Why could I not see them?

In the very beginning, I was not even aware that I was in hospital. In fact, once I had realised that I was in hospital, I had been aware for quite a while, but it was not for several years later, when my time in hospital was a faint memory, that I understood what it had felt like to go to hospital for that very first time. Freewheeling my bicycle down a hill on the way to the doctors, I— The sound of the spinning chain is the last thing I remember. A local resident, who called the ambulance and placed my bike in his shed for safekeeping said I rode straight into a lamppost! I was knocked out cold, but the crucial thing is that I was conscious as I was driven to hospital. I remember a large abrasion on the palm of my right hand. I remember moving my right thumb to each finger in turn to prevent the hand seizing up. I remember a nurse called Mercy. However, what I never remembered was why I was being taken to the hospital in the first place. It is very scary.

Other than this bike ride, which I mostly remember, the several dreams I had in hospital are not complete enough for me to remember fully, and I often wonder whether they hold any relevance. The dreams and images I retain from that period could well have occurred in the Trauma Unit, but no doubt I dreamt when I had been transferred to Royal Ward as well. Consequently, it is impossible to discern where I was when my various dreams occurred, or even if there was a purpose behind them.

However, there was one hazy memory that occurred to me sometime in the first month that gave me a reason for continuing my life. I can remember seeing myself lying in a bed. I recall glancing around what appeared to be some kind of room. Though I cannot remember seeing very much it seemed that I was lying in what looked more like a corridor than a room. Was this an out-of-body experience? It did not feel like one, but then again, do *you* know what one feels like? While lying there I started a conversation with myself – an old habit when there was no one to talk to.

'Where am I?' is the standard question one asks in these situations. It is something of a cliché, and I doubt my first thoughts were any different. 'It looks like a hospital... it must be a hospital,' my thoughts continued. There was a slight pause while I considered the full implication of these thoughts. 'I must be ill then... Well, I don't want to be ill!'

I did not know why I was in hospital, but I wanted to get out sooner rather than later; it did not really matter why I was there. It never occurred to me that there might be a perfectly reasonable explanation for it. I did not even look for a reason. I was there, wasting time, skiving off work. What other reason did I need?

These early thoughts were simple. There was nothing complicated in their meaning. However, they implied far more than I initially realised. Before I knew it, I had promised myself that I would get better – I almost forced myself. In a word, I was stubborn. Depending on where they are used, negative attributes can have a positive meaning, and my stubbornness turned out to be very positive. Without this ability to fight against the world, often with no regard for my own safety, and having the will power not to listen to any of the experts who said I would never walk again, I have no doubt that I would, at the very least, be in a wheelchair without the ability to walk. My own will was strong enough to carry me through my accident and deposit me a long way above the best that my consultant could ever have hoped for. I can certainly be thanked for a lot of my recuperation. Truly, it doesn't really matter how many people help you or what they do, unless you have the will to get better, they may as well give up. My rehabilitation was very successful and a lot of it is due to sheer determination. The promise I made to myself while on that hospital bed did not allow me to give up, regardless of any pain I felt.

Having said that, the Trauma Unit did me a lot of good; it brought me back from the brink of a lifeless existence and thrust me headlong into the real world, where the possibilities are endless and I now have the ability to do anything I want. Certainly, it would seem that someone who had been through his third major car accident and only had a small scar on his elbow to show for any of them, appeared to have the ability to do almost anything! My horizons were a long way off. I could reach out and grasp hold of anything that I wished.

In later weeks, my father was to voice his concerns over my ability to get better and if I had it in me to go up against this insurmountable wall that was the severity of my accident and somehow scale it. I replied with a presumption that I do not think he will ever forget.

'Don't worry,' I retorted – words that are understood to make the calmest person panic. 'If I was going to give up,' I told him, 'I would probably be dead by now.' I said it in a very matter-of-fact way and, thinking back, it was probably very true as well.

Awakening

Slowly I improved; each day was a milestone. It was even a miracle that I was there at all. Yet, given the care of Sonja and Jo, and the expertise of Ros and Jackie, I could only improve. They were too well trained to let my life proceed in any direction other than forwards. I could not help but get better. True, I had relapses, but I was being well looked after. Once, there was even a power cut to the Trauma Unit. Obviously, a room catering for such sick people has its own standby generator; it is able to kick in if the power ever failed. This process takes an interminable number of seconds; meanwhile, all the ventilators, monitors and other electrical equipment cease to work. As soon as the power stopped alarm bells rang, nurses jumped into action, diving across beds to reach the manual pumps so that life-giving oxygen could be pumped around our bodies by hand. We had our moments.

After my tracheotomy tube had been removed on 28 December, it was thought that I had progressed to the stage where I did not need round the clock care and would be able to cope relatively easily on the main ward. Besides, this four-bed unit was intended for very severe, traumatic intensive care and I simply did not belong there any more. It was time for me to give up my bed to someone who was more deserving than I was.

My surroundings changed; it must have been a happy, pleasant change of scenery. The Trauma Unit was a dark, dreary place, full of tubes, monitors and flashing lights. It was quiet, there was little commotion… It was almost sombre. By contrast, Royal Ward was bright and airy with the hustle and bustle of nurses and therapists going about their business and had a row of large windows at each end.

The bed I was first in was brought down for me from the Trauma Unit. This 'Flexicar Clinitron' bed, like most hospital beds, had bars on the sides that could be raised to stop a patient falling out. It also had a special air mattress that could be inflated to different pressures over different areas of my body. It was designed to prevent bedsores developing without having to turn me every few minutes.

The bed (Bed 8) was positioned next to the windows, allowing me to look out if I wished. I had spent much of the previous ten years out of doors, and perhaps it was thought I might appreciate being near the environment. After all, the doctors said I was conscious. They were half right and some days I was very good and looked relatively well. Maybe I could have looked out of the windows, but I was normally asleep. Even when awake, I was not aware of my surroundings and cannot truly remember any events during that period of my life, other than the hazy images that may or may not have been real. It was a further two weeks before my memory returned to me fully and these half-images of my dreamlike state receded back to my sleep where they belonged.

The main difference between the ward and the Trauma Unit was that the ward did not have one-to-one care, and the nurses had to be shared between several patients. Having no memory of the events that had preceded my entrance to Royal Ward I did not notice this lack of 'personal' nursing and did not really care either. I was not in a state where caring was at all possible. Certainly, I did not think of my cats for several months. When I did, they were long gone. As my parents were unable to keep pets at their house, my cats were sadly given away to the Cats Protection League and found new homes. Having heard from Julie about the unmanageable siblings of my adorable kitten, I feel very sorry for his present owners! That said, it seems the speed of my recovery can probably be attributed to my love of animals, especially the horses I had looked after. My intention of getting back to Willowtree to see them was a sufficiently powerful image to help me crawl back from a disabled probability to the now able-bodied possibility.

> 'I wanted to see Phil, but how would he look? Could I cope? David and I arrived at the Royal London - there he was, by the window. He appeared as if sleeping, perhaps peacefully. I cried again. Phil looked calm, no outward marks. David remarked on how the human brain acts in a logical fashion in shutting itself down in such an emergency. We talked about everything and nothing - we kept Phil company.

'On our next visit, he seemed less peaceful; his left arm was moving in what appeared to be involuntary movements in the space around him. Although deeply unconscious he showed signs of being uncomfortable, trying to pull his catheter out of position. This was distressing for visitors but, in a way, was a relief, as it seemed perhaps a positive way forward. Slowly, the way moved forward, progressing with each day.'

Cynthia Matthews, family friend

Then came 30 December. Life in the ward had been ticking over in the usual manner for two days and I had done my best to do nothing, seemingly only able to lie there. As I was soon to prove, lying there was not all I could do; but at the time I was prone and somewhat incapable. One day a nurse was gently washing my hair, and as she was coming to the end, some other nurses called for assistance to help them turn one of the patients not on an air mattress. My nurse rushed over to help, failing to do up the bars on the side of my bed in the process.

Maybe I suddenly thought back to when I was a child when I dived off a top bunk, landing on my head, and ended up in an A&E department... That was then, though, and this was now. I had just had one head injury; a second one would not have been too clever. Yet, if I had the sense knocked out of me in the first accident, maybe another blow to the head might knock it back in? It is a theory Mother will not be swayed away from even now. Maybe that first bedroom dive over fifteen years before was exciting, and I wished to have another go. Maybe I simply fell out of bed, the lack of bars predictably unable to prevent my wriggling body from leaving the edge of the bed it was lying on. However, it happened, I nosedived onto the floor.

If all I was doing was trying to bring attention to myself, not having the 'personal' care my body had been getting before, attention it was I got. The loud noise my head made when it hit the floor – by now the sonorous, ringing thud becoming known to those who happened to listen – caused nurses from far and wide to come running, find out what was going on and offer assistance. The things people have to do to get attention! My trouble this time caused a small cut to lie engraved onto my left eyebrow, not dissimilar to the now disappeared indentation to my right eyebrow received from the bus. All that remained from this original injury was a small white scar running across my temple. This newer, small cut may have been bigger than I anticipated, requiring six stitches to put right; yet now I had the evidence to show I had been in an accident.

My horrific car accident left me with hardly any visible signs that I had ever been involved, let alone one of the principal participants. Other than the small graze on my left elbow and the almost invisible scar from the bruise on my right arm, the scars are all hidden well away out of sight. I did not even have broken bones that would have given friends the pleasure of writing on the cast. I would now have an obviously visible scar, though. So what if it could not be directly attributed to the accident? Having a plaster covering the stitches over my eye gave visitors the opportunity to pose questions – even if I was not able to answer.

Proof I now had, but with it came irritation. The stitches were fine when I could not feel them, but as I grew more aware of my surroundings and unfortunate situation, I started to be able to feel the signals given off by the remaining nerve endings that still fired. Those that fired impulses from my left eyebrow made their presence known with great enthusiasm. Every time I had nothing to occupy my thoughts, my eyebrow itched... and I scratched. It was a vicious circle that was self-defeating, yet very hard to break; my parents were forever telling me off for scratching, but how could I stop?

Although unorthodox, my methods were very successful. I had a work colleague, Karen Newlyn – a hospital veteran herself, having given blood for many years – who loves picking spots and scabs. Though these were mainly off dogs, cats or horses, there was always a hope she would attack me with similar alacrity. I was in hospital far longer than I ever thought possible and my scar healed long before I saw Karen again, but I stopped scratching.

I cannot blame anyone for my falling out of bed. It happened simply because there were fewer numbers of nurses than should be available to cope adequately with the volume of patients, an unfortunate by-product of the society in which we live. Mind you, although my 'probability of survival' would have been 94 per cent in the USA, a probability of 91.2 per cent in the UK shows that we do have the expertise, even though there is not the financial support to back this up. It could also be said that I was relying on someone else to do a very personal necessity. The trouble is I had to, and so cannot condone the actions that brought about my injury. Even so, it was useful, helping to form a determination to wash myself.

The Royal London Hospital was then undergoing refurbishment, and space was needed. I was the 'star of the ward' according to staff nurse Doug Jones, and in spite of my recent setback, it was decided that I ought to be placed at a hospital where the need for acute care was not so paramount. Northwick Park may have taken me for rehabilitation, though they were full at the time. Unfortunately my family's local hospital, the Lister, did not have access to neuro-rehabilitation. Against the hospital staff's wishes it was decided that I should remain at the Royal London initially. Anyhow, I had to show them that I could live up to Doug's expectations.

As time progressed and my body started to improve and my muscles became stronger, I soon found I was flinging myself around my bed, my good arm pulling me along in a determined crawl, much in the same way to the Terminator chasing after Sarah Connor in the film. I became so adept in my bed-bound acrobatics that I was soon threatening to throw myself off the bed again. The nurses had to do their best at being inventors and came up with a marvellous solution. I was moved from next to the windows to next to the nurses' station (Bed 11) and a couple of mattresses were spread on the floor, held together with a large sheet. The walls were lined with more mattresses. There are several people who will swear that I am crazy, but did I really need a padded cell?

As it turned out, though, this was a very good idea. I had the habit of spinning around the mattresses, trying to play in a similar fashion to a puppy chasing its tail – I was 'dangerous'. A lot of people find this hard to believe yet 'my' wonderful idea has now been borrowed by the hospital and I believe they are adding a special padded cell specifically for people like me. Some people do believe it since they had the misfortune to see me on the mattresses. My uncle, David Ross, on the only occasion he visited me in hospital, saw me there, as did my brother's future wife, Claire McDermott. I say misfortune, since I was inadvertently horrible to them all, often turning my back on them in an attempt to ignore them.

'I decided I would like to visit you while you were in the Royal London Hospital. After the initial shock of hearing about your accident, the next few weeks were a period of great worry, and family instincts came to the fore – it just seemed right that as many people as possible from friends and family should see you and talk to you. By the time I visited you were out of danger and on the ward... I came on my own, not knowing what to expect. The nurses were washing you so I waited until they were finished. You were in your "den" with mattresses on the floor and lining the walls. I remember going close to you and saying who I was, and when I said my name, "David", you gave a clear sign of recognition, turning your head towards me.

'I don't think you took in much after that, but I carried on talking to you, feeling rather self-conscious at carrying on a one-sided conversation. I just didn't know if you were hearing and understanding anything of what I said, but I just carried on talking in the hope that my prattling would provide some stimulus to you. Most of the time your eyes were closed and you seemed half asleep, but some of the time you seemed restless and moved around on the mattress, using your legs to manoeuvre yourself around sometimes with your feet on the mattress "walls" and your back sliding around on the mattress "floor". You went into one of the corners with your back to me and I thought that this was an unsociable way to treat a visitor! I came further and further onto the mattress and tried to keep close to you while I was talking.'

David Ross, uncle

At this stage my presence was beginning to be known by people other than my immediate family. At the yard where I worked they all knew something had happened, since the police had come about my car. On New Year's Eve, my second night on the mattresses, two parents of children who owned their own ponies at my yard, Brenda Aldis and Sheila Sproul, came for a visit. Although they had been a couple of times before – they, in fact, were the first people to come and visit me, other than my family – this was the first time I would have had any hope of remembering their visit... not that I did. I loved them coming and they brought a smile to my face; mind you, how can you not smile when two married, middle-aged ladies say they will try and get into bed with you! They were joking, of course, but how was I supposed to know? I kept that smile for several days on those mattresses.

Brenda and Sheila are a couple of busybodies from my yard and, although best of friends, were forever having a go at each other. For someone who was having difficulty coping with his own existence, was it a good idea to be faced with other people's problems? Was it, in fact, pleasant to see them? There is one point that has to be understood about any hospitalisation: it is good to see anyone, often whether you would have wanted to or not, and Brenda and Sheila are no exception. They do have conflicting views that not everyone agrees with, yet they also like a laugh and a joke and both have very good spirits. They have the ability to brighten up any situation and were able to give me first hand knowledge of the continuing life down at Willowtree, laced with their own particular style of humour. Some of the things they joked about with me are unprintable!

Someone that I took for private horse riding lessons, Danny Davies, came in to see me around this point, and joked that I had fallen off my horse and he was getting away. He was saying that I ought to get up and go and retrieve him before anyone else got hurt. As he was relating this story to me I was getting more and more frantic and he soon had to stop. Whenever I tried to get up, not surprisingly, I kept falling down in a heap shortly afterwards. This extensive animation could simply be put down to the fact that I was beginning to feel better. As I improved, I failed to understand why my limbs were not doing as they were told and were simply acting on their own. More truthfully, I had no idea my limbs were not doing what I told them; my spinning around in a circle was not my doing, since I was unaware that I was doing it.

Jane White, a very good friend of mine, wanted to come in and see me as soon as she heard about the accident. She was advised not to, since only my family would have been allowed in to see me in the Trauma Unit. Even though she had a steady boyfriend, and his child, she was going to come in saying that she was my girlfriend just to see me. She never did, coming in for her first visit with Danny instead.

As these early days moved into weeks, I started to reclaim my old self. I would never be the same person again, but at least I had a suitable template onto which I could build a new person, someone different onto which parts of my old self could be attached. My memory was coming more and more into its own with each passing moment and I was becoming far more aware of my surroundings. When my cousin, Lara Salter, came to see me in the first week of January, she talked to me continuously, often holding my hand, as anyone would in a similar situation. I cannot remember her speaking, but she swears that I was listening to her, following her voice with my eyes and even responding to her. Chances are I knew who it was, much in the same way that it is said a person in a coma can hear, and benefit from, music – though maybe we are not supposed to know all matters of this nature.

A photograph taken of me while she was there certainly shows my dipped eyes straining to see where this recognisable voice was coming from. If I was able to remember what I saw then the image would no doubt have been very hazy; as it was, I could only see movement to the left. No doubt due to my sight becoming worse, my sense of smell improved. I can now stand a foot away and smell a flower as skilfully as anyone else sticking their nose in the petals. There was a nurse I remember who I never saw, so she may have been a therapist or a doctor. It is a shame I never saw her since she smelt wonderful, my head followed her around the room. I have always said I am good at following my nose!

All the nurses from that span of my life remember the mattresses as well as the fun I used to have on them. In July 1995, five months after leaving the Royal London, I went back for a visit to the helipad. While being taken around the ward by the HEMS Rehabilitation Coordinator, Julie Baldry Currens, one of the nurses saw me and scratched her head. Julie went up to her to ask if she recognised me, when she suddenly squealed, 'Bed 11!' Although not able to remember my name she was able to remember the 'bed' number where the mattresses had been.

By 10 January I was out of this comfortable nest for ever and back onto a normal bed, though my position remained next to the nurses' station, a position I stayed in until I left at the end of the month. A request was made for me to have speech therapy since there was 'no vocalisation' and I was given an initial assessment by the dietician. Luckily I had started solids since I was still pulling out my NG tube. Even though this fine bore NG tube had been inserted on 26 December, I was still not used to it and I did not like it. Thankfully, NG feeding was only continued until 16 January when that unloved tube was removed for ever.

Unfortunately, I was still not tolerating fluids and I was not receiving all the nutrients that I needed. It was recommended that I be given supplementary feeding of semi-solid Fortepuddings. I even had a thick, high-energy drink – 'Ensure Plus' – that tasted like nectar from heaven. As I used to cough on liquid, all fluids were thickened, from a glass of water to gravy. A favourite topic of conversation between the nurses was which food thickener to use. They had all developed their favourite and did not like using the competitors'!

It was on this bed that I started to consciously remember events, everything passing previously existing in a foggy twilight before I knew what was happening. I became aware of my neighbours, and two of them are hard to forget. One of them refused to swallow. Many times he would take a mouthful of food and chew it, then smile. 'Have you swallowed?' he was forever being asked. He just smiled; he would not talk, thereby showing the food still in his mouth. Swallowing is a direct response of food hitting the back of the throat. Quite how he bypassed this involuntary reflex, I do not know.

My other neighbour was a gentleman of oriental extraction who did not speak much English. One word he did know, and used constantly, was *oxygen*. Every couple of minutes there was a cry for more oxygen, usually followed by the nurses politely telling him he could not have any more, as the doctor had set a limit and he had reached it. I could not understand this politeness, but could not speak to say anything. Even so, my mind kept screaming out that too much oxygen would eventually kill him. Why would they not tell him?

This period of my incarceration also marked the point where I seemed to have more visitors. Whether I had more or not I am unsure, but I certainly began to remember them coming at this point. My riding instructor, Viv Howie, came down, as well as Rosemary Regan, one of the riders from the Monday night. I even had Mrs P over with Fiona and Melissa, accompanied with my favourite snack of jelly babies. It was especially pleasing to see them, since they were probably the last people to see me before my accident.

Thinking back, the change in my confidence began at around this stage in my hospitalisation. All my visitors were very pleased to see me, amazed that I looked so well considering my accident. Their style of greeting, although unusual in Great Britain, was polite when given to someone who is in hospital. There were kisses aplenty. What is more unusual is that before my accident I used to run for cover when anyone showed me any sign of affection. It even took me until I was twenty-two before I found Alison, my first girlfriend (or if truth were known, she found me). Exchanging kisses with friends – unheard of in the British ideal – was unreal and took several months to be accommodated. It started to change my confidence, since it was unnatural for me and I had to change who I was to encompass the ability.

Karen Lawley, a wonderful singer/actress whom I used to teach to ride, was one of the few people who came regularly to all three hospitals. She also started to come in to see me at this time, as did Vicki. Occasionally coming in with Vicki was a good friend of ours, Leigh Fellerman.

'Leigh went to the Royal London Hospital before me, only to say that Philip was drifting in and out of consciousness and didn't really recognise who she was. I waited until he was able to take notice of his surroundings and, unsure of what to expect, Mum and I went to visit him. He recognised me, but I couldn't believe the difference in him. He was thin and his limbs, usually so animated, were hanging loose. His eyes were empty and his speech incredibly slow and stumbling. [Vicki first came in to see me after 18 January, the day I started to speak.] However, he was alive and the nurses were confident he would get better with time and with lots of physiotherapy.'

Vicki Blake, friend

Leigh, in fact, came in three times. Once she came in with Jane, armed with a blue, cuddly lion. They decided that the lion should be called Pest – after me! It was a joke I joined in with, though I was only half-aware. I always enjoyed seeing Leigh; I used to go down to the yard on a Saturday since she worked then, often giving Sunday a miss since she did not. She is one of the few people I can easily and happily talk to for hours about any subject, regardless of the passing minutes or the cost of the phone call. Her blonde hair, eyebrows and blonde eyelashes fascinated me. It nagged at my zoological training and made me intensely curious. What is more is that, other than finding her very pretty, I was really attracted to her personality, sense of humour and maturity, though I never had the confidence to say anything at the time.

Other visitors included Alison (though we had split up she was still a good friend) together with her best friend and co-rider, Debi. They came in on several occasions, usually armed with packets of crisps, chocolate bars, and more jelly babies. Once they even came in with several bags of chips and the contents of a local Kentucky Fried Chicken takeaway. They would come and stay for a few hours, covering all the topics that you chat about in situations of this sort. How did I find the therapy? Was the food nice? Did I have any pain? They probably even mentioned the weather!

Once though, when I could talk, they were chatting about when next we could all go out together and hack some horses through the countryside. They wanted Vicki's telephone number so they could ask her to come, and were pulling their bags apart trying to find address books, when I just blurted out the number off the top of my head as though nothing had happened that might affect my memory or my mind.

'We should have known to ask you,' they said; but surely they can be forgiven for not thinking I might remember? Yet, I could not forget; after all, Vicki had 'made' me remember it – and even now I still can, despite our misfortune.

It started to dawn on all of us that I did not have much wrong with my mental faculties, and I appeared to have come through my accident as though I had never been in it. It was obvious to anyone who knows me that I had changed, but it seemed like most of the changes had been for the better.

'If I had to sum up Philip in one word I think it would be "determined". Ever since his accident he has never stopped fighting, and this shows in how quickly he has recovered. There is still some way to go and I'm sure that the longer it takes, the more frustrating it must become. But he never seems to let it get him down.

'I haven't known Philip very long, about two years, and until his accident he was just someone who came for a drink after horse riding. I think to hear about anyone who has had a major accident is shocking, but when it happens to someone you know, even slightly, it's hard to comprehend. I don't know why but I just wanted to go and see if there was anything I could do, even if it was to sit and talk to him, which is in actual fact what I did.

'I don't think I was really prepared for what I saw. Philip was lying in a corner bed, on his side; his eyes were open quite a lot of the time but there was nothing behind them. I held his hand and talked to him but got no response. It's funny what you talk about in situations like that, nothing really, but anything is better than nothing.

'I must have stayed for an hour that first time and as I left the ward I just broke down and sobbed. I couldn't believe that one moment of haste could completely destroy a person's life like that. I really felt that he would never come out of this nearly vegetative state, that he would be like a baby for the rest of his life. How wrong can a person be?'

Karen Lawley, friend

A great deal of time was spent carrying out my own rehabilitation. I became very good at using my left hand. It started to become dominant and, if nothing else, my left side is now stronger than my right. Yet I naturally used my right hand to clean my teeth and brush my hair, the processes being habitual. There was an element of safety involved and after a shower a nurse always used to comb and blow-dry (ugh!) my hair. Wet shaving was another function best performed by someone else and was normally done for me by a nurse, either male or female. Eventually I had to shave myself – using my right hand – and with help from staff nurse Doug, I went about it. He gave me lots of encouragement and pointed out the areas I had missed. Before long I was shaving like an expert, especially after my parents had, at Doug's insistence, brought in a mirror for me. Unless I wanted a beard, shaving was an essential function, and I practised regularly, at least every other day. My father helped me one day, telling me areas that I had missed. When I thought I had finished, I looked at him and smiled a victorious smile.

'Very good,' he said. 'Only, you haven't done anything.'

On closer inspection it was found that the razor blade was blunt – I would have had more luck shaving with a piece of paper! Quite why I assumed the razor blade was changed every day, I will never know. You would have thought that I would have noticed the lack of nicks, but I was invincible so why would I have thought a razor blade would cut me anyway? Later, Dad brought in a pack of razors and I did the job properly.

Even though I was – just – able to shave on my own, I still needed help in the bath. It somehow required more dexterity and concentration – after all, I could not cut my throat with a blunt razor! However, someone with no balance could quite easily slip in a bath, bump their head and drown. Often, especially in the early days, I was pushed down to the bathroom in a wheelchair and transferred to a hoist. This was then used to lift me up into the air, swing me over the warm pool of water below and, rather like a digestive biscuit into a mug of tea, dunk me so that I could be washed. What was pleasant about my time in Royal Ward was that the patients were able to have a bath or a shower every day. It gave me lots of opportunity to practise washing myself, and kept me very clean! The practice was not wasted and there soon came the day when I would use it.

That day was one when I was told I had physiotherapy. This was fine, but I was told quite late. I had to get ready quickly, even though I was not able to move very fast; but with help from another nurse, Alan Tate, I managed. He took me down for a shower and left me to it. He sometimes made a few verbal suggestions, but would not lift a finger to help. To give him his due, he did occasionally hold the shower head for me when I used the shampoo or soap, but most of it was up to me.

I have to say that I hated him for it then, or at least would have done had I the sense to do so. On reflection, it is one of the finest things that anyone has ever done for me. It was my first bit of rehabilitation, and showed me that you never know what you can do until you try. Alan is a very good nurse and only made me do this since he had a fair idea that I could cope. In fact, I could cope with most difficulties then; I could even stand soap and shampoo in my eyes. Unfortunately, the shower head was an entirely different matter. It was 'alive'! The power as the water came out was stronger than I anticipated and, when I held it, the water did not all come in my direction. Alan was soaked. Unfortunately, the water made his uniform turn translucent and stick to his skin. I was oblivious to the events unfolding around me, my mind not being aware of anything remotely sexual until March at the earliest, and then not properly until April – but at least it cheered up the female members of staff!

The End of the Beginning

By the start of January, I had begun to walk, or at least the physiotherapists walked while I swung my left leg – the good one. This was swung very well, but it was not able to propel me very far and I had to rely on the physiotherapists to place my right leg. Being unable to feel the leg, I had no idea where it was supposed to go. Besides, after catching the full force of the car, my right leg muscles had pretty much given up anyway and could not swing the leg, had I known where to place it. Fortunately, I had plenty of practice at walking; although there were days when I used a commode, a nurse or a therapist often walked me to the toilet.

All things considered, my posture was very good, as was my balance when sitting. Ros had been making me sit correctly since my time in the Trauma Unit and by now I was relatively good. By 30 December I was even able to manage the impressive feat of sitting independently for ten seconds. Ros, with my main physiotherapist, Jane Manners, tried to improve upon this by making me change from a sitting to a standing position without falling over. In the first few weeks they had to hold me while I stood up since I was not very adept. Practice makes perfect, and I soon got the hang of it, though I often had to hold on to the chair.

I remember one occasion a few days later when Jane had me standing up; she became sidetracked, so I waited. Soon I was applauded by Ros, who said that I had completed that week's aim of standing unassisted for ten seconds. Neither Jane nor I had planned for this. Not long after that, Jane, once again, asked me to stand. She was interrupted and was asked a question by another patient. After a few moments I started to wobble and reached out to grab hold of a large mirror (positioned in front of me so that I could check my posture) to give me stability and prevent me from falling. I should have just sat down, but I had not been told I could stop standing. This act of politeness on my part meant I was simply told off for not asking! They were talking, though, and I was too well behaved to interrupt them. This mask of politeness is not expected nor wanted in hospital and it soon fell away. A couple of months later I was butting in on conversations, interrupting and generally being facetious (all done with a splash of humour, of course).

Another important part of my physiotherapy was attempting to straighten the bend in my right arm from the accident. Due to the flexion in my biceps, it was too painful to straighten. The physiotherapists tried for weeks to straighten my bent elbow, but it was not budging. They had me moving beanbags and rings with both arms, forever trying to get me to straighten my right elbow. Most fun of all was when I went into 'four-point kneeling' when they would physically push my arm to get it straight. As I had no balance, we had a hilarious time trying to get me to kneel in this position. When I first tried, two physiotherapists ended up on the floor with me – and it was not by choice!

There were certainly days like that, which were full of humour. Naturally, there were also days when I was not very happy. Being the talkative, happy-go-lucky person that I am, I spent most of my physiotherapy sessions trying to talk; yet on one occasion, I would not mouth a word, despite bullying. Occasionally I was agitated and uncooperative. One day I even refused to open my eyes! It is unlike me, but I did occasionally misbehave. At times like that I did not know what I was doing or why I was there. I doubt I even knew I was in physiotherapy.

With this lack of knowledge comes fear, not a fear about 'will I live through this trip to hospital?', but a simpler, much more basic kind of fear. You know that you partook in some dire and drastic event, but you do not have the faintest idea what it was or why it happened. To begin with you have no notion how you arrived to where you now lie, yet as time passes your memory snatches images out of your forgotten consciousness; you begin to piece together what happened and you start to rationalise what actually occurred. Some of your immediate past comes back, but much does not and you fill in these blanks with what you hear and with the knowledge about whom you are, but the image still does not, make complete sense (why was I on a bus?). You wrestle with your thoughts as you try to come to terms with what you *think* happened, but ultimately no explanation makes good enough sense and you simply have to try to forget something you cannot even remember. Unfortunately, to forget you have to remember – it is very frightening. Fortunately, having encountered people like me before, the therapists knew they needed to have patience, and allowed me to work through a lot of the problems myself. Put simply, they gave me space. I owe these nurses and therapists my life – and I don't just mean survival.

Somehow I knew that my arm should be straight so I set to work myself, though it was not until my last few days at the Royal London before I really got the hang of it. Most of my leisure hours were spent attempting to wedge my arm in the chair seat and force it straight with my leg, much in the same way the physiotherapists tried to do. It took me several weeks since the arm bends round many joints, making it very hard to keep it straight. I continued and eventually found a way that would work. I pushed it in spite of the pain and kept pushing until it had stopped hurting. I did this twice then went to sleep. The next day, my last, the physiotherapists came round to say goodbye. I showed the previous night's work to Jane and she was surprised, but my biggest triumph was when I showed Ros. 'I have just written my physiotherapy report saying you can't do that,' she said. 'Well, I'm not changing it now.' To my amazement as well as theirs, I had ironed out the kinks in my arm and I was able to straighten it.

What was it that possessed me to carry out this arduous physical torture on myself? Many of the people who have had a head injury that I know have a permanently bent arm, since it really hurts if they try to straighten it. Why did I endure the pain in order to have a 'normal' arm? What was it that the physiotherapists said that made me force my arm straight? Certainly I went about it with a demented attitude as if I had no choice, as though my life depended on it. I am not sure what it is in my make-up that made me battle against the pain, but I am very glad it is there. I would have coped with a bent arm, but it is amazing how much easier my life has been using two arms when compared to people I know who have an arm still locked in flexion unable to be straightened. Everything I did, like this, was designed to get me better. A lot of it hurt like hell, but I did not want to be ill or in hospital. I would not stop pushing myself to the limits, and beyond, until I was better. By punishing myself like this I was discharged much faster than anyone expected.

Most of the rest of my 'lessons' were in speech therapy. It's odd when you realise that to begin with I could not speak, although, being unaware that no noise was coming out when I 'spoke', I thought people were just not listening. Once the speech therapist, Jacqui Hester, had come to see me after I was referred, she gave me a short assessment noting that I was alert and cooperative, though I had a short attention span for any tasks I was told to do. I became restless and fatigued very easily. My 'receptive language' appeared functional and I responded appropriately to simple commands. As the days passed and I regained the ability to speak, my 'expressive language' was noted as functional at a single word/short phrase level, though my high-pitched voice was impaired by weak breathing.

When Jacqui first saw me, of course, I could not speak. It was annoying for me since I have always been a very talkative person. Before I uttered my first words I was already trying to talk, seemingly in an effort to make up for lost time from the days when I was not in a fit state to try and say anything. My mouth worked nineteen to the dozen in an effort to try and say as much as possible. It was hard since I would normally 'talk till the cows came home', yet I could barely grunt. For once I was silent.

Communication is an art and is one of my greatest pleasures. Consequently, this lack of communication was rapidly becoming one of my greatest fears. Through the skill of the nurses I was able to keep my sanity. Simply through years of experience, they seemed to have an understanding of whatever it was a patient wanted, and they were able to interpret my gestures. I suppose my mum had become used to me telling her precisely what I meant, and whatever empathic connections she had had with me had withered and died many years before – she was hopeless. She tried very hard to understand what I was trying to say, guessing at odd words in the hope she might hit on the right one. She even drew up a keyboard and asked me to point to the letters to spell the words. I moved my hand so slowly that it was infuriating trying to follow what I tried to spell. I would gradually move my hand over the keyboard and then back again. Trying to find a particular letter often passing over the one I wanted. My hand was also not very accurate, and this inaccuracy became more evident as each week slipped by.

Mother often used to play games of 'Noughts and Squiggles' with me in order that I could keep my mind as sharp as possible. A squiggle was about all I was able to do in the crosses department, and as for doing a circle! We could also only play with a 'fibre-tip' pen. We did try a biro, but I could not press down hard enough to usher out any ink. Considering I never usually lost at this game, learning at an early age that it is impossible, I played very badly. Mother always used to win and I could not understand why.

Unable to understand me, she often left me very infuriated, especially given the linguistic excellence of the nurses. Only that morning, 17 January, it was noted by the nurses that I was mouthing appropriate words such as 'Hello' and 'Thank you', yet to my mother they were just random lip movements. I was so cross at her not understanding my mouthed words as I repeated, over and over again, 'Make the most of the quiet,' that sound was produced. The word 'quiet' interrupted the buzz on the ward as I 'screamed' it.

Nurses came running from all sides, astonished that words had been voiced and congratulated me. They were amazed since my silence had been complete and no one was able to get a sound out of me. We were faced with the awful probability that I might stay like that. It did not really affect me, not having the mental capacity to appreciate that I should be speaking aloud or even maybe that I could. Coupled with this was the innate idea that there was a characteristic that was wrong and that I should be putting it right. After a while I suppose I realised that I should be speaking without ever consciously realising that I was not. After all, I thought I was speaking; how was I to know that no noise was being produced?

It was such a strong inherent feeling that I simply acted automatically without ever thinking about it. All the weeks when I mouthed words as though I was speaking was simply governed by instinct. I could not understand why no one could hear me, especially when the nurses acted as if they could; to my mind, my mother was behaving very stupidly and it is not surprising that I grew angry. She was overjoyed that I had spoken and told me that she did not mind the noise and wished I would keep talking.

> 'The incident that sticks out in my mind the most has to be when Philip spoke to me the first time. He was sitting up in his chair with his dinner in front of him, and I sat down and started waffling on as usual, when he leaned forward and said, in a whisper, "I can talk now".
>
> 'I nearly fell out of my chair, I was so excited. Those four words proved that he was going to be OK but also showed just how much work had to be done.
>
> 'An experience like the one that Philip had has to be life changing. It is up to the individual whether those changes are positive or negative, and Philip has done his best to see the good in what has happened. I think he will grab more of life's chances now and use his "new life" well.'
>
> Karen Lawley, friend

In further speech-therapy sessions, Jacqui tried to increase my volume. My whisper was all very well, but people had to strain their ears to hear. She spent most of the lessons making me shout. As my recuperation progressed I was increasingly told to talk quietly – basically to stop shouting! In those far-off days, Jacqui did not mind what I sounded like – all I had to do was produce sound. Thankfully, I was able to. There was no physical reason why I could not speak aloud. Maybe I was beset by a fear of talking, or rather with the fear that there might have been a physical problem preventing me from talking. Or was it that my vocal chords were not receiving information from my brain, the cells that sent the impulses no longer existing? In those simple days, noise was good and people wanted to hear it.

> 'Voice quality improving. No longer whispered but consistently voiced. Hoarse, strained quality affecting intelligibility making Philip use telegrammatic speech [i.e. speaking in reduced phrases omitting function words, to improve intelligibility].'
>
> Jacqui Hester, speech therapist,
> 19 January 1995

Thankfully I enjoy talking, and one of the first things I did was phone my grandmother to let her know that I could now speak. The telephone, located snugly on a little trolley, was wheeled over and plugged into a socket on the wall next to my bed. This, and other telephone calls, gave me plenty of practice talking. Mind you, speaking was no real problem and from a speech-therapy point of view I was cured (by as early as Christmas 1995). Voice therapy however, needed working on, since I had a long way to go to get back to normal, or at least a quality I considered normal. Unfortunately, although I could speak, the voice I used sounded weird; I could not whisper (strangely), scream or mimic different dialects as I was able to before, except the accent which had 'taken over' my vocal chords – Welsh/Italian according to Mother. It should be realised that instances of this are not uncommon. After her accident, one lady from South-east England now speaks with a distinct Scottish accent. Another lady reported on *That's Life* several years ago, left England speaking with a characteristically English accent and emigrated to Australia. Unfortunately, a while later she lost her voice. When it returned she was speaking with an Australian accent. My voice, though not quite English could be used now and I used it; even speech therapists have commented that I talk too much! Mother now realises how profound my first words were.

Talking and walking took up a lot of my time, but the therapies that involved these took up no more than two hours a day and usually far less. I had at least twenty-two hours to do what I wanted. Naturally, most of it was spent sleeping and that did me good. In the succeeding months I was sometimes up most of the night and was often moaned at for not getting enough sleep. In those early days with not much to do; I needed a lot of sleep, and I wanted it.

Yet sleep only involved part of the day. Thankfully, washing took a long time, so a good couple of hours were 'wasted' every morning cleaning my teeth, shaving and brushing my hair, not to mention the hours that would be spent having a bath. Much of the rest of the day was spent eating. Once I was on solid food it took me hours to eat. Cutting food with your left hand when you are naturally right-handed is not easy at the best of times and doing so one-handed is nigh on impossible. Often, Mum or Dad would be there to help me eat, even if only to cut the food for me.

This hospital food was very good. I am told that when my eyesight was poor and my taste buds had yet to improve fully I used to eat whatever I was given, whether I normally would have done or not. I even had onions, of which I despise the taste, and even smell, and the odd cup of tea, which I stopped drinking fifteen years previously. Perhaps more unusual was that the tea only had one teaspoonful of sugar, compared to my more normal four! I can also remember that there was a lot of food, often as much as you could eat and, just like at school, the puddings were absolutely fabulous.

It is impossible to understand quite what goes through a person's mind after being involved in an accident like mine. Throughout your life you have learnt to do things in a certain way. Suddenly, everyone else is dictating what you have to do and how you do it, as if you never did it correctly in the first place. Not being in a state to understand why you have to obey the commands, you naturally disobey them. It is a very human reaction.

When not in physiotherapy, for example, I was told to sit in the chair and read or listen to music or... or whatever. I could not see well enough to read so I mainly tried to stand up – not that this should ever have been attempted on my own without help from a physiotherapist. You can't keep a good man down, and I was forever trying to get up. It ultimately left me falling back down again, landing on the chair with a crunch, but I was not to be deterred.

Before long I got the hang of standing up by wedging my legs against the chair legs for stability, since my legs could not take my weight. I am living proof that 'having a go and seeing if it works' can really work. Until you have a go you will never know if you can do it. If it does work you continue doing it and try something a little harder. The more you push yourself to the limits, the further you will overtake them.

The nurses, whether I had not noticed or could not care, knew of the dangers of what I was doing and tried to restrict my movement by sitting me in a wheelchair and clipping a table onto the front. Their early attempts were futile and I spent many moments of pleasure unhooking the table and letting it clatter to the floor. Other people's infantile attempts at preventing me from trying were not going to stop me from having a go. Somehow I knew that I was only going to get better by doing things. Sitting there, letting the world pass me by and acting like the sick person I was supposed to be, was not going to do me any good. Only by fighting this complication and not giving in would I be able to overcome it. Because of my wants and need to (in their eyes) threaten my own existence, the nurses learnt quickly and were soon somehow able to lock the table in place. I still tried to move it, but was unable to, not being able to see well enough to find out how they had clipped in the table. After finding it easy to remove to begin with, I became increasing frustrated, as the table would not move. Hours would be spent bending, twisting and forcing it, but it would not budge. I was somewhat annoyed.

One other activity I was not allowed to do on my own was get in and out of bed. However, I was allowed to get *ready* for bed on my own. This was not very difficult – I wore pyjamas all day long! Once in bed, though, I spent a few minutes removing the pyjamas from underneath the bedcovers, though to begin with I never knew I was doing this. If I wear clothes in bed I sweat a lot and get tied up in the pyjamas; it is natural for me to sleep in the nude. It was the cause for the odd red face in the morning, I'm sure, and it took the nurses a few days to get used to it. Although I was far less confident than now, it was not me who had a red face either; hospital helps eliminate any shyness you have about your own body and can leave you with the attitude that it does not matter who sees what. There is no room for modesty when your life is on the line and your future lies in other people's hands. Besides, nurses are well trained and are used to seeing everything. No doubt they eventually reach the level where they cease to 'see' anything. Even so, I do remember one nurse who joined the staff at the hospital sometime in the last two weeks of January. When instructed to get me up, she was told she needed a new pair of pyjamas. Since my urethralcatheter had been taken out on the 18th, she probably thought I was still incontinent!

Being put to bed has its merits, but once I was not put to bed and it seemed like I had been awake for hours. I was very tired and my chair seat was quite comfortable. I slowly slid myself off the chair so that I half-lay on the floor. I nestled my head in my hands, resting them on the seat and attempted to go to sleep. Over the years I have slept in some odd places so that position was not uncomfortable. A nurse rushed over, pulled me up and put me to bed, muttering that if I was tired I should ask to go to bed – though my lack of confidence prevented it. I rapidly fell asleep.

I awoke to find food coming around and wondered what breakfast cereal I was going to get on this new day. After a few minutes I realised this was not breakfast, but supper. The few seconds of wondering how I had slept through a whole day passed quite quickly and it dawned on me that I had had a quick nap before supper. I spent several minutes in a daze, not really knowing what time, or even day, it was – nothing unusual there! By that evening I felt as though I had lived through a very long day that had never seemed to end. Time was effectively warped. This was not a unique experience, but an event that would happen in all three hospitals, although it did lessen after I borrowed a watch from Mum.

Also on the 18th, I had some VIPs come to see me at 1.30. I did not know who they were or why they were there, yet what they thought of me would determine my whole future and would have a significant bearing on how my treatment was going to continue. It was an assessment where I had to show that I could achieve a great deal.

The Regional Rehabilitation Unit (RRU) at Northwick Park Hospital in Harrow, where it was suggested I should go, had sent along the Head Speech and Language Therapist, Mary Oliver, and the nursing sister to assess me, along with a staff nurse, Mandy Spencer, and a student nurse. Demand for spaces there is high, so they came to assess me to see if I would be a suitable patient. Thinking back, it was a marvel to see them this early. I was still not able to walk without assistance and I had only begun to talk the previous morning. I seemed to be in no fit state to see anyone. However, when asked questions, I showed that my memory was surprisingly good by saying that I had been 'hit by a car', and that I was at 'Whitechapel Hospital'. According to these VIPs my speech was 'strange in form – hoarsish, but normal in content'. That did not seem to matter though; I told them that I slept 'fine'. However, I could not tell them the date, or the day. Given my somewhat eccentric understanding of time, this was not unusual. All seemed to go very well, despite my complaints that my eyes were poorly. Even so, when asked to read a name tag from 'three feet away', I seemed to have no problem, bad eyes or not. Mind you, being asked to stare at a women's breast is a pretty basic stimulus and I was obviously not too ill for that!

By the end of January, the procedure to merge the Royal London and St Bartholomew's hospitals was well under way. Throughout the month, Sophia Ward, the adjoining ward to Royal, had undergone extensive refurbishment for the merger. Royal Ward was next, and they wanted to clear out as many patients as possible. I was stable and doing fairly well, so I was one of the first to be moved, my stay at the Royal London Hospital coming to an end. Before leaving, I had five swabs taken to see if I was infected with the bacterium MRSA (Methicillin-Resistant *Staphylococcus aureus*), swabs that had previously been taken on entry to the Trauma Unit.

Throughout the centuries of medical knowledge, bacteria have been slowly mutating against our resistance to their deadly assault. One of the most recent mutations to become apparent is MRSA, a bacterium resistant to standard antibiotics. Once infected with this bacterium, patients are not able to fight against subsequent infections, since their immune system has been compromised. Due to the inevitable presence of various infections in a hospital, an outbreak of MRSA can be devastating. Consequently, separate disinfected cotton buds were gently rubbed over my eyebrow, wrist, anus, pubic hair and the back of my throat, and cultures produced. If I had been infected, I would need to be isolated to prevent inter-hospital transference. Thankfully, I was not.

On 25 January, Carrie came down once more to see how I was. She took Mum and me out for a pizza as a treat. What was astonishing was that I was let out of hospital. I had been fully conscious for less than a month and they let me out, away from their control. Heaven knows what could have happened – yet they 'knew' nothing would. Of course it helped that Carrie was a hospital sister. A wheelchair was brought, and I was wheeled out, along Whitechapel Road towards the nearest fast-food restaurant, as though it was done every day. I have to say that it was marvellous.

> 'On my last visit, I met up with your mother and you were off to Physio - how the physiotherapist at 5'1" managed to stop your lurching gait landing you on the floor, I'll never know - past the decorators into Physio where Lynford Christie would have been worn out! Anyway there were two priorities for Phil - hand/eye coordination and mobility. Phil, you were moderately happy but so determined despite the misery of pain. However, that first trip out to the pizza parlour... well, it was worth it.'

> Carrie Ross, aunt,
> hospital sister, Wessex Nuffield

Unfortunately, the pizza did not do me any good and I ended up having diarrhoea. I was ill for about two weeks, it finally leaving my system after I had transferred to the new hospital. Mind you, having been through what I had been through, I could deal with whatever life threw at me. Besides, I did not know what diarrhoea was really like; I did not realise there would be much of a problem. This confident viewpoint lasted for only the few seconds it took for the feelings of not being well to become actions.

Two nurses dealt with me, one changing the bedding, and the other giving me a bath – the best bath I had had for a long time. It was so good being scrubbed and washed, and I returned to my pristine bedding feeling cleaner than I had done for ages. As the nurses left they told me to shout if I felt ill again, but I was gone. Feeling as tired as I did I quickly fell asleep. Moments later I awoke suddenly. Unfortunately my growing confidence had not developed fully; I was too insecure to shout and the nurses were forced to reappear to repeat the whole process again. They were not very pleased – but I thought I was kind in giving them something to do! Eventually, I was put to bed and was able to pass the rest of the night quietly.

In spite of these recent events, I felt quite cheerful. So cheerful was I that on the following morning my parents organised for me to go up to see my two nurses from the Trauma Unit. It would be gratifying for them to see my progress and wonderful for me to put faces to their names and to thank them personally for their help. It may only have been a job to them, but it was my life and I was thankful. So it was that on 27 January, only five days away from my discharge, I went up to the Trauma Unit and saw Jo, Sonja being away that day. I said, 'Hello, how are you?' and other pleasantries.

'We thought that might happen to you,' she said, telling me of a South African night nurse who used to chat to me before I went to sleep. My voice had apparently gained a South African quality that she and Sonja presumed I would pick up off the nurse; though, at the time, I was still getting used to speaking again, and who cared what I sounded like – I could not recall my own voice anyway. It was excellent seeing her, and I was able to show off standing in the wheelchair. I even turned round – very difficult to do in those days without falling over! She was amazed, and glad to see that her hard work had accomplished so much.

Having not seen Sonja, I popped up the next day to see her. Just like Jo the day before, I saw her chin hitting the floor (well almost). No one could believe how fast and well I had recovered. Jo and Sonja gave me a wonderful insight into what happened when I was first there and what was done to me. When I arrived at the unit a question surfaced in my thoughts and demanded to be answered.

'How bad was I when I first got here?' I asked hesitantly, revealing the lack of confidence that was still present. I thought it a fairly reasonable detail to want to know. Hearing some of the tales about me in those first days and having looked at the photographs of me that Jo had (sensibly) suggested my parents take, I felt it only fair that I should know quite how bad I was. The answer I received was not what I expected. It was given to me as it happened, straight down the line; the blow was not softened in any way. Sonja closed her index finger over her thumb as she formed a circle. The gap was very small, her finger and thumb almost touching.

'About this far away from death,' she said, as matter of fact as you might tell a friend the weather report.

The 27th was also my last speech-therapy session before my discharge. My voice quality had improved and I showed consistent voicing, though I was still dysarthric. My speech was already showing signs that it could improve almost back to normal, but my reading was not so good. I had:

'...difficulty following lines; missing words and lines; good understanding of what is read.'

Jacqui Hester, speech therapist,
27 January 1995

My last two days in hospital drifted by and I barely remember their passing. My penultimate day was very quiet and, having nothing much to do except the little physiotherapy I did before being passed on to a different physiotherapist at a different hospital, I asked various nurses if they had a pair of scissors I could borrow. I assumed that they all should have scissors as part of their uniform, but it was very difficult to get hold of a pair. Finally I did and set about cutting my fingernails, much to the surprise of the sister, Chris Reavely. She relented, but kept a close eye on me, maybe secretly hoping that I cut my finger; at least then she could come and be a nurse, relieving her boredom on this very quiet day. My toenails, on the other hand, were a near impossible task, and I had to await the hospital chiropodist. In my time in hospital, I would see all manner of doctors who would heal me from head to toe.

On my last day, when an ambulance had been organised to come for me, I was not taken down to Physiotherapy, since they did not want to be interrupted in mid-flow. I hated the idea, since I knew the physiotherapy was doing me a lot of good; but I sat and waited, watching patients come and go, and was even able to say goodbye to the physiotherapists as they went home at the end of their day. I had to sit all day and had nothing to do – I was still not able to read. Thankfully, Mother was there as she had the intention of travelling in the ambulance with me to the Lister (for her, it was on the way home anyway), a bed still not being free at the RRU; she stayed with me all day. At least I had someone to talk to if nothing else. Unfortunately, by five in the afternoon Mother had to go home to cook my father his supper, leaving me to once more find something to do. By nine o'clock in the evening the ambulance arrived and I was able to transfer between hospitals. The ambulance was supposed to have arrived before noon!

The London ambulance trip can only be described as interesting, lying on my back, strapped in so as not to fall out, with only a small window to look through to tell me where I was. Mind you, in the dark it was hard to see outside, anyway. It was so dark I could only see when a bright light shone through the window, glaring at me.

Darkness is normally sleep inducing, but I could not sleep. My mind was clawing at the inside of my head as it tried to comprehend this most unusual experience, not that I was in any hurry to repeat it. The journey was made worse since my head was quite high, lifted up by four pillows, and I was slowly choking on my own phlegm. It was not fun, but I was too insecure to protest, constantly telling the ambulance attendant that I was fine when he was kind enough to ask. Such insecurity is a trait most of the people I knew at the RRU, both staff and patients, will find hard to understand.

This ambulance trip was between my first two hospitals and I was still less than two months into my second life. Hospital gave me a chance to radically alter my life and the opportunity to completely rebuild myself from the inside, making fundamental changes that would affect my very spirit. This rebirth took several months through my time in hospital. My only difficulty was to hold on to enough of my 'prebirth' (the person who came before my rebirth) to keep me, me.

Kish Mattu agreed with me when he was interviewed for the Channel 4 programme, 'Living with Brain Injury' on 13 March 2000: 'The person I was before was very strong and had good sense and he helped me a lot.' I, for one, am glad I'm not the person I was before, but without his strength I would not be the person I am now.

The ambulance made its way to the Lister Hospital in Stevenage, Hertfordshire, passing through a part of London I do not know very well. The window was small and my not brilliant vision was obstructed by the angle of my head on the pillows.

Despite these problems I was able to see part of the route we took, although it was dark outside. I became concerned at one point as we passed one building because I thought it had the words 'University of Kent' outlined in neon down one side. I placed my trust in the ambulance driver that we were not travelling in the opposite direction to that which we should have been taking, yet, to this day, I do not know what that building was and why it was there.

On arrival at the Lister I was taken via the A&E department along several corridors to the main building. From there I was taken up three floors and deposited in a side room off one of the wards so as not to wake my fellow patients, by now long gone to sleep, and adrift in their dreams. While the ambulance attendants sorted through their paperwork, I lay for several minutes not daring to sleep, knowing that it was not over yet. For all I knew we might be in the wrong hospital! Karen Warn, a pleasant staff nurse, did pop in to see that I was all right, and I had a chat with one of the house doctors, Josh Brombecker, so I was made to feel welcome. Yet it seemed as if I'd been left alone in a strange place without even a watch for comfort. Once the paperwork was completed and the ambulance crew had left, I was checked in, given a new ID bracelet and asked several questions. I suppose they had to make sure they had the correct patient! After quite a while I was finally left alone to settle and go to sleep. It was past eleven o'clock at night, after all.

I think it was when I woke up the following morning that it dawned on me that I was no longer at the Royal London Hospital. I was not quite sure what to think, though my initial feeling was one of hatred. Up until the day before, I thought I was going off to the RRU at Northwick Park and saw no reason why that should change. It was rather alarming to be at the Lister Hospital, seemingly a halfway house, a stepping stone on my way to something better. My relationship with the hospital started off on the wrong foot and I never really got over it. It took several weeks to get used to the Lister, by which time I was on my way to Northwick Park. I treated the Lister as I found it: a stopover, a roof over my head while I waited for a bed at the RRU. It took a month before a bed was free, yet I was glad. I was never treated by the therapists at the Lister as though they had a deadline to stick to. They were therefore very thorough and did what they thought was right at the time. They progressed as I did.

I thought I was fine when I left the Royal London. After all, I had to live up to being the 'star of the ward'. However, thinking of the line 'We can rebuild him, we have the technology...' from the start of *The Six Million Dollar Man*, it was plain that I could be vastly improved. At the Lister they added bits that were missing and 'tightened a few nuts'. I was new and improved when I left. Physiotherapy there was excellent under the watchful eye of Kate Morrisey; the occupational therapy I had with Michelle Hamilton, helped by Georgia Donovan, has been the best occupational therapy I have ever had, anywhere. I am now very glad I went to the Lister. I realise that whenever I changed hospitals I felt pretty good. With the hindsight that only experience can bring, I realise how incorrect my initial feelings were and how much further I could go.

Therapy at the Lister was second to none, and I liken their work to building a large castle for me to live in. Even though the castle was built very well, it was boring. Yet, without good foundations the castle would soon collapse. My physiotherapy at the Royal London seemed unremarkable to me; often I wondered whether it helped me at all. I went there not being able to walk and I left not being able to walk. I could sit, though and even that I could not do properly in December. Thoughts like this made me realise quite how remarkable these therapists were. Without the solid foundations they had created for me at the Royal London, no amount of therapy afterwards would have done any good. At Northwick Park, they were able to make my boring castle exciting, raising a drawbridge, portcullis and setting out all the pretty banners and flags. Each part of my rehabilitation was not quite good enough on its own. The complete picture, on the other hand, was a masterpiece.

A Moving Experience

I now know my life at the Lister Hospital was very beneficial, but back in February 1995 I could not be told that; I did not want to know. All I knew was that I had been taken away from a hospital I had grown to love, and from the people I knew, halfway through the week. The move was not even left until the weekend so that I could get used to the idea and say goodbye to everyone. I was whisked away from my beloved East London for no more important reason than the hospital wanted to do some redecorating. It was not even as though I was being taken to Northwick Park's rehabilitation unit. Though it had a very high reputation, I was sent to a regional hospital of no great relevance to the recovery from my accident save that it was near to where my parents lived.

However, the one big advantage of going to the Lister, as was revealed to me many months later, was that when I was discharged and my life as an inpatient was finally over, the therapists there already knew me, so going back as an outpatient was comparatively easy. Unfortunately, back in February I did not recognise the value of the move. It was hard to understand, having been through what I had, why I should be doing other people favours. If nothing else, Mother's daily lunchtime trip from work would quickly come to an end. Although I had the opportunity to see both my parents more or less every day, I had to wait until the evening, by which time I was often quite tired, having been awake all day.

So it was, on Wednesday, 1 February 1995, I was removed from the Royal London Hospital and obliged to undergo my 'ambulance journey through hell' towards God only knows where. Arriving at the Lister as late as I did, I could not do any therapy until Thursday. That was close to the weekend, so the therapists did not wish to start me off and then have a break for two days, so my therapy would begin the following Monday.

Having no therapy on the Wednesday as well gave me a five-day break, which, wanted so badly by most people, annoyed me more than I dare say. I had nothing to do and my physiotherapists from the Royal London had not considered that I would need any exercises.

My first days at the Lister were designed so that I could take it easy and settle in at my own pace. For the average person this would have been fine, but I wanted to get better, and I needed my therapy to do that, especially since I was not allowed to practise any therapy on my own.

Having mastered standing up when at the Royal London, the obvious next step was to try and take… the next step! Of course, the nurses were worried in case I fell over, and I was forever being told off if I tried to walk around my room. Even so, I secretly tried to do this on a regular basis. It is a shame I was not allowed to do so. Once I had been transferred to the RRU I was allowed to move around, while at the Royal London I did not want to go out and about. At the Lister I wanted to move around, yet was neither able to properly nor allowed to try; I felt confined, as though in a cage. Instead I was simply supposed to take it easy, relax for a couple or days and do what I wanted, except try and walk. Unfortunately, I still could not see well enough to read and, when not eating or sleeping, I was sitting down with nothing to do for a very long time. At least it meant that I was able to adapt, breathing in the air of excitement, since I had little idea as to how this new hospital operated. Everything from the therapists and nurses, down to how the food was given and getting ready in the morning, would be new and had to be learnt afresh.

One of the biggest changes was the disappearance of daily baths or showers and their replacement with a bowl. Although patients were allowed to have a full wash whenever they wished, providing the bathroom was free – easy for me as I had an ensuite bathroom – most of the morning's washing, whether shaving, brushing one's teeth or a bed bath, was courtesy of this bowl. This was hard to begin with: the water rarely stayed in the vessel it was brought to me in as I sloshed the liquid around, spilling it everywhere. Although I quickly got the hang of preventing the water leaving its confines, my biggest problem was with the bowl itself. It was kept on a shelf in a cupboard about six feet off the ground. There was no way I could get it down and had to ask for a nurse to help me, even though I needed 'no help'. Yet having to ask for that help was beneficial, and I managed relatively well that first morning when I had a wash, from the bowl.

Before I knew it, the weekend had arrived and was spent in hospital. This was all well and good, but I still had nothing to do. Generally, I hate Mondays and have no love for mornings. That Monday morning was going to be very good, and I had looked forward to it for several days, so much so that I cannot even remember the weekend. I could at last have the therapy I so desperately wanted and needed. The trouble was that the therapists did not know me and had no basis for determining my capabilities. (Ros's physiotherapy report had temporarily gone missing.) To ascertain these I had to be assessed. This took two days so my therapy was not really going to start until half way through this second week.

My first assessment was for physiotherapy with Kate, who saw me on the plinth and the mat, and even asked me to try a little walk – not my most comfortable activity in those early days! Once Kate had carried out her assessment of me, she asked my mother and me what my problems were, as she had not yet received my notes from the Royal London Hospital physiotherapists; neither of us could give a satisfactory answer.

'Never mind,' she said, 'I'll find out.' Then she very professionally started my physiotherapy as though she had always treated me, quickly ascertaining my problems.

Kate turned out to be a very accomplished physiotherapist, and the therapy I had from her was as good, if not better, than that received from the teams of therapists at the Royal London and Northwick Park hospitals. Her instruction was fabulous and she was a wonderful person. Yet I seem to remember having misgivings when I first met her. There was nothing wrong with her, though, and it was not her fault. It takes me a while to warm to people and she was in the unfortunate position of not being Jane, Jackie or Ros. The physiotherapists I had grown to love and respect were gone, and in their place was this changeling. Initially, in a way, I was disappointed, but this did not last.

Michelle and Georgia, who I saw next, had a slightly easier time. I had not known any occupational therapists at the Royal London, and had no one with whom to compare these new people. There were also more of them, so any antipathy I felt could be divided between them and diluted. They were also very clever in playing their trump card right at the start. Michelle had a student working with her, who I thought was quite pretty. It was clear in my mind that my 'monastic thinking' of the previous two months was coming to an end.

Another important aspect of that particular Monday was that it was my father's birthday. He was overjoyed to see me when he came to visit that evening, never thinking the day would come when I would knowingly partake in such celebrations. I was very happy as well since he and Mother brought in a few items from home, many of which were vital for keeping my boredom in check and my insanity at bay. After they left I went to sleep, having already had my supper.

Following breakfast on Tuesday I had my first session of speech therapy. My therapist, Audrey Canadas, had a student, Sue Fields, with her. If I did not mind, I could choose to be seen by someone unqualified and in turn help her with her studies. In no way was I averse to this suggestion as was to be shown throughout my hospitalisation. Sue was very helpful and asked many questions. I hope seeing me was as helpful for her as she was for me.

After speech therapy I had little to do until my brother Simon came in for a visit with Claire. It was wonderful to see them and, as he always did, Simon was continually trying to make me laugh. He did this, not entirely out of love, but essentially because it was funny – especially when I had just taken a mouthful of water, ending up spitting it all over the floor, chair or bed. Once I accidentally spat water all over him! Served him right, though I cannot wholly blame him; because of the problems I had with timing my swallow, I normally ended up coughing and spluttering water everywhere anyway. Mind you, he could have been a little more charitable.

Very little of anything constructive was done in my first seven days at the Lister, but at least my assessments were finally over.

With any luck I would start therapy properly, and life at this unloved hospital would become more exciting. Before it could though, I had an unwanted stowaway from the Royal London to contend with.

Throughout the day on Thursday, 9 February I was not feeling my best and by the evening I felt very nauseous. I lay on the edge of my bed fighting the qualms of sickness as though I could handle them. Normally I should have been able to, but the diarrhoea I was afflicted with after my evening out from the Royal London had not been entirely vanquished. There were still some of the bacteria biding their time before coming to the fore. They did not wait for long either. I half woke in the early hours of Friday morning feeling dreadful – my diarrhoea was back! I tried in vain to prevent making a mess of the sheets. Moments later the sickness hit me and, tilting my head over the edge of the bed without a care for my slippers awaiting my feet on the floor, I vomited. I did feel better. In fact, I felt so good that, after wiping my hands on the sheets in my half-asleep state, I dozed off again for the rest of the night. Thankfully for the nurse, I did remember to warn her in the morning!

When I awoke properly on Friday I was glad for the purging my stomach had undergone and was looking forward to the joys I hoped this new day might bring. To begin with, my floor, bed and I needed to have a wash. While the housekeepers dealt with the floor and changed the soiled bedding, I was lowered into the bath, where I wallowed for a few moments before washing my hair and having a good scrub. I also brushed my teeth and wet-shaved – all by myself, of course.

When I was out of the bath, (not that I should have left its confines on my own) and was dry and respectable, I rang the bell and waited patiently for the nurse to come to help me back to the chair so I could get ready for therapy. After waiting a few minutes I rang again and waited once more. This continued five times. I had 'promised' the nurses that I would always wait for help and never try walking on my own. Unfortunately, I never did like waiting and was getting fed up sitting in the bathroom until help arrived. In despair, I got up and walked. Not a very good walk, it has to be said. I started to realise how little different we are from apes and monkeys. Since my legs could not support my weight, I had to take support from stationary objects if I did not want to hit the deck rather rapidly. I practically swung from one object to the next by my arms, using windowsills, doorways, my table and my bed until I finally made it back to the chair. Once there I quickly dressed and made myself ready for therapy, just in time for my porter, Don Bissett, to collect me and wheel me down to the occupational therapy department.

I always had a good giggle in occupational therapy, since Georgia and I would constantly try to make each other laugh. That Friday was no exception as I was asked to lift hoops up over Georgia's head while she was standing on a chair. Easy until you remember that I was still in a wheelchair, something I believe I would have stayed in a lot longer had I not been constantly trying to walk. Michelle must have invented this at the last minute, because Georgia was wearing a skirt. No matter how hard I tried not to, I kept getting the hoop caught on Georgia's skirt and hitching it up. This was very funny, and she and I were in fits of giggles. The more I laughed though, the less able I was to lift the hoops cleanly up in the air and kept banging them against Georgia's head.

Giving up on this exercise, I was presented with an electronic wobbleboard – a board one stood on that wobbled to the left and the right depending on which leg was taking more weight and which way one was leaning, gleefully bleeping whenever you were slightly off balance. I was not very good. I was so bad Michelle had a go herself, only to find that this particular board was broken and I had to use the normal (non-electronic) one instead. On this board I was much better.

Therapy over with, I was taken back to ward 5B just in time for my consultant's rounds. I complained about my eyes to the consultant and was promised I would get to see the ophthal-mologist. Unfortunately, it took them several days to fix me up with an appointment, and when they finally did, a staff nurse told me they would not see me until mid-March. Although I was seen before the end of March, it was not until after I had left for the Northwich Park Hospital.

Unlike my unhealthy morning, Friday evening was fun.

Karen, who had (while driving past) already tried the Royal London, came for a visit. She was armed with good cheer, pleasant conversation, some books to try and read, and a packet of jelly babies: the knowledge about my love for this flavoured gelatine having rapidly spread from one friend to the next. It had been her birthday the day before and I had great pleasure in presenting her with a birthday card. She was taken aback, since I had managed to buy her a card even though I was in hospital, but more to the point I had remembered; after all, I did not know her well then, our friendship only evolving over the five months of my hospitalisation.

When she had left, the evening continued with lots more food. Unfortunately for me 'lots more food' is a misnomer. A menu was brought around the night before and patients marked their preferences for lunch and supper for the next day and breakfast for the day after, as well as their preference for a small, normal or large portion. At the Royal London you were given quite a lot of food, though no choice, whereas at the Lister patients were given a choice, but I had to endure 'starvation rations'. The hospital was full of older people who did not eat very much and my 'large' portion was nowhere near large enough for me.

Thankfully, they did provide bread and butter, and I had a jar of Bovril at hand brought in by my parents. Moreover, many people brought cheese in for me as well, so I was able to supplement my diet to some extent. Topped up with several packets of crisps, biscuits and sweets brought in by visitors, I was able to keep my intake of calories relatively high, as long as I ignored this unhealthy diet! It was important for me to have a high calorie intake, something that had been acknowledged at the Royal London, as I have a very high basal metabolic rate. Because of this I burn up food as heat very quickly. At least it means I stay warm and do not get fat.

Over and over again I asked for a 'proper' meal with a sufficient amount of food. On many occasions no one listened. I even had the sister, Sharon Denham, phone down to the kitchens for me. She was not listened to either. Several empty days followed her request and, at long last, something happened. I suppose Sharon's request had finally filtered to the ears of the minions below and, by Friday, 3 March, I had a visit from the dietician. After I'd been checked out and we'd had a discussion, we finally agreed on a cheese sandwich at breakfast and a baked potato at lunchtime, as extras. This was to start on the Monday. Predictably this turned out to be the Monday I left!

Heading back across the gulf that separates these thoughts from my trivial lifestyle where I had nothing to do, we travel back three weeks arriving on Friday night, 10 February, with a crunch. Finally I was to go home for the weekend, something I had not even considered initially. A few days before, though, Georgia was talking to me and spoke as though I was already going home at the weekend, so in a way it was her idea. Kate and Michelle (the other occupational therapist) both mentioned it as well, telling me I should go home. Both of my parents liked this amazing idea, as long as my doctor agreed. Further to this, I had a short chat with one of the nurses who said she would have a word with Josh, the house doctor, and see what he said.

Mother phoned the next day and he said it would be fine, but to try and limit it to a day at a time to begin with, spending the night at the hospital. At long last I could try to walk around, and possibly fall over (though I never did), without troubling the hospital staff. I could also – finally – listen to my CDs or watch videos, eat a sufficient amount of 'healthy' food and be taken out for a drive to friends' houses, the countryside or simply the local pub. By my second weekend at home, having endured the first so well, Josh relented and let me home overnight; in truth, an hour away from the routine of being in hospital was enough of a break, so it was magical to be away for the whole weekend.

Going home provided me with a break for two days a week where I could do what I wanted, but for the other five days I was reliant on visitors to come and amuse me. Having visitors is the only variety in many patients' existence and is a window to the outside world – the institutionalised version of an evening down the local! It did not matter who turned up since it was pleasant seeing anyone. Obviously it is best when people you know well turn up – people where there is no doubt you want to see them. One was my uncle, Colin White, who came for a visit on the 16th. He was bored – his wife, Laura, and daughters had gone on a skiing holiday. Having decided to come over and see his parents in Dorset, he thought he would pop in and see me as well. It was wonderful to see him and he brought me a gift, bought in the duty-free shop on the way over: a large, round, black clock with moving hands – silver hands that moved up and down, rubbing its belly!

Mum and Dad came every day, of course, and I saw quite a lot of Simon and Claire before they started back at university, usually coming armed with a McDonalds' burger and fries. Cynthia was also wonderful, coming in about once a week and bringing blue cheese and jelly [though obviously not together!]. Other than Karen, who was marvellous throughout my five months incarceration, I had few of my friends come to visit, as I was forty miles away from them by this stage. Debi and Alison also from Willowtree, did intend coming, but the car broke down at the last minute.

'A few days before Christmas 1994, my husband told me that Philip "was not very well" – another of these typically English understatements. Having asked why he was "not very well", I learned he had been hit by a car. Another silence, and then Colin, very quietly, added that Philip was unconscious in hospital! Now it was my turn to remain silent.

'After the initial shock, my first reaction was to call Rosemary... Her control over herself was amazing, as usual, and quite unlike me, a Russian, she retained her calm and composure throughout the conversation...'

Laura White, aunt

An Occupational Hazard

After my fairly tedious first ten days at the Lister, the second complete week dawned with a much more promising feeling. I was beginning to get used to the hospital routine and had finally recovered from my original apathy towards the move. On the Tuesday of my second full week, thirteen days after my move (i.e. on the 14th), my habits changed radically and I woke up early. It was very unusual for me, and I had no reason to wake up early and had every excuse to remain asleep for most of the day. It was seven in the morning and I was not used to the idea of early mornings. By the time I reached Northwick Park it had become a habit to wake early, but in the beginning it was very peculiar.

While I lay there not really wanting to move and, in doing so, admit to myself that I was awake, Staff Nurse Heather Brent came round and asked me if I wanted to sit up. Although she only meant in the bed, a process I could have achieved myself had I wanted, I thought she meant for me to sit in the chair, so I helped myself up and, with her 'unnecessary' help, sat in the chair. Once there, I washed, and dressed for breakfast.

This turned out to be important, since I ate slowly and physiotherapy was relatively early. Moreover, Don, the porter, was always very prompt and usually had to wait for five minutes while I finished off getting ready. Once, a couple of weeks later a nurse had just run a bath for me when Don turned up a good quarter of an hour early. My luxurious bath was reduced to one of just over five minutes, with a promise that I could have a proper bath on the next day. I was so rushed I even combed my hair while Don took me down in the wheelchair! Although physiotherapy was very good on this second Tuesday, I cannot remember what we did, even though Kate was surprised at how well I carried out the exercises.

Praise such as this always cheered me up, and I was flung into a very good mood that I carried with me straight through lunch. It

An Occupational Hazard

then continued into the afternoon when Don wheeled me down to occupational therapy. This was always a good laugh and I soon started to really enjoy it and to care for the therapists, although at the start of my recovery, when physiotherapy reigned supreme, I never understood the purpose behind this strange activity. It took a further six weeks before I began to discover the real purpose behind occupational therapy.

A few days later, it was Michelle who braved standing in the hoop on a chair, maybe thinking Georgia went through enough the first time. If only she knew how virtuous my thoughts had been! Even so, being sensible, she wore a pair of trousers, but I still found it funny. Mind you, it did not help with Georgia also being there telling me not to laugh. There is nothing more likely to make me laugh than being told not to – my imagination takes over and I start thinking of things that are funny. By the end I was in fits of giggles and I was not able to keep my hands still. Whenever I laughed, my hands shuddered, making the hoop bang against Michelle's head. This, unfortunately, made me laugh even more. It was about this time, amid my apologies for giggling during physiotherapy, that Kate impressed upon me the philosophy that it was better to laugh than cry. I fully agree and have cherished that thought ever since.

Once my giggles had subsided and my therapy was over, Georgia wheeled me back to my room, since she was on her way up to the ward anyway. She arrived a trifle early for her next appointment so she and I ended up having a chat. Since she was interested, I showed her the photograph album that Mother had been collating about the aftermath of my accident. We became so heavily engrossed in our conversation that we did not notice time passing (not unusual for me), and Michelle had to come and prise Georgia away so that she could go about her business.

All occupational therapy was like this and was always very pleasant. My sense of humour was similar to Georgia's and we used to always set each other off laughing. When we weren't laughing, several items were used in order to advance my abilities of manipulating my fingers, increase the strength in my forearms and hands, and check the functions of my brain and my ability to remember. A lot of the rest of occupational therapy involves functional activities (washing and dressing, cooking etc.), therapy which Northwick Park prizes itself in doing. However, I had been washing and dressing ever since Alan 'threw' me into the shower at the Royal London and I had a great deal of practice at the other tasks on my weekends at home. Thankfully, most occupational therapy at the Lister came in the form of remedial studies, where we played physical games and took physical tests. It was the type of help I needed a great deal, and was something which North-wick Park would, it turned out, be unable to offer me.

At the memory tests I was very good, remembering everything that Michelle asked me, whether it was photographs of people's faces or pictures of objects, repeating a route she had walked, retelling a story she had read, or asking a question at a designated time. At the start of one of these tests she showed me a picture of someone as well as letting me know her name, telling me she would ask at the end of the session. I remembered her name ten minutes later at the end of the test. By contrast with the few physical problems I had, my memory was very good.

Other treatment included screwing bottles onto their lids, which were fixed onto a piece of wood, and carrying objects with my feet. This strange practice involved using tins containing different weights. By hooking your foot under a webbing loop attached to the lid and trying very hard to balance, it was possible to 'pick' them up and move them. Games of 'Noughts and Crosses' could also be played with your feet using large wooden 'counters', also with a loop across the top. I played 'Solitaire' with my feet where I grasped the wooden pins between my toes to move them. Sometimes I would pull a tyre towards me by twisting a rod with a rope attached to it, the other end being tied to the tyre. I also had to bend down, pick objects up a foot or so away from me on one side and transfer them to the other while balancing on a wobbleboard.

Putty was used continuously, as it was useful in its ability to be rolled out, though its solidity provided some resistance. Clothes pegs were also often used, since they had to be pinched to open them. They were designed so that different strengths had to be employed when pinching them. Throughout it all, several tools were used to measure my strength for gripping and pinching, as well as 'pegboard' tests for measuring the fine control of my fingers and my speed and accuracy. Although my speed was not that bad, I was not very accurate (less on the right-hand side). However, it was not until ten months later that I realised there was little feeling in my right hand, and what there was confused my mind and sent me warped and misleading information.

Occupational therapy at the Lister was heavily dependant on physiotherapeutic factors. Although fun, it was not always easy and it took a long while to perceive the changes, but they were coming – just like British Rail trains! It was abstract and general and the kind of care that I needed. The specifics for personal care, often needed by so many people, were far below my abilities. As Alan, the nurse at the Royal London had shown me, I could do anything I wanted if I only put my mind to it.

At the Lister, this confidence and ambition was tempered with the knowledge that was provided through the work that the therapists carried out. They strived for excellence and whatever they did was carried out to a high standard and with an enormous amount of care. In many respects it was annoying, I did not need a lot of the care. If I was sitting on a plinth, for example, and the therapist had to leave for a moment, she would not go until someone was sitting with me. If I had to be left alone she was forever looking back to make sure I was OK. I knew very well that I could sit (Ros taught me well) and I did not like it thought that I wasn't able.

On one occasion, however, the actions of the occupational therapists may well have been validated. A pillow had been placed on the floor in front of a table with a device on it consisting of a box of clothes pegs and a vertical metal rod. There were four strengths of clothes peg of differing colours and I had to clip them onto the rod in the same order until I ran out of pegs. This was to be done at a stretch while kneeling on the pillow, both left and right-handed, using all four fingers (with the thumb), with weights on my wrists so as not to make it too easy. As I was preparing to kneel on the pillow the therapists were asked a question by someone else. Being the impetuous fool that I am, I refused to hang around and wait for them and descended on to the pillow myself. The move was slightly faster than anticipated towards the end, causing much consternation among Georgia and Michelle, who were convinced I was going to headbutt the table – mind you, my head was moving fast in that direction! That's where impatience gets you – but how was I supposed to know they were going to help me?

As they were unhappy about the bend at my right elbow, which was still slightly present, the occupational therapists also regularly splinted my arm to help straighten it. I was told it would make it easier, straightening my arm as I moved objects, but I cannot remember if it did or not – all I can remember about the splint was that it hurt. However, I had learnt that pain often did more good than was realised and I started to welcome it. There is nothing worse than knowing part of your body exists and not being able to feel it. Many people's inability to put up with a small amount of pain in the short term often leads to them having far longer-term problems, usually accompanied with a great deal of pain. Through a certain ability to suffer pain, I was able to straighten my arm when in the Royal London, so that I can now use it properly, even if it is still not quite perfect. I smiled at the pain, telling myself that it must be doing me good.

Naturally, all of these exercises, be they as 'mundane' as screwing a bottle onto its lid or as treacherous as nearly losing my balance on the pillow, were treated with a humorous disposition – Georgia and I normally had a good giggle at everything. In a certain way Georgia's attitude in constantly seeing life in a funny way may have been considered unsuitable. Yet life was normally funny and she probably only saw events as humorous because I did. Had I seen everything with a serious attitude, no doubt Georgia would have been somewhat less light-hearted. Perhaps Michelle could have been considered as not being forceful enough, in letting us 'mess around' rather than just doing the therapy. In fact, they both took the correct attitude realising that seeing life light-heartedly allowed patients to recover far more quickly than if they took life too seriously. Humour involves the release of endorphins from the brain, much in the same way as sex or chocolate, the latter being something I no longer really like... but thankfully, I find life constantly funny!

As the weeks at occupational therapy went by, everything had become much better. My speed and accuracy were improving, as I was able to place the pegs into the pegboard in their appropriate holes much faster than when I was first transferred. All my grips had increased to not far short of twice as good as the initial tests at the start of the month. This pleased me, since to begin with Michelle and Georgia were both much stronger than I was, in spite of the fact that men are naturally stronger than women. When I was ready to move hospitals again, I was happy to see that I was on the way to being stronger than them. In fact, because of the accident, despite being right-handed, my left side had become far stronger. I had started to improve and still am; my body was healing and my intelligence was fast returning back to normal. Unheard of confidence was evolving from the remnants of my past life; I even started to make some friends.

On 13 February I met Liz Salisbury, who introduced me to her daughter, Lisa Stringer, another patient who had been involved in a car crash; hers was so bad she was cut out of her car. Lisa and I got on very well and, for both of us, it was marvellous to have the other there as a friend. She had also been to North-wick Park, where I hoped to go, so was able to tell me all about it. Lisa was a demon at the game 'Connect 4' and our respective occupational therapists used to bet on who would win when we played each other. Lisa was made to stand (in a frame) to get her legs used to her weight, and I had weights on my wrists to make my arms work. I will use the excuse that I was too busy thinking about the weights on my wrists: Lisa won, often by more than five games to one. She was very, very good, always thinking ahead for the next several moves, in the same way that you should when playing chess. I played each move as I came across it and therefore could not help but dig the grave that eventually buried me and my game. However, in the countless games I played with Lisa in the succeeding weeks there were a few I did win – but usually only when she let me!

Like occupational therapy, physiotherapy at the Lister had also been a delight. Once I had overcome the initial dislike of Kate Morrisey as she took over from the therapists at the Royal London, I very quickly began to enjoy the treatment she gave me. I remember one of the sessions we had, in the side room off the gym, when a neighbour, Ann Birkenhead, popped in to see me. Ann was a trained physiotherapist and worked very near the Lister, so it was somehow natural for her to come in, something she did on several occasions for the rest of the month. After my discharge, still three months distant, she was to prove very helpful, giving me lifts to various appointments once I was an outpatient.

> 'The look of gentle, wry amusement which greeted my rather precipitate arrival in the Lister Hospital gymnasium was rather typical of Philip, as our developing relationship was later to reveal. Flanked on the left by his physiotherapist, Philip was being put through his daily paces in balance, control and gait. Clad only in shorts, he was not in the slightest bit put out by the appearance of this total stranger and only too ready to demonstrate his progress in my presence and that of his mother, Rosemary.'
>
> Ann Birkenhead, neighbour

Just like in occupational therapy, which involved doing the same procedure over and over again, physiotherapy was continued until I instinctively knew how to do various actions. Many of these actions we take for granted, but they had sadly become lost to my brain and I simply did not know how to do them. Obviously there were some physical problems as well; the dislocation of my right shoulder restricted its movement and my leg muscles had wasted so badly that my legs were no longer able to support my weight fully, though they improved rapidly. Mostly, though, I had simply 'forgotten'. Like the area concerned with talking, the area of my brain that had initially learnt how to walk when I was a child now lay as a charred, empty wasteland of dead neurones and I was 'forced' to relearn. My balance, for much the same reason, had also been thrown into turmoil, and the only way to teach me was to repeat an exercise until I finally realised its purpose.

One day Kate wrapped her arms around my chest and, being so thin and weighing as little as I did in those days, she tilted me back against her, and swung me around one way then the other as though I were a rag doll. In a way, this was good physiotherapy for her as well – she was several inches shorter than me! The idea was that it would give me the same sensation as falling over. It should have been instinctive for me to stick out my leading leg to prevent me from falling. Sadly, I lifted my leg, bending my knee, and would have ended up in an unfortunate predicament lying on the floor had Kate not been holding on. She repeated this for several days until I instinctively knew what to do, and now there have been several occasions when I have fallen rapidly to one side, but prevented myself from sustaining any injury by sticking my leg out first.

Kate's other idea of fun, designed to help me obtain a real sensation of balance, was to sit me on a large ball and rapidly move it left, right, forwards and backwards; the aim was simply to make me fall off. As I improved, I would be able to keep my upright position, no matter how erratic the movement of the ball. Once, after I had coped with Kate's antics very well, she happily revealed that she had been very cruel, really trying to get me off, though obviously not very hard.

Another major aspect of physiotherapy was simply making me stand up from a sitting position and sit down again. This 'simple' exercise is much harder than you might imagine, made more so by being attempted 'one-legged'. My other leg was injured so badly it could not support my weight, at all and it was similar to trying to stand up resting one foot on a balloon, a feat they made me do many months later whist I was an outpatient. Sitting down, on the other hand, though much easier, was far more violent. Sinking down to the last six inches was fairly simple, but it was somewhat rushed over the last few inches and I usually landed with an undignified thump on the chair or whatever I was alighting onto. One other problem I had was with perception, and I always thought someone had moved the chair, since I was unaware of its location, adding to the precariousness of sitting.

Kate spent a little of every week making me stand up and sit down properly in an attempt to teach my mind the correct actions so that I would perceive them instinctively and would not have too much of a problem performing these actions. On and on she instructed me, slowly and controlled, standing up and sitting down, until it was natural. It did not take long before I was getting up from a chair without holding on to anything. Sitting down properly took longer, but eventually I was able to do that as well.

However, it took a great deal of confidence to 'know' that what I was going to sit on was still there and it would not move! After several days practice, I was finally able to stand up and sit down all by myself without relying on holding on to the chair. Getting from the chair to the bed, though, was a skill in itself and often I alighted face first like a child, my legs following after I had landed in a crumpled heap.

Though I soon learnt not to land on my face, it was not until I went to Northwick Park that I was taught how to go to bed properly. Mind you, it was a wonder I could go to bed at all – and so what if I ended up on my head first; at least it would not hurt! Kate would not rest, however; once I had started to get the hang of moving properly, she continued until I could move straight, helping me lose the 'banana shape' that I was developing. Ultimately, that could all have been blamed on the problems I had with my vision, but that was an enigma all its own.

Standing up, sitting down and sorting out my balance were all very useful, but Kate had a bigger plan, a greater ideal for my recuperation. She firmly believed that I would be able to walk unaided and, quite correctly, knew that she had the abilities to help me aspire to this goal. A lot of her time was spent teaching me to walk. It started simply where I walked between two plinths with my hands on them so as to walk in a straight line. When doing this Kate was mainly concerned that I placed my feet in the correct place and learnt how to step accurately. As I progressed she told me to place my hands on her shoulders and we moved away from the plinth. It was then that she realised I was pressing down very hard and using the tension in my arms to keep my balance. Making life very difficult, though trying to improve my walking, she positioned me back between the two plinths and made me rest my hands on two large balls, the idea being that if I pressed down on these they would spin away and I might fall over. In other words, by not pressing down I would not fall.

As these simple steps became better, I was trusted to go out into the gym and walk around 'normally'. Not on my own: Heaven forbid that I would be allowed to behave so perilously! Kate would stand behind me with her hands on my hips so that she had some control, could feel my movement, and could see how my pelvis moved as I walked. Sometimes she would do this on her own, though she normally had help from a selection of physiotherapy assistants. It was useful having all these helpers around both from a physiotherapy point of view and also for my confidence. As the weeks progressed various incidents happened that helped chip away at the bricks of the cell imprisoning my confidence. So much so that I even welcomed the presence of an A level student who had come in to see me (a patient – anyone would have done) and ask a few questions, since she was interested in studying physiotherapy at college. I was very happy to be of assistance.

When Kate had me walking, it was usual to have two assistants helping standing either side of me, each one placing one hand on my chest and the other holding on to my hand. By this arrangement they were able to keep me upright and support my weight, allowing me to swing my legs. Being pinioned by the therapy helpers, I could obtain the stability I needed without having to rely on the furniture and 'swinging' from one piece to the next. While I was being assisted, I was told not to think about walking, when I did it became much worse: walking should be natural and 'mindless' – it is instinctive and, for the most part, reactionary. When I stopped thinking about it, my walking improved tremendously. The more I emptied my mind and did not think about the action of walking, the easier it became; as soon as I thought about it, I started to stumble.

After a while we progressed to trying to walk faster, and Kate, who had been very pleased with my walking, suddenly figured that I might as well have a go on my own. She told her assistant to 'drop me' a second, to which she reluctantly assented. Kate continued to walk with me, however, with her hands on my pelvis – not for support, but to feel the movement. We walked two lengths of the gym – not bad for my first proper walk in ten weeks! It was wonderful to be able to walk again; there was no stopping me now.

A few days later, a different assistant and I took a little walk, which was not at all bad; Kate was so impressed with my improvement that she told me to have a go on my own, with no assistance what so ever. I was suddenly free from all constraints that had been imposed upon me and my walking became easier and more natural (even if it was technically not as good, being jerky and mechanical). As the weeks wore on, I became stronger and stronger and was soon walking longer distances, getting faster every day. Consequently, I was told to practise walking carefully at home. Unfortunately, walking at home had significant problems that taunted me and tried to block my progress and advancement: stairs.

When you first think of them they do not appear that difficult, but they are. They are on a 'hill' for a start; there is a greater chance to trip up the stairs – very common for me – or slide down them, now an unavoidable danger. It was further to fall as well. I did not like them – my first adventure on them at home necessitated my ascending them on my backside one by one, and heaven knows how I came down! Kate soon had me on the stairs in the gym, and after the first ascent was so impressed that she was satisfied I had the ability to climb the stairs at home, providing there was someone there to watch me. Annoyingly, this would make me feel somehow smaller than I was, as if I didn't know what I was doing. I understood the safety, but it was still demeaning.

I had several tries at the stairs during my last few days at the Lister and it was during one of these that Kate, seeing how much I had improved, mentioned that it was a shame that we did not have a video of me from before the treatment. For that matter, it was a shame that no one had taken a video of me right from the start to show how much I had improved over the several months of my hospitalisation. Hindsight, being the wonderfully enlightening entity that it is, stuck its ugly nose in to sneer at us, as it rose up in the air to emphasise its indignation: Ros had told me that she wanted to video me at the Royal London. My instinctive discomfort soon changed to acceptance and I was quite looking forward to the experience. She was going to start filming in the following week, but that was the week I found I was being transferred to the Lister. No sooner had Kate thought to video me than I was told that Northwick Park had at last freed a bed and I was to be moved once again.

At last I was to be taken to the RRU and I was to leave this unloved hospital. Finally I was to be receiving the care that I needed and would get all of the therapy, all of the time. Meanwhile, I had still not been immortalised on video, something I believe should be done as a matter of course. For me it was soon to change. I would have misgivings, however, leaving a hospital that I did not like and going to Northwick Park, in that I was also saying goodbye to the nurses and therapists with whom I had become quite friendly.

Going up and down stairs marked one of the last main objectives that Kate had in mind. To the unrefined extent that I had achieved this, she had finished, though the final polishing still needed to be attained. I was not as good as I was to become, but was very good nonetheless. Kate had converted the uncouth individual with whom she had been presented into a cultured person, though she never had the time to convert my unrefined state into the 'gem' I was to transform into.

There was no way Kate could have known that I was to be transferred after the first month and she had never treated my therapy as though there was a time limit for my duration at the Lister. She carried out her treatment of me to the best of her ability, adapting and evolving as I did. In the few days we had, unknowingly, left to us we managed several other, finer feats. She had me walking backwards and sidestepping, using a pole as support, as well as endless work on the ball, the stairs and some more normal walking. She was forever concentrating on my neck, with the memorable words, 'Chin in!' as it jutted forward, not unlike a caricature of Bruce Forsyth. One of our best-remembered sessions involved a game of football. It was a simple version where the ball was rolled to me and I kicked it back, both left and right-footed. It was not designed to turn me into Pelé, but it would increase my reactions by having to move to the ball, kick it back and recover. I was not very good; the physiotherapy assistants were kept very fit, as they ran all over the gym chasing after the ball wherever I kicked it, but that did not matter, I was exercising my legs and beginning to use them properly.

In one of my last sessions, I did everything that was asked of me and it all seemed OK. Unfortunately, Kate was not very impressed; she insisted that I was tired. I denied this saying that I felt fine and it seemed like I could keep going all day. She was adamant, stating that my muscles were tired, whether I thought I was tired or not. I just wish if a muscle felt tired it would inform my brain! She said that people are fine at the beginning of the week, yet they tend to tail off towards the end, so it was nothing unusual. She told me not to bother about the exercises she had been giving me and to concentrate primarily on having a good rest and getting some sleep during the coming weekend.

HELICOPTER EMERGENCY MEDICAL SERVICE

HEMS Dr: _Hem_   Paramed: _GAARSH_   Amb C/S: _N 401_

Incident date: Incident time:

Location: _CATFORD_   HEMS arrival: _1_

Patient name _PHILLIP WATKINS_ (M)/F   Age: _27_

Mechanism (Blunt)   Penetrating   Burn   Inhalation

Description _RAN OUT IN FRONT / CAR_
MINOR DAMAGE TO CAR

RTA   Vehicle _P/BIKE_ vs _CAR_   Speed _25_   Seatbelt Y/N
Driver   Front pass   Rear pass   (Pedestrian)
Entrapment   Ejection   Cab intrusion   Assoc fatality

Clinical Injuries   _HEAD INJURY_
(R) HUMERAL #

Interventions (Oxygen)   (collar)   OETT   NETT
Surg airway   (IVI x 2)   Cen/fem IV x   Cutdown x   Chest drain x
Splint x   to   RED   MAST   DC shock x

Fluids Hartmans _1000_ ml   Gelofusin _____ ml

Drugs   _ETOM 18   ANAT 150_
SUX 100
PANC 8

Time	Pulse	BP	RR	E/4	V/5	M/6	GCS	Satn%	Temp
08·35	85	120/80	20	1	1	4	6	90	
08·55	92	137/80	25	—	—	—	—	100	

Reason for triage decision: Signed:
QUICKEST NEURO

What the doctor did, when he did it and who am I anyway?
8.55 a.m., 9 December 1994

TRAUMA PATIENT INJURY LIST

Name: Philip Watkins

Number:

Date of birth

Admitting general surgeon ___CROSS___
Admission date _9/12/94_ Time _9.0⁼_
Helicopter patien: (YES)/NO
Cause of Injury _Knocked down by_

Anatomical Region	injury	Consultant
1. HEAD	For CT scan	Chowdhary
2. FACE	contus by (L) eye	
3. NECK	C-spine - NAD on plane films	Chowdhary
4. THORAX	NAD .	
5. ABDOMEN/ PELVIC CONTENTS	USS - NAD, DPL postponed until CT scan	CROSS .
6. SPINE	NAD ,	
7. UPPER LIMBS	# contus on (R) upper arm .	
8. LOWER LIMBS/ BONY PELVIS	contus (L) knee .	
9. EXTERNAL	(L) contus over lat aspect (R) upper arm	
COMPLICATIONS .	(L) contus (L) knee . + effusion (R) knee .	
	(R) contus by (L) eye .	

Where it hurt
9.03 a.m., 9 December 1994

Name of Patient...... LIMATU, unknown / Philip WATKINS
(BLOCK CAPITALS)

CROSS / HEMS.

DATE		
9/12/94. 0907	TRAUMA CALL (HEMS)	21C
	RTA: Pedestrian struck by car	
	TOI: ~ 08¹⁵ ?	
	MOI: ? Ran in front of car (25 mph).	
	AT SCENE: GCS 6/15 (E1 V1 M4)	
	Head injury + ? # ® humerus	
	Pupils 6 + eyes deviated to ⊖.	
	P120 BP 85 RR 20	
	⟶ intubated & ventilated (etomidate IV, pa	
	1° SURVEY	propofol
	A: intubated & ventilated.	
	B: no chest deformity	
	equal movements	
	AE good ® = ⓛ	
	C: cardiovascular stable	
	P 80 BP 140/80.	
	well-perfused.	
	D: pupils = ® 4 ⓛ 3, not reactive.	
	sedated.	
	2° SURVEY	
	HEAD: 2cm laceration superolateral to ® eyebrow.	
	no blood from nose/ears/mouth.	
	C-SPINE: in rigid cervical collar	
	CHEST ⎫	
	ABDO ⎬ NAD	
	PELVIS ⎭	
	UL : large abrasion over upper lateral ® humerus.	no clinical indica...
	LL : minor abrasion over ® patella	whether it was ...
	?? small effusion of knee	
	LOGROLL. NAD.	
	PR · ® tone ® prostate position.	

A general survey
9.07 a.m., 9 December 1994

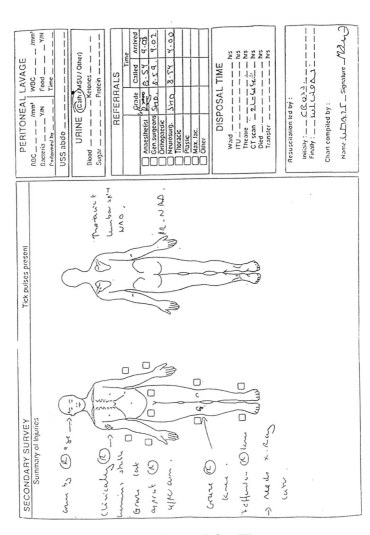

Summary of injuries before CT scan
9.44 p.m., 9 December 1994

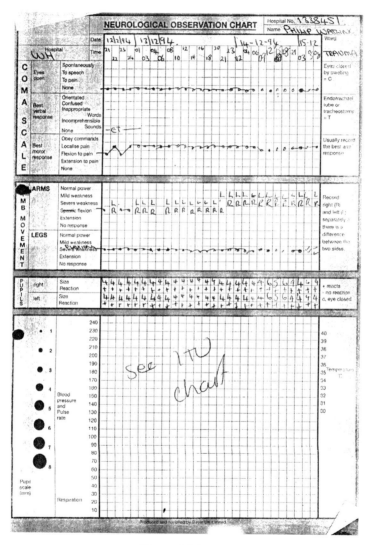

Trauma Unit notes
12–15 December 1994

DIARY:

<table>
<tr><td colspan="7">PHYSICAL ASSESSMENT OF CONDITION / NEEDS</td><td colspan="7">GOALS AND PLANNED CARE</td></tr>
<tr><td colspan="7">Respiratory   1   ①   2   3   4   5</td><td colspan="7"> ①   2   3   4   5</td></tr>
</table>

Respiratory
Tracheostomy size 10 crap via the
ventilator at 15 cms. Tracheostomy
continues to irritate the trachea
causing violent coughing. Sputum
mucoid small amount.

- Tracheostomy dressing
- Ventilator observations
- Humidification
- Suctioning as required
- Regular ABG's
- Tracheostomy emergency equipment

Cardiovascular   1   2   3   4   ⑤
Monitored in SR Normotensive
Peripheral pulses palpable Afebrile
IV ABS continue

- Hourly rhythm and rate
- Palpate peripheral pulses
- Hourly temperature
- IV AB's

Pain / Sedation   1   2   3   4   ⑤
Nil pain relief given

- Assess levels of pain and if
  required review analgesia state

Neurological   1   2   ③   4   5
PERRL Spontaneously moving
left limbs and flexing right limbs

- Neurological obs hourly
- Contact neuro team of any
  changes immediately

Gastrointestinal
tube insitu alimalyte at 100/130 mls/hr
2 hour periods. Bowel sounds
able. Bowel motions loose and
great. BSL's 58 mmol this morn

- Check NG position
- Alimalyte infusion hourly
- Regular BSL readings
- Auscultate bowel sounds
- 2 hrly H2O rest.

Renal   1   2   ②   3   4   5
C insitu. Urine output adequate
and Na+ stable. Bowels opened small,
ear amounts twice today

- Urine output hourly
- K+ and Na+ levels
- monitor and document
  bowel motions
- Auscultate bowel sounds

Mobility / Wound care   ①   2   3   4   5
Full nursing care. Regular eye and
uth care. To sit out with the aid
a physio. Turned regularly. Tracheostomy
using daily. Inspect regularly
as insitu.

- Full nursing care as per protocol
- Regular eye and mouth care
- Turn regularly
- To sit insitu
- Tracheostomy dressing
- Inspect all wounds

Psychological and / or others   1   2   ③   3   4   5
Family visit and aware of condition

- Support, educate and
  reassure family and
  others as required

Rehabilitation
Police aware progress

- Liase with Police as required

Excerpt from Trauma Unit notes
Christmas Day, 1994

Excerpt from Trauma Unit notes
Christmas Day, 1994

DATE	
26-12-94	Gen. Surg.
	Stable
	Apyrexial
	CXR to check position of new Tracheostomy tube.
	Check FBC/U&E.
	Continue ...olyte
	HOCKEY
	SHO 1789.
	Resp WD
2/12/94	LwR N/S
	Deep corneal (L) side
	opacities eye growing
10.30am	fell out of bed.
	No LOC.
	cut to (L) eyebrow
	O/E P.E.R.L.
	no other scalp wounds.
	Still deep corneal (L) side
	laceration
	not down to bone
	sutured c 3.0 nylon suture
	for R.O.S. 5/7.
	S Chatterton
	SHO
	1122
31-12-94	Nsulk
0am	GCS 804 BNR 5 BNR 2
	Otherwise stable
1-1-95	Nsy
11am	TPZ/IW stopped yesterday
	one temp spike line
	now apyrexial
	c/w Rx

I fell out of bed
30 December 1994

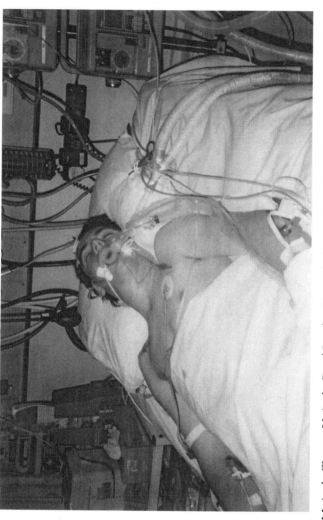

Me in the Trauma Unit, the Royal London Hospital, showing the camino ICP monitor above my right eye.
December, 1994

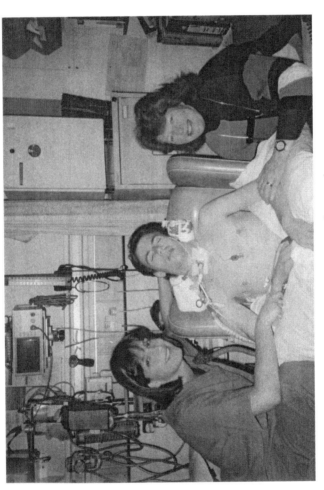

Sonja Downey, me and my mother
Christmas day, 1994

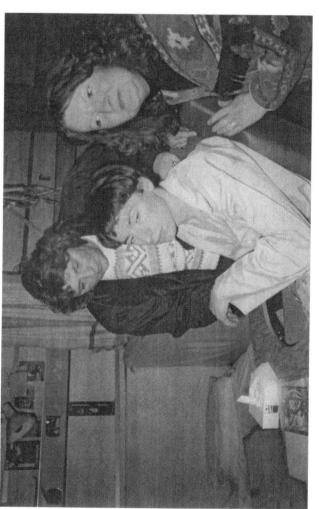

Friends Brenda Aldis and Sheila Sproul visit me in my 'padded cell'
New Year's Eve, 1994

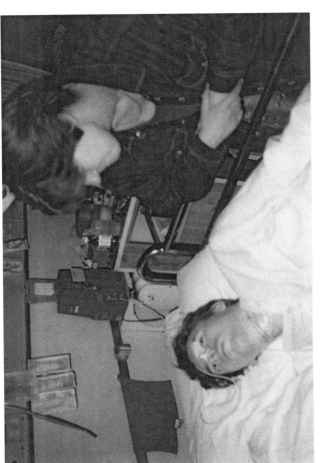

I see my cousin, Lara Salter
January 1995

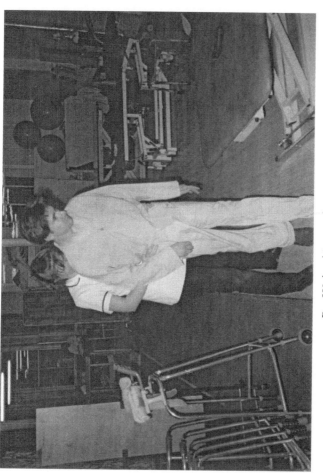

Ros Wade taking me for a walk
January 1995

My parents and I visit Jo Fresson before my hospital move
27 January 1995

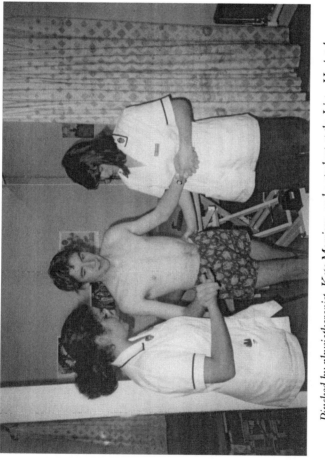

Pinched by physiotherapist, Kate Morrisey, and a student at the Lister Hosiptal
Febuary 1995

Pelé beats physiotherapist, Kate
Febuary 1995

My grandparents, Marie and Gordon White, visit me at the Lister Hospital
2 March 1995

Paul Rudd, me and Alastair Wilson on the Royal London Hospital helipad
25 July 1995

Taking the cows for a walk near my parents' house
August 1995

Georgia Donovan instructs me on how not to fall off a wobble board. Outpatients at the Lister Hospital October 1995

Sonja Downey, Dave Gurney BSc. and Captain Ian Field at my celebration
9 December 1995

Jumping Ernie at the Bradbourne Riding and Driving Centre
July 1996

Chapels of a Previous Life

Therapy at the Lister was very pleasant: I enjoyed it all. I had finally reached the point where rest was not enough and I wanted to do something. The longer I was out of my room and doing therapy the happier I was. In a way, though, it was unfortunate that I wanted therapy so badly. For very obvious and reasonable grounds the nurses did not wish to have me trying to walk around the ward in case I fell over and acquired an additional injury, putting my recuperation on a back burner until this new problem was cleared up. The nurses meant well, and what they said made sense, but it did not stop me trying; besides, nothing did happen and I doubt anything would have done, given that I was blessed with these bones that do not appear to break. Consequently, I was forever trying to walk around places. It was harder in my room, since it was small. I needed the large space that was in the gym to walk 'properly' in those early days. Besides, in the gym Kate or somebody else was there to help me if need be, even if only to tell me what not to do. Yet she was not going to be there for ever shouting, 'Chin!' I had to adapt to walking on my own. I was always trying, but had to time it when the nurses were not watching. There is no doubt they knew I was trying to walk, but I was clever in not getting caught. There was an advantage to having a side room where no one else could interfere with my progress!

After all, I knew that walking was something I had to get used to at some point, and trying there and then was as good a time as any. My legs were not very strong and I had become reliant on the strength in my arms to provide me with balance. On this basis I devised a way around the room to the toilet and back, using the fixtures in the room, swinging from one to the next, hoping that my legs would eventually become strong enough. Once, though, I was coming back from the bathroom, 'illegally', when I walked into the wall next to the doorway. Cursing, I sidestepped, using

Kate's technique, and went through the doorway – a small space, something still too difficult for me to negotiate safely.

Appreciating my need to get better as quickly as possible, Kate was very helpful in providing me with exercises to do on the bed twice a day. In fact I kept them up long after I left the Lister since I knew they were doing me good.

One therapy I never really understood was speech therapy. There is no doubt that I needed it or that it did me some good, but I never gained a firm idea of what it was I was supposed to be doing. Having physiotherapy exercises I understood, but I never saw the value or the consequences of any voice exercises. I simply did not know what to do and nobody told me why I needed to do them. I sounded funny, that was apparent, but nobody was sure precisely why. Apparently, my accident may have damaged the vocal chords, causing the strange accent and the 'breathlessness'. Audrey was not trained in voices, though, so referred me to a colleague who listened to me, but was not sure either. She said that I would be sent down to the Ear, Nose and Throat (ENT) clinic for a proper examination of my larynx. This I was told towards the end of February, Audrey not knowing that I would be disappearing at the beginning of March.

Unfortunately, doing therapy was far from being a constant activity and took up only about three hours a day at the most. Most of my experiences at the Lister came from within the four walls of my room. Although not detrimental to my rehabilitation, it did require a different viewpoint as I tried to extract any use I could obtain from it. One experience that was very unusual for me came courtesy of the chaplain; he and others were praying for me all around the world:

> 'In my local hair salon where I had been known for many years, one of the girls, Moira, pushed me hard saying, "What's the matter with you? You're never this quiet."
>
> 'She is a staunch Catholic. On hearing the problem, she said, "Prayers daily from the whole church will be offered up… Keep us informed of his progress… What is his name?… Where is he?… What happened?… We will pray… We will let other churches know…"
>
> 'A very dear friend who believes deeply in spiritual healing, on hearing of Phil's situation, took a similar line – "Where? How? What?" etc.

'Who knows how you came through it, Phil? Who cares? It worked, something worked.'

Carrie Ross, aunt,
hospital sister, Wessex Nuffield.

Thank you everyone who prayed for me: though I did not, you believed it would help, and that might even have made a difference.

All this religious intercession from other people, yet I do not believe in God. I have no faith to aim in that direction and was very content with my own abilities at getting better. I have always viewed life with a happy and untroubled air and have no need for any religious intervention or a compassionate ear to listen to any of my problems – I simply do not have any. I did not need, nor in any way want, the chaplain or any service he could offer, and yet he came. Whether he heard a voice crying out for help (!) or something else I am not sure, but he was forever coming to see me. I may be wrong, but there is a plausible explanation for his visits: there were many people who do need him and whom he had to see. From experience I have noticed that some of these people are fervent moaners and are continuously complaining. By not complaining or moaning and always having a smile on my face, viewing each day with an open mind and a sunny disposition, maybe I made it important for the chaplain to see *me*. Perhaps he needed to see me in the same way that others needed him to see them... or am I just being big headed?

Just like these encounters with the chaplain, I learned to treat every aspect of my hospitalisation as therapy, and I changed a great deal. I have always been charged with self-confidence, something that no doubt played a large part in my very fast recovery. Unfortunately, around other people, especially strangers, I lacked confidence and had been shy most of my life. I had a great deal to learn and, strangely, hospital turned out to be a great teacher. But to go up, you have to first go down. I had to understand the disadvantage that a lack of confidence could cause before I would be in a position to do anything about it.

My first lesson in this respect was food – I simply did not get enough. The more food I asked for, the less merciful the kitchen staff seemed to get. I was living off my own food when I should have been getting it from the hospital. That is what I paid my taxes for, after all.

On 1 February the housekeepers brought some scrumptious food – roast lamb, one of my favourites, with all the trimmings. I had just settled down to eat this when Ann popped in to see me. Although I had only met Ann a few days before, I, (almost literally) welcomed her with open arms. I was so busy chatting to her that I failed to notice one of the housekeepers creep past to take away my half-finished tray. As was normal for me I had 'saved the best bit till last' and had eaten all the vegetables and some of the potatoes. As the tray had disappeared, so had the roast lamb. This annoyed me, all the more so considering they never gave me enough food to begin with. Three months previously I would have stayed silent and put it down to experience. Now I was livid, though, and submitted a polite complaint, mentioning that I was a growing lad! Someone, somewhere must have listened since I was (accidentally?) furnished with two suppers, which made up for my loss.

Sometimes it does work if you complain, although never complain too much. You have to be polite or people will not be generous in return. I learnt that complaining once in a while does no harm. In fact, it occasionally does some good. In spite of this unfortunate incident, I am not one to complain and at least there was a choice of food. Most of it tasted fine as well, though they did have a tendency to overcook the vegetables – probably to soften them so they could be eaten by old people with false teeth. It just made me more insistent upon going home so I could have some home cooking.

I could have coped with the small amount of food if I had to, but it was marvellous seeing the dietician on Friday, 3 March and being granted extra food. It was just unfortunate he left it until three days before I was transferred. The person who moved into my bed that first night after I left was probably on a diet and did not want my extra food! While I missed out on my extra food, I began to learn to stick up for myself. I think in the long term I won.

'This was an animated, smiling and confident Philip I saw before me – in total contrast to the inert form captured on the photographs while he was still in the Trauma Unit. As he shared them with me, the one constant which struck me was his sheer determination and sense of self-responsibility for his recovery. OK, he received the best possible care, but this can only bear fruit if the recipient of that care does his bit. And Philip did more than his bit; never looking backwards, always to the front, with an eye on his next small gain in balance, gait, fluency of speech. I would see him practising his exercises out in the paddock adjoining the houses where we live. He showed dogged patience and determination to recover physically, but in tandem with this came the mental stamina and robustness of heart and spirit to handle disappointment over loss of livelihood and independence. The humility, grace and good humour with which he pursued his ultimate goal and the reliance on the goodwill of friends and neighbours to ferry him to various appointments reflected a strength of character so rare in a young person.'

Ann Birkenhead, neighbour

It was also while at the Lister that I started my early morning regime. As it is natural for me, I was forever going to bed late. It was normally well after midnight when the lights in my eyes shut down for the night (morning!), but I was not naturally able to wake. This was no problem in hospital as the nurses willingly came round to rouse us from our slumber. What is unusual is that I woke up immediately, and did not seem tired, either. This was remarkable, since these late nights, coupled with early mornings, prevented me from getting much sleep. Even more remarkably it started to become a habit of mine to wake up early, often over an hour before I was 'woken up' by the nurses. Initially, this was very frustrating, as it did not matter how awake I was I was not ready any earlier since I was not allowed to get up without a 'chaperon' – a ridiculous idea, but not going anywhere would have stopped me falling over! Though I believed I would have been all right, the nurses were adamant about me not getting up without someone there. It may seem like an important notion, but less than a month later (at the RRU) I was told to do everything on my own. Perhaps their insurance policy allowed patients to do more?

I learnt very quickly that I had to do something so, not being allowed to get up, I fished my clothes out from my bedside cupboard and was half dressed when a nurse came around to wake me. Surviving on the five or six hours' sleep a night that my body seemed to allow me obviously caused a few problems. Once, I fell asleep in the chair, feeling very tired. Usually my level of tiredness was very low, but occasionally I 'crashed-out', for no apparent reason. When I woke up I thought it was about 6.30 in the morning. Nobody had woken me – not even for supper (!) – or to put me to bed. Quickly I undressed, and hopped into bed (even though I was not supposed to on my own I was quite capable) for the five minutes that passed before the nurses found me and woke me for supper. Heather suddenly asked, 'Are you going to get up, you lazy devil, and have some tea?'

Naturally, I got up and was dressed and in my chair when I realised that indeed it was 6.30 – in the *evening* – and was now supper time. Memories of falling asleep on my chair at the Royal London came flooding back.

I also had to get used to boredom. I couldn't go anywhere and had little to do. To begin with my eyes were so bad I found it very difficult to read. It took Josh a fortnight before he agreed that the seizures I had had while unconscious were not bad enough to stop me watching television in hospital. Of course, I could watch television at home, and by this stage I had watched plenty during my weekends away from hospital, to no ill effect. It was all right for me to have an epileptic fit at home with no one to care for me, but I was not allowed to have one in hospital surrounded by doctors and nurses! Because of this I was not allowed a television until they considered there was very little chance of my having a fit.

My time was my own and I could do whatever I wanted, providing I did not move from the bed or chair and try to wander around the room. In effect this did not leave much for me to do, and I spent most of the time thinking – the simple pleasure of tossing ideas around my mind, happily realising that I was unable to find any holes or crevices where these ideas could become lost or stuck. I discovered – though I half-knew already – that there was not much wrong with my mind or memory, or at least no more than I knew was already wrong with my mind! I also played patience with a deck of cards, listened to my personal stereo and stared out of the window wondering what could be happening in the other rooms I could see. Once, Becky Teacher brought some plasticine along and told me to build something. I decided to build a model of the HEMS helicopter, but it was accidentally squashed that evening when my room was cleaned.

Simon was very kind one day when he brought in some physiotherapy tools which athletes used to strengthen their hands and fingers. One, a tightly wound metal spring that could be gripped and squeezed, belonged to him and I borrowed it, the other he bought specially for me after my accident. This one was a jellied substance in the shape of a face. You could build up the strength in your fingers by squeezing it, twisting it, and... well, doing anything you like to it really: when left for a few seconds, it miraculously returned to its initial shape. Simple things – for simple minds! – all designed to keep me occupied and my boredom was diluted to a certain extent. Even so, there was still little to do; hence one reason why I enjoyed therapy so much: like going home, it gave me the opportunity to remove myself from within the enclosure of my four walls.

During my third week at the Lister, I was returning back to my room from occupational therapy when I noticed the bed was littered with *Horse and Hound* magazines and various packets of sweets, including packets of the by now infamous jelly babies. As Don, the porter, helped me out of the wheelchair (I occasionally did what the nurses told me), I was informed by a nurse that some people had been up to see me, but had now gone. I don't remember if I knew whether someone was expected or whether I had sensed something with my psychic powers, but in desperation I scoured the room and noticed some movement through the crack into the bathroom, since the door had not been fully shut.

It was therefore not a total surprise, but it was fantastic to see so many people from my yard. Mr and Mrs M, Jan and my colleague Jane came up to see me. It was especially pleasant seeing Jane since, although she had come in to see me several times at the Royal London, I did not really remember her visits and I did not recall seeing her since November the year before. It was lovely hearing the gossip down at the yard as well as the low-down on what had been happening with Shannon and the other horses, the dogs, cat and various other animals. They remarked that they thought I was doing much better than they had anticipated, and Jane said that I was much improved. I had an enjoyable chat with them, though it was mainly Jan and Mrs M – I hardly said a word to Jane. Thankfully, she came up to see me again (later, when I had transferred to Northwick Park) and we were able to have a proper talk.

> 'We can remember that day very well. It all started very quiet, and then there was a commotion; we did not know what had happened. Then the helicopter came and landed close by. We realised someone had been hurt, but we did not know who it was.
>
> 'Later, we heard about the accident on the local news and found out how badly you had been hurt.
>
> 'The helicopter is a marvel; you hear of an accident where you are sure nothing can be done, then the helicopter comes and you can survive. It's amazing.'
>
> Rosa and Arthur Massey, ex-employers

Shortly after the Masseys' visit, Mother tried to organise a trip for me to visit the stables where I had worked. I loved the idea and became very excited. We had a word with a staff nurse, who gave no indication that she was going to prevent my trip. In fact, she also thought it was a wonderful idea saying that it would give me a radical change of scenery. Upon receiving Josh's consent on Friday night, I went home with an air of expectation: Saturday, 25 February could not come soon enough.

Although I went to sleep relatively late on the Friday night, I awoke early on Saturday morning and was ready long before my mother had anticipated. I was washed and dressed some time before she got up so I watched *The New Adventures of Superman* on television. All of my efforts were towards a very good cause. After 2½ months I was at last going back to the riding stables that I loved so much. Having thought of everyone at the stables a great deal when I was in hospital, and finding the images of my own horses bobbing in and out of my mind, willing me to survive and to go and see them, I considered it my duty to go back there. In my mind it held an importance for my recuperation. Even so, thinking of them was not going to get me there, and I had to wait for Mother to rouse herself from her slumber before she and Simon were able to take me for a visit. It seemed to take her for ever, but finally she was ready and we made our way down to South-east London.

Mum did not know the route, but I, strangely, was able to remember it and give her directions. As was constantly being proved, there was not much wrong with my memory, apart from those five or six weeks surrounding my accident. We were doing very well and were early. Unfortunately we arrived through Upton Park at the same time as the football ground gates began to open in preparation for a match involving West Ham United Football Club. There were several hundred fans, and many of them, like us, were driving west along the A13, causing a traffic jam that took about twenty minutes to ease. Thankfully, we were not held up for very long, and were soon on our way heading for the A102 (M), the Blackwall Tunnel and the A20. Later, after negotiating the chaotic road network south of the Thames – getting Mother totally lost – we were at last on very familiar roads heading towards Willowtree.

As we drifted up to the main gate of the yard, I had my first surprise. Mr and Mrs M had tied a banner to the gate with the message 'Welcome Philip' inscribed on it. There were balloons there as well to mark this joyous occasion. At the end of the day I took some of these balloons back with me to the Lister. They hung in my room for several days, where they gradually dried up and shrivelled. Inevitably, they all started to burst, causing nurses to come running from far and wide to find out what was happening. It was funny.

My second surprise came as I was wheeled in through the gate by my brother. Since Jane was a very good friend of mine, she would have known how I was feeling and, after saying hello, she rushed off. She was gone for a few minutes before she returned with my horse, Shannon. He must have been having too rich a feed in my absence and was recovering from laminitis. His feet hurt, and he could not understand why he was being dragged out of his warm, comfortable box and compelled to walk over the cold, unyeilding concrete. It all changed when he saw me and something remarkable, yet beautiful, happened.

Suddenly a whinny broke the silence as I reminisced, revelling in nostalgia, so I looked up to see what it was. There was Shannon with his ears pricked forward and his eyes wide with happiness as he strained at the lead rope, trying to come and see me; there was no doubt he had missed me. It is an image that I will treasure for the rest of my life. Obviously I had also missed him, and I'd brought two packets of Polos and several parsnips (his favourite treat) to give him. As he approached I noticed he had a red, first prize rosette attached to his bridle – a presentation to me for surviving my horrific accident. Even though I had brought his favourite treats he was extremely pleased to see me and kept nuzzling and nibbling me. We were really fussing over each other for several minutes. Then he smelt the parsnips and kept trying to pinch them off me. Being polite, I gave him some, and he happily sucked them until he realised that his teeth hurt too much as well and he was not able to bite into them, continually spitting them out in despair. Not wanting to be refused at this early stage in the relationship, I cut the parsnips into small pieces to make them easier to eat. Thankfully, he devoured them. Then, 'good girl' that she is, Jane disappeared again.

After returning Shannon to his box, she went off to get Captain and Chelsea, my two mischievous miniature Shetland Ponies. They were also pleased to see me, but in contrast to the devotion shown to me by Shannon, they were more interested in the food. I was happy to give them some and they, at least, were able to bite into them – once they stopped trying to bite my fingers, that is! Like all the horses, they were after any food they could find, and were always trying to dig through intrepid visitors' pockets and play with their hands to see if they were hiding anything edible.

Most people, naturally, pull their fingers away from a horse's mouth in case they get bitten. I have been around horses for many years and instinctively trust them. I firmly believe that they trust me and would not wish me any harm. Whether it is a lack of fear around them or a careless feeling towards any danger I might be in, I am always stroking their muzzles and risking getting bitten.

If they wanted to nibble my fingers they could; I would have moved them fast enough if they tried to bite, since I tended to know when they were going to nip before they sank their teeth into my frigid flesh.

There were lots of people down the stables that Saturday, including regulars like Brenda and Sheila, and many of the weekend staff whom I knew, including, of course, Leigh. Debi was there, as she had found out I was visiting and came down to see me. There were some others whom I had not expected to see. Mrs P was down there with Melissa, and I approached her with a question. I simply wanted to know why they had come down, since they were not normally there on a Saturday, favouring a Sunday. Mrs P's reply was one that warmed my heart and I shall never forget it. She told me, very matter-of-factly, 'We heard you would be coming for a visit, so of course we are down.'

It was a simple reply, yet I could see that it was coming from the heart. For me, too, it was wonderful seeing them as myself, rather than the animated cadaver I had been when they last saw me at the Royal London. It was also pleasant seeing all the other people who had come down that day just because I was there. It was fun seeing all the girls again, including some I had never met. There were also two horses I had not seen before, and it was pleasant making their acquaintance. Shannon very kindly, through me, offered these new horses some of his Polos, so they, and a few other select horses and ponies, partook in some of the treats that I had brought down specifically for him. It would have been greedy for him to eat all of them without offering some around, so I was happy to comply with his benevolent wishes! Being the thoughtful person I am, I even went up to every horse and gave him or her a Polo personally.

This is awfully difficult to do from a wheelchair, and the ground around the yard was very muddy, making Simon use all his muscle power to push it around – especially when laden with me. Whether I should or not (probably not at this early stage given the attitude of the physiotherapists later on at Northwick Park) I stood up and walked. Of course, Simon was there just in case I lost my balance, and to lessen the panic state that slowly rose and bubbled in Mother. Mind you, it was certainly easier walking around, even though I technically was not supposed to be able to walk. The yard had not been designed with wheelchairs in mind and, even without the mud, it would have been hard to negotiate the unevenness of the ground and the various other obstacles, whether they were brushes, forks or brooms, wheelbarrows or their drivers. In short, the yard was not big enough to cope with a wheelchair. Whatever one's views on the matter, it was definitely easier feeding the horses from their head height rather than my hip height.

It was amazing to be back, but I knew I would not survive the day there without some lunch and I was, very willingly, dragged into the caravan to have some refreshments. My employers generously provided lunch and I happily ate. Julie could not be down that day, robbing me of the opportunity of having a philosophical discussion with her, but she had very kindly baked me a carrot cake and sent it down to me with her apologies and best wishes. It was wonderful realising how much I was loved, whether by people who came to see me, many of whom I had not expected, or in Julie's case when she sent me the cake... or, indeed, by the horses themselves. All in all it was a very enjoyable day, and put me on a high that lasted for several days.

On the Sunday morning, though I had little sleep on the Saturday night due to all the thrills during the day, Simon and Mother came to the Lister early to give me a bath. Though I could manage on my own, the nurses insisted on me having help getting in and out. Having become used to pretty young female nurses giving me a bath, it was somewhat alarming having the burly and hairy form of my brother lathering the soap. For the most part I kept snatching the soap and shampoo away from him and washing myself, continually trying to picture a pretty, young lady.

While they were there I asked Mother if she could cut my hair. It had been over three months since I had last cut it and it was getting a bit straggly. This she happily did, and I was for once presentable for any visitors who might drop in. This was fortunate, since some family friends came in to see me. It was lovely to see Sarah and Alison Hume and, as always, we had a jolly good giggle. They very kindly took me down to the coffee shop, fighting over who would have the privilege of pushing me in the wheelchair, and treated me to a glass of orange juice and a doughnut. When I was still in the Royal London I found I had to drink using my left hand, my right having so much ataxia that the glass was shaken so much on its passage to my mouth, sloshing the liquid around and spilling it everywhere. By my move to the Lister, the ataxia was getting much better in my right hand, and I tried to drink the glass of orange juice using it.

Later, Becky, who was driven in by her stepfather, Jim Webb, met up with us just after we had arrived at the coffee shop; it is a miracle we met up at all. We all sat down and had a chat for a few minutes before Jim disappeared for a moment and bought us all a bar of chocolate. After he returned, we chatted some more before Sarah and Alison went on their way. My guests were depleted by half but I did not mind; it pleased me a great deal seeing Becky, as I had become used to seeing her at least once a month and it had become very comforting and familiar. She was (and is) a very good friend and I enjoyed her company. We had been through a lot over the years and knew each other very well. Unfortunately, I had not seen Becky since our last meeting that fateful Halloween so many months earlier.

At last, I was able to have a proper chat with her, though it was a ridiculous way of maintaining a friendship. Surely a simpler route would have been to have called her in November and meet up somewhere? 'If I knew then what I know now…' and other thoughts make their presence known at times like this, as people think about different ways they should have treated their lives. Yet we cannot live our lives thinking of the ifs and buts, and regretting what actually did come to pass. If so, we would never progress and would spend our lives living in yesteryear. Such antics lead to stories of mad uncles and dirty old men: tales to frighten small children.

When the Humes had left, Becky took over as my wheelchair driver, showing off the skills that she had learnt when she had done a bit of nursing a few years before. I quickly showed them what I knew of the hospital before I was pushed back up to my floor (five) via floor four. Now, it sounds stupid, but none of us could remember which floor was mine! We soon realised our mistake and I was on my way. My visitors stayed for at least two hours and it was a very pleasurable way to finish off my weekend.

During my penultimate weekend at the Lister, and before I considered myself ready to say goodbye to everyone, Mother took me shopping and we bought three boxes of chocolates – one for each group of carers. I presented the first to the occupational therapists, thanking them for all their wonderful help. They were all very pleased and assured me that the chocolates would not last very long, remarking, 'Are you trying to get us all fat?' I ended up with having a joke with them. I was in a really happy mood, but why not – life is short!

After overhearing a conversation Kate had had with someone the day before, I gave her her box of chocolates and joked with her, 'You know that diet you're not on... that's good, because here you are!' I had only just started speaking when she said she was on a diet, although she had denied this to her friend the day before.

'Women are always on diets!' she insisted, though she took the chocolates readily enough, promising to share them with her colleagues. The third box of chocolates had been bought for all the nurses, and I presented them to a very grateful nurse.

As a new month began and my time at the Lister was drawing to a close, I found I had settled in very well and, once again, though in a different hospital, I did not really want to go. My opinion about the Lister had been turned on its head and I had begun to like it there. Of course, I wanted to go to Northwick Park and I knew that I would get better much faster there. Even so, I could not help but feel a little sad about having to move again.

Before I was able to go, though, I had to be checked for the presence of MRSA. Northwick Park staff are very diligent with trying to keep themselves uncontaminated with this deadly bacterium. As a consequence new patients often have to go into isolation after transferral to show that they are not carriers once the incubation period has passed. Throughout the duration nurses and therapists have to dress up in gowns, boots and hats so as to prevent skin-to-skin transferral. Once out of the isolated room and stripped of their potentially infected outer garments –

to be taken away for incineration – several minutes would be spent scrubbing their hands with strong disinfectant. The swabs taken at the Lister, just like those from the Royal London, came back negative; I was never placed in isolation.

Thursday, 2 March marked the end of the snow-free days that we had been graced with since the winter the year before. It started falling and would not stop, never wishing to bid us farewell; my maternal grandparents, Gordon and Marie White, who had come up from Dorset to see me in hospital, feared they would become stranded in Stevenage and I became concerned about my move. My grandfather hated hospitals, but was persuaded to come and sit in the coffee shop by the entrance. Leaving him drinking his tea, Grandma, an ex-nurse, came up to see me and find out how I was. Unfortunately I was preparing for physiotherapy, so was not able to accompany her to see Grandpa. Before I went to physiotherapy I bid her farewell as she and Grandpa went home, promising to return in the afternoon.

> 'We cannot tell you how distressed we both were when your mother rang to tell us the bad news, and though she refrained from stressing the gravity of it to us, the details came out gradually and gave us great concern.
>
> 'We have always regarded you as an exceptional lad, very intelligent, and entertaining, although perhaps a little eccentric as regards to your feeding times and the variety in your appetite; however, the considerable quantities that you devour in your meals has never put any additional weight on your streamlined figure.
>
> 'When we visited you at hospital in Stevenage we were greatly pleased to see that you were showing good signs of recovery.'
>
> Gordon and Marie White,
> maternal grandparents

In physiotherapy, I had a very controlled walk between two plinths resting my hands on the two large balls. Unfortunately, Kate would not let me have a 'game of football' since I was experiencing a certain amount of 'limb-jerking'. Before I left, I informed her that, as I was going to Northwick Park on Monday, she would have to write my physiotherapy report before my transfer, the occupational therapy report having already been written.

My depression at not playing football in physiotherapy soon disappeared as my grandparents returned. Once more Grandma came up to see me, leaving Grandpa trying not to be noticed downstairs. From this point on Grandma took control. She sat me in my wheelchair and, not acknowledging anybody offering assistance, pushed me to the lifts where we travelled down two floors before she pushed me the length of the hospital to the coffee shop, where I devoured two muffins and a glass of orange juice. My grandmother was then eighty-nine.

I do not remember much else happening at the end of this week, my last at the Lister; Friday was to be the end of my therapy and I went home at the weekend as per normal. It had become so much of a habit, with my parents living in a village near Stevenage, that the nurses at the Lister took it for granted that I would not be there at the weekend. It amazes me, the trust these people had. While at home I was allowed to do whatever I wanted, and had not reported back to the occupational therapists with a list of problems. It was assumed (naughtily, but in this case correctly) that I had no problems at home, and did not warrant a home visit. It may be unusual, but I never had a home visit from anyone. Once at Northwick Park I had been home several times without any problems, and I suppose the therapists there assumed I had been visited at home by the therapists at the Lister. I was fine at home; I was coping very well and would have called for help if I needed it.

Being in hospital taught me to have a go myself and I have been climbing the sheer cliff face of adversity ever since. I think I would have somehow resented any home visits from people telling me how to look after myself or carry out particular tasks. Besides, I did not do much anyway, especially those activities with which I might need help! This was the frame of mind I started with, but it changed within a couple of weeks. I could not keep up the pretence for very long and was soon helping out around the house with activities ranging from assisting with the cooking and cleaning to carrying out many minor repairs and DIY. Although I was soon to begin to carry out activities at home, little would be achieved at the end of this week.

This certainly rang true for Saturday where I was relatively quiet and I did not do very much. However, Sunday was busier as my parents and I had a little adventure. As it had, for several months, been decided that I ought to go to Northwick Park, it was suggested that I should make a visit, to scrutinise the locale and see if I could get a feel for the hospital. The trip had been planned for several weeks, long before we received information that I would be transferred there on the Monday. Undaunted by this sudden good news, my parents took me to Northwick Park anyway, although we understood that there would be no therapists there at the weekend, and the number of nurses would be greatly reduced. This was useful to know, since it was very quiet at the hospital and the inactivity could well have been taken the wrong way.

As it was, we were warmly welcomed; after all the nurses probably had little to do themselves, most of the patients having gone home for the weekend. Mandy Spencer, who saw me on my assessment while I was at the Royal London Hospital and Linda Ryan, a jocular Irishwoman with a love of horses, were very friendly and helpful. They gave me a lot of the ins and outs of the care that was available there before giving me a tour of the ward. After that, I was introduced to a couple of the patients who had not gone home for the weekend. They were able to give me a complete and subjective rundown of everything that went on, rather than the somewhat glossy overview given to me by the nurses.

During the couple of hours I spent there, I received much warmth from the experience. If nothing else, it gave me a stronger feeling that I wanted to go there; I hoped it would be my last hurdle before I was able to return home for good. I had been on this silly holiday for too long shirking my responsibilities, and I ought to return to the real world and do something normal. If only I had realised how much longer it would take me.

The Beginning of the End

The irony oozed through the day: a thick, sticky substance, making its presence known to anyone who cared to think about it. Having taken a short outing from the Lister the day before, my arrival at Northwick Park carried a hint of expectation. Maybe my move would be somewhat easier than my previous transferral, I might even arrive when patients still lay awake in the warmth of their bedding, so that I would not be greeted only by night nurses.

Even with this strange turn of events, my move was little different to that from the Royal London. I was told the ambulance would arrive during the early part of the morning. Anticipating their arrival, I was packed and ready to leave as soon as breakfast was finished. As I should have expected they arrived late, but they came to pick me up in the mid-afternoon rather than the late evening as before. Maybe my day trip did hold a destiny.

The nurses received the phone call to say the ambulance was on its way, so I was made ready to go down to meet it. I was mostly ready, so it did not take me long, and I was soon wheeled down to the A&E entrance by an agency nurse. Once there, I was unceremoniously dumped by the nurse while she continued on her duties and I quietly awaited the ambulance's arrival.

There was a bit of a wait, but they soon arrived and, needing to make sure they had the correct person, the attendants spent the first few minutes filling out some paperwork. That completed, they had a quick look at the map and we were off. Feeling more confident now, and not wishing to choke, I sat up in the ambulance and chatted to the ambulance crew.

Northwick Park in Harrow is a very big hospital, well known and clearly signposted, placed at the corner of two intersecting main roads. Naturally, we got lost! After driving around the town centre – more than once – the ambulance driver gave up on his abilities at finding the correct route and flagged down another vehicle to ask directions. By a strange twist of fate the vehicle we pulled over was another ambulance, whose drivers could sympathise with us in our predicament. As is always the way, we were told that we were practically on top of the hospital; it was just that we were facing the wrong way... on a dual carriageway! Once we had extricated ourselves from our unfortunate difficulty, we were soon on our way to Northwick Park Hospital. From this point on, the ambulance journey was very easy.

Arriving at the A&E entrance of the hospital we had our second surprise. Putting it mildly, it was miles away from the wards. My two 'escorts', since it was taking so long, kept thinking they were going the wrong way and kept having little squabbles as to who was driving and did that person know where they were going. I just lay back, smiled and prayed that at least one of them was driving. Their antics reminded me of watching a slapstick comedy for the in-flight movie on an aeroplane and I found it very entertaining.

Eventually we arrived on the sixth floor, at the Regional Rehabilitation Unit. As with my previous journey between hospitals, I arrived long after supper, though sounds did still emanate from the various bays, since not everyone was asleep. Arriving late did not bother me as I like late nights and was used to eating late – I was certainly very hungry. The nurses were extremely kind, and after they had checked me in they found some scraps of food for me to eat. To begin with I was in a side room all on my own adjacent to the ward.

Once I had been checked in properly, I was moved along the corridor and taken to one of the four-bed bays that branched off the main ward corridor. Once in Bay C, a nurse helped me put all my things away in the various drawers and wardrobe that are available for each of the patients. My bed was next to a large window that overlooked the nurses' station. I could see everything that was going on and listen to any gossip, if I chose. I thought it would be convenient since I could attract a nurse's attention if I needed to, but this need was superfluous since all the beds were equipped with a buzzer – not that I ever used it for myself. Although complacent this first night, the following morning I was a trifle annoyed at arriving so late the day before, when I found out that I had been booked for a physiotherapy assessment, had I arrived early enough.

The first full day at the unit, Tuesday, 7 March, was all mine, giving me the opportunity to settle in properly and sleep on if I needed. It had been designed so that I had a free hand in what I did when, as long as I followed the constraints of my timetable. I only had one thought, to get better, and to do so I needed therapy. Bearing that in mind, I wondered how I was going to fill my days until therapy started properly.

The rest of the week continued in this fairly sluggish manner. One day, while deciding whether to start with nothing or do nothing second, my occupational therapist, Samantha Eaton, came over to introduce herself and discuss the kind of things we would be doing. She mentioned using the washing machine and oven (both of which I had used during my weekends at home) and the important consideration that must be given to 'washing and dressing'. As this was something I had been doing for myself ever since Alan refused to help me in the shower at the Royal London, I did not see the need for this therapy. Obviously I realised the importance that this must be for many people, but I also perceived its superfluity for me. I asked if there was any therapy along the lines of what I had been doing at the Lister. I was told that the occupational therapy performed in the RRU was designed to get patients used to functioning on their own again. I was already doing this, a fact that Samantha would inevitably discover, and I soon came to realise that most occupational therapy at Northwick Park would be somewhat pointless for me.

By now, feeling more confident that I was somewhere I should be getting all the therapy I needed (though I was slightly dubious about occupational therapy), I settled down to life on the unit. I was brought a fair amount of paperwork in the form of my weekly timetable, showing what I was doing when and the menu for the next day so I could choose my food. Unfortunately, there was no bread and butter, and you were not supposed to have biscuits, sweets, chocolate and other delicacies in the RRU to ward against getting fat, due to the inactivity associated with lying in bed not taking any exercise; it was a rule I soon learnt to bend slightly. However, there was a greater quantity of food, and I was finally off the starvation rations I had been getting at the Lister.

Although I eventually discovered lots of activities that could keep me occupied, I started my incarceration at this new hospital with little to do. I merely sat quietly and waited expectantly for my physiotherapy assessment, though I did have a chat and quick assessment with the consultant. That went very well and she seemed fairly confident about my potential for recovery.

After a few moments, and not a moment too soon, or else I would have left, came the love of my life – physiotherapy. It was the therapy I had been doing the longest. I really enjoyed it and it was very good for me; so soon after my accident, it was the therapy I needed most. I had been looking forward to physiotherapy since the Friday before, when I had said goodbye to Kate, and was glad when this assessment finally arrived, with my new therapist, Elaine Gates. She showed me the correct way of getting out of bed. This instinct had been eradicated from my mind due to my accident, and from all the months of lying in bed, unable to stand, it seemed as though I had forgotten. She even showed me the correct way of putting on my shoes, a process I apparently had been doing incorrectly throughout my life. Simply by crossing my legs and lifting my feet to my torso, it enabled me to keep my back straight, and prevent any pain that may develop if I continued to crouch down.

Although I had a few assessments, this was a slow week and I was able to do whatever I wanted for most of the day. However, I still found it hard to read, and I had not yet discovered the delights of the computer room. I had not been given any exercises for physiotherapy, either – except the exercises which Kate had given me while at the Lister, which I still practised – nor was I fired with the enthusiasm for discovering any exercises on my own. To start with, I considered wandering aimlessly around the ward, but soon decided it was hard to wander in the wheelchair, borrowed from the occupational therapists to discourage me from walking outside the bay, and doing so aimlessly was impossible; everything about my existence seemed to have a purpose. Thankfully, I was able to play cards and had some music to listen to, but ultimately would become bored with no one to talk to. My roommates were not very talkative. Two or them could not, and the other preferred screaming!

My luck was in; someone was answering my prayers. It was not in the way I wanted, but I suppose it was predictable. Quite what I did in hospital I do not know. I had the chaplain around for a visit, though I never asked for him. He listened to my pleas of sanity and 'religious contentment' and he never came back again, much to my gratitude.

My luck ran truer as my second visitor came to see me, shortly after the chaplain's departure. Cynthia Matthews and her husband, David, had been family friends for thirty years. She had been wonderful visiting me at the Royal London and the Lister, and continued at Northwick Park. As Blue Stilton is one of my favourite cheeses, she was very thoughtful and brought me some. Like all blue cheese, it has a high fat content and was probably highly 'illegal' to have on the RRU. Working on the principle that what they did not know would not hurt them, I kept very quiet about it, although I have no doubt the nurses realised my little devious ploys at getting extra food far sooner than I ever would have anticipated.

Not long after Cynthia left, my supper arrived, quickly followed by Mother. Since mid-February she had managed to time her arrival with that of my supper, probably to make sure she was offered a cup of coffee that came around at the same time as the food. She was more than welcome, especially when you consider I do not drink coffee.

Mornings at the RRU all followed a similar routine. Regardless of the time that I went to bed the night before, I had developed the habit of waking up early, before the nurses arrived to do the dirty deed. It was for no apparent reason and was probably a form of conditioning. Although the nurses did not wake me up terribly early, I slowly discovered that it was not particularly pleasant to be woken by the nurses and then having to rush to be ready for therapy, so I roused myself early and took my time. Having spent many years finding it very hard to wake up, this was an incredibly strange sensation. To further confuse myself, I had misplaced the ability of staying in bed once I had woken up, maybe rebelling against having to stay in bed while at the Lister. I had to get up, regardless of the time.

Once up I had to keep myself occupied, so I washed, often having a shower. There was a small problem, though, in that I was still, supposedly, reliant on a wheelchair. Nevertheless, it had become more natural and instinctive to wash myself, and it felt necessary; although still taking longer than I wished, it was certainly much easier. Even having a shower was no great problem as I simply transferred – yes, on my own! – to a chair and showered while sitting. I then dressed and was frequently able to do another job before breakfast arrived.

Continuing from my early mornings, there was a great deal of variation in the therapies I had and the therapists I saw. My time on the unit would bring a lot of changes and surprises. However, it took me several weeks to find my niche in the RRU, and initially I was easily bored, seemingly having nothing to do. Although lunch was enjoyable, it was also tedious: an hour's break when the therapists were not troubled by patients. It was a barrier to the physiotherapy that I needed and its presence was a trifle annoying.

Soon I had my first proper physiotherapy session, and its arrival heralded a slight problem: not being used to the ward at this early stage, I set out in the wheelchair from my bay and turned the wrong way to the gym. I soon realised my mistake and, hoping nobody had noticed, wheeled around and headed back to the gym. Thankfully, Elaine had not noticed my slight delay and carried on with the physiotherapy as though my mistake had never occurred.

We spent the whole hour concentrating fully on the right-hand side of my body. This was very important, since that was the side that received the full force of the car, while it was the left side of my brain that received most neural damage, further affecting my right-hand side. We did quite a bit of walking, though now it was done correctly, putting the weight evenly on both legs, rather than the list I was developing by carrying most of the weight on my stronger left leg... I tried, anyway. (Of course Kate taught me properly, but after being transferred from her care I quickly picked up bad habits, not wholly knowing the correct way of walking.) By now, it was becoming particularly obvious to me that I was not going to fully get better on my own. There is no doubt in my mind that I would have improved left to my own devices, but to get better properly I needed help from these wonderful therapists.

Later in the same day, the senior psychologist, Clare Owen, came around for the standard initial interview to see if I needed any counselling or psychological input. My answers were very good, considering, and on the whole very positive. She decided that I did not need any help and never saw me again, until I asked to see her several weeks later. She also gave me a form for my parents to fill out, which they did quickly. After worrying about me for three months, they were taking a well-deserved week's holiday to Madeira.

More therapy came with the help of Samantha, who arrived early on Friday morning, telling me to stay in bed and not to have a wash or get dressed until she returned. This I found hard to do, but I gritted my teeth and waited patiently until she came back. This delay to my morning's ablutions was all in aid of the primary occupational therapy care that was offered in the RRU: 'washing and dressing'. Samantha came into the bathroom with me and watched while I had a shower to make sure that I could cope. She then came out with me into the bay and made sure that I could dress myself without too much difficulty. I thought that I had shown that I was fairly proficient in getting myself ready in the mornings when Samantha turned to me saying, with a surprised tone in her voice, 'I've got you down for this again next week; I will have to cross it out though, you're too good.' It was not meant as a compliment, merely a statement of fact, but it did make me feel much better, in that someone else had noticed that I was greatly recovered.

My other treat for the day was being weighed to see if I would put on weight during my stay on the RRU. A comparatively easy exercise, but I never saw the point – I was never weighed at the end of my stay. I weighed just over ten stone at the start, my pre-accident weight, but now all of my clothes had become a little tighter. I eventually realised that although no heavier, a quantity of my muscle that had been developed over the years had been converted to a larger quantity of the lighter-weighing fat, so in spite of my weight being about the same, I was bigger.

At the end of the day, my father came to see me, bringing with him a brand new television. Although I was of course pleased to see him, his presence also heralded great joy in the existence of the television, as it would alleviate a large proportion of my boredom. Coming so soon after my transferral to Northwick Park, this was vital as I was still a few weeks away from waking up to my new life and finding something other than therapy to keep myself occupied. While we were chatting, the Staff Grade Medical Officer, Dr Natasha Hoddle, came and introduced herself, welcomed me to the unit, and let me know that if there were any medical matters that I wanted help with, not to hesitate to ask her for information.

Shortly after that one of the patients came zooming around in his electric wheelchair to deliver that week's newsletter. He was halfway through packing for his trip home at the weekend so he soon zoomed off again. Dad was also midway packing for his holiday with Mum, so he went on his way leaving me with nothing to do. While I was pottering about trying to think of what to do with myself, Barbara Kane came to take me to speech therapy, since I had forgotten all about it. The session was very enjoyable and we went through a questionnaire about the state of my memory! Notwithstanding my difficulty in remembering the times of my therapies from my timetable (has time ever meant anything to me?), I was so good at answering this long list of questions that Barbara kept telling me to slow down, since she was not able to write fast enough. It didn't help that since my accident I slurred my speech when I talked quickly, making it hard to understand me anyway.

My life at Northwick Park Hospital only really began in the second week after I had moved in, which gave me most of the first two weeks of March to get used to the idea of moving and get settled. My first weekend in hospital passed without incident; indeed, from my point of view, nothing happened. Monday, 13 March had to be more interesting, in the sense that it wasn't possible for it to be any less.

After getting ready on Monday, I had a long chat with Linda. I had great pleasure in showing her the photograph album of me that Mother had been compiling regularly. She was fascinated at seeing the changes and said she could not believe it when she saw a picture of me lying on a bed with tubes emanating from every orifice. We talked for what seemed like hours (though a few minutes is probably nearer the truth) and it was a great way to start off the week, though it would be hard to top those few moments of pleasurable relaxation. After delaying her from her work for long enough she made her excuses and left me to my physiotherapy.

Elaine and I spent the whole hour running through some exercises that I was advised to practise for my own benefit. This gave me a spark of an idea to do circuit training every day, which soon burst into a flame so that I could fill all my spare hours. My free time would now be spent stretching and bending, exercising muscles, tendons and ligaments that would rather rest and not do any work that might bring any pain. Yet damaged neurones had to be shown new pathways so I could relearn various activities.

So it was that I entered into my lunch break feeling much happier, and I was positively ecstatic when it came to my speech therapy after lunch. I also met some new people: two speech and language therapy students joined in the day's session so as to help them with their studies. These two students, Rachel and Debbie, were going to test me for dysarthria – a study of how well the muscles that are used in speaking are functioning. Although I have not seen the results, I did have a sneak look at the test paper while they were noted and saw that 'good' or 'normal' was being ticked against most of my responses. This seemed odd to me, considering that everywhere I went it was noted that I was dysarthric, even though I was shown not to be. Whatever the reality, once more a test aimed at discovering why my voice was so bad ended up being normal. This happened to most tests that were carried out on me be it for my voice or otherwise. I did not know whether to be happy or sad since, although there appeared to be nothing major wrong with me, I had no explanation for what *was* wrong with me or why.

During my enjoyable speech therapy I realised that a 'head injury' could not be put forward to explain every fault, although it was this that had instigated all my present imperfections. Later, while wondering what was definitively wrong with me, a medical student came round and asked if she could have a look at me and ask a few questions. Other than helping with her course I have no idea precisely why she was there, but I was not going to let that lack of knowledge prevent me from participating in helping her with whatever information she would like to know. Shortly afterwards, her colleague arrived to remind her that they had to leave. Although in a rush, she was so interested with what she was told about me, she could not help but have a look at me herself. Naturally I was not going to complain, and the prospect of these two young women prodding and poking me was not altogether unwelcome!

After they left, an old school friend of my father, Alan Soloman, who had heard about me in one of the scholarly magazines, popped in to see me. Although I had never met him, a life revolving around the here and now was a good home for a passing acquaintance. It was very interesting seeing him, to hear that I was becoming infamous in certain walks of life. Certainly, the realisation that people who had never met me were thinking of and asking about me left me with a greater resolve to get better than I already had. It was now I realised that by not getting better I would do more than just let myself down.

With this inspiration hovering over me, threatening to haunt me if I did not listen, I started doing the peculiar things that were soon to become my trademark at the RRU: after everyone was fast asleep I started some more exercises. With only the night nurses left awake, carrying out the few duties they have to do before settling down to a night filled with tedium unless there was a cry for help, when they would all scramble, hoping to be the one to answer first and break the monotony, I decided to stand to one side of my room and balance on one leg. Although walking was still very difficult, standing was becoming easier, but would only improve with practice.

This strange habit not only helped sort out my balance, but it also strengthened my weaker right leg, so that it got used to carrying my weight again. One of the night nurses, Grace Bentley, came around and, being a little concerned, asked if everything was all right. I said I was fine, but with not much to do and still wide awake, I was slightly bored. She sympathised and invited me out to chat with her and the other staff nurse, Antonia Christos. I can still remember the surprised look on Toni's face as she saw Grace strolling back with a patient in tow. She showed no annoyance and in all the times I came out to chat with the night nurses I was never reprimanded and always welcomed with 'open arms'. So enjoyable was this extra-curricular rehabilitation that I did not notice the time passing (no revelation there) and I finally went to bed long after two in the morning, only leaving a few hours to sleep.

These passed without incident, and once I had woken up later on the Wednesday at a respectable hour, I was to discover a day filled with new challenges, as well as a seed of an idea that would blossom over the next few months and eventually alter the way in which I would treat the world and the people in it. It would teach me things, furnish me with ideas and give me a further reason for living, a final destiny – I was introduced to the computer room.

I was assessed by the technician, Matt Demus, who showed me a passage from a magazine and told me to try typing it. Having become quite proficient at typing over the years, I went about this comparatively easy exercise with great gusto, making several mistakes. I still did not have the fine control in my hands and fingers, functions I lost in the accident, and was forever hitting two keys at the same time. Matt told me to type slower, and instigated a computer programme whereby the response of the computer was slowed down and the keys had to be pressed for a large fraction of a second before the computer would respond. There is no doubt that this drastic intervention worked, but I still pressed the space bar as fast as normal. All the words were joined together and there was no space to be seen; somewhat like trying to find a parking space on a Saturday morning in a busy town centre!

Thursday was an uneventful day, except for the chastisement given to me by Elaine when I walked to physiotherapy. It was clear in my mind that I could walk by this stage, and I saw no reason why I should not. Unfortunately, I was not walking properly and the therapists did not want me developing any more bad habits by trying to walk too soon. I was allowed to walk in the bay for practice, but if I ventured over its threshold I was told to sit in the wheelchair, until they decided I was able to walk out on my own, without developing any bad habits.

One event that did happen on Thursday was the nurses happily informing me that I would be moving bays over the weekend. At the time, I was slightly shocked that I was to be moved so soon after I had become settled. Later I realised that the staff was being very generous in telling me, and with three days' notice to get used to the idea as well. Thinking about it, especially with the snub nose of hindsight poking in again, moving could not do any harm, and I decided that it would be pleasant meeting some new people.

Later that night, I was aiming to go to bed when I noticed that Toni was out by the noticeboard altering the main timetable for the next day. Having discovered I was allowed out at night-time, I decided to take a chance and go out and chat to her and Grace. I really enjoyed these forays out at night, getting quite a reputation for myself, though I do not know of any nurse who resented my presence. Unlike my first flit out into the dark world inhabited by night nurses a few days before, I went to bed slightly earlier, though it was still after midnight.

I am not sure quite what power Elaine had over me to make me do what she said, but unlike the majority of people, whose words go in one ear and make a similar departure, she made me listen to her. After telling me off for walking the day before, by Friday 17th I had relinquished this primal right and made my way to the gym in the wheelchair. There, I did my circuit training in order to get it out of the way before Barbara came down to take the introductory admission video of me. The RRU has a system whereby a video is taken of each patient on arrival and discharge to provide a before and after view that they can keep for their records. I was glad of this, since it had been suggested for three months that there should be a video of me. At long last it seemed I would receive an enduring memento. It is just a shame I have never seen it.

Once completed, I discarded the morning and welcomed in the afternoon. First thing after lunch I was taken down and shown how to use the exercise bike, and it was suggested that I should use it every day to help with my therapy. After that came my last physiotherapy session with Elaine before she went on her two-week holiday to San Francisco. Later, I packed some things that I might need on my two-day holiday, when I went home for the weekend.

After the first few days of lethargic indifference, I altered my realities once home and decided to help around the house in the same way that I had during my weekends home from the Lister. After all, I was trying out many more activities to see if I could do them while in hospital, so there was no reason why I should not at home. Over several weeks I amazed myself with all the things that I achieved, just given the belief that I could do them. To begin with I did not achieve a great deal, though I was able to sit there and cut the vegetables for supper. I found it hard carrying out many activities simply because I was stuck in a wheelchair, though I generally got out at home. I was not in a wheelchair for long enough to really get used to the position. I marvel at the way 'disabled' people carry out their lives from the seat of a wheelchair, often doing a better job than many able-bodied people. Compared to experts like these I did little, but I achieved far more than I initially thought possible. It was with a well-formed opinion that I returned to the RRU, looking forward to the discoveries that would be associated with my new bay.

The first, and major, discovery was the people I met in the new bay, who were very pleasant. They, in fact, turned out to be the best bunch I shared with in my two months and my discharge brought the realisation that it had been my most enjoyable time. Another small problem on my return was that I was very thirsty, and the nurses, probably not realising that I would be back in the evening, had not got around to putting a jug of water out for me. Wanting to quench my thirst I went out and had a quiet word with Grace to see if she could get me some water. She gave me an indignant look and joked with me, 'I see! So you go away for the weekend, and when you come back all you do is start moaning!'

I would not have minded, but getting the water for me should have caused no problems for her. Had I realised how the nurses did it, I would have done it myself: very simply, she filled the jug up from a tap by the sink in the room – not hard, really, though I probably would have spilled it! I thanked her very much for the water and, by now very thirsty, drank it all. Feeling satiated, I finally drifted off to sleep.

Laughter is the Best Medicine

A new week, a new physiotherapist, and a new bay, Bay A. This week also opened up new adventures for me. Along with another patient, Chris Hyde, who transferred a few days after my move to Bay A and occupied the bed next to mine, I was instructed to go shopping for the staff if they wanted anything. Many of the nurses and therapists did not have sufficient time to visit the shops, even though there were some situated in the hospital. Nonetheless, many wished to have some light refreshment during the day. Quite why the occupational therapists trusted us over and above the other patients I do not know, but we now had a job designed to increase our confidence and to give us some exercise. Their original intention was that Chris, who could walk, would push me, but I made a steadfast refusal. I would propel the wheelchair myself: why settle for the easy option? What the therapists did not realise then was that this show of companionship would help to radically alter the way I was beginning to view the world.

As my new therapist was away for a couple of days and Elaine was having a couple of days off before her holiday to the USA, I had a temporary stand-in. When Maria Purl – who had, coincidentally, also been Lisa Stringer's therapist – first saw me on Tuesday, 21 March, she brought a colleague who mediated between the hospital and the Riding for the Disabled Association (RDA) stables in the area. She had heard that I used to work at a stables and suggested that I might like to go and do some riding. It was pointed out that exercise of that nature would do my pelvis far more good than hours of physiotherapy, and from my work I knew how important horse riding is for disabled people. I said that I was very interested, so she rushed off to make a few phone calls and try to book a lesson for me. After she left, Maria and I occupied ourselves with a lot of stretching around my pelvic area, continuing until after four o'clock; to my delight she kept me in for an extra half an hour.

Later that day I prepared, perhaps stupidly, for an early night (by which I mean before midnight!) Experience should have told me that I ought to go to bed after midnight – I tended to wake up earlier feeling refreshed. If I went to bed early, I would toss and turn for hours, desperately trying to get to sleep and then wake up feeling terrible. That night was no different: I was restless, so I rolled over to make myself more comfortable. Unfortunately I rolled over slightly too far, the bed soon ceasing to exist underneath me, ending half a roll earlier! Lying on a bed that is not there is very tricky, and I ended up on the floor with a quiet bump. I was up very quickly hoping that no one had seen my embarrassment. There was no pain, I was not hurt so I got back into bed and went straight to sleep. The following morning, I was, stupidly, relating the sorry tale of strange things going bump in the night to one of the nurses. After all, I thought it was funny.

'You should have told someone,' said the nurse, rather annoyed.

'I was all right,' I countered.

'So! Why didn't you tell someone?' said the nurse getting more and more irritated.

'I was tired,' I said. 'I went back to sleep.'

'But you could have had a head injury!' By now the nurse was getting flustered, but not argumentative enough to get her point over to me.

'I've had one of those,' I said. 'I know what they feel like.'

As far as I was concerned, that was the end of the conversation. Thankfully, my apparent lack of brain damage was proof enough for them and I was able to 'live another day'. Lucky for me, since about five weeks later another patient also fell out of bed. He was sat down and fussed over, told not to go to therapy that day and was given various tests and X-rays. This would have annoyed me. Thank heavens I never had to undergo that!

I was to prove that my fall caused no serious after-effects when I went to 'current affairs'. It had never been my favourite topic; I never read a newspaper or even watched the news on television. Even so, in the RRU it was enjoyable, and I was able to have some proper, intelligent discussions with people, even though I usually did not know about the topics that had been on the previous night's news. In spite of my apathy, these sessions always stimulated a great deal of discussion. As was normal, I never said very much; I spent much of the session sitting quietly and listening to the points that everybody else brought up. After all, the details of whatever was being discussed were usually a mystery to me. In doing so, I did not waste my words, and when I did say something it was very apt, profound and insightful. I actually paid attention during these sessions and even found them quite enjoyable. What made it easier was that the therapy assistant was very pleasant. Carol Lee had a good sense of humour; she was intelligent, well read, eloquent, and attractive into the bargain.

Even after three months, I still could not quite figure out what speech therapy did for me, though I am sure it did far more than I realised. Thankfully I always used to find it enjoyable; my apologies became more evident as I started to find these lessons more and more funny. In despair we soon stopped and instead Barbara asked a series of questions designed to check the condition of the 'artistic' right-hand side of my brain. Finding life slightly too logical, and given that my brain worked in an illogical fashion, I relished answering these questions. I had always found mental escape easy, and thankfully still did, even after a potentially fatal accident. At least physical escape was also becoming easier by this stage and I could get off the unit to go to the shops, although I was still chained to a wheelchair.

Another escape came on the Thursday morning in the form of occupational therapy in which Samantha showed me around the kitchen. While considering what complex recipe I might do, I was asked to make a cheese sandwich. I realise this task could be complex for people with certain disabilities, but for someone with no 'apparent' disability (acknowledging the assumption that the wheelchair was only temporary), who had been cooking for twelve years, making a cheese sandwich was rudimentary; I was even somewhat embarrassed, but I made one nonetheless.

Maria, who was going to take me for physiotherapy at 11.30, walked past the kitchen at one point and made a jocular complaint that she did not have a sandwich. Later, when she came to get me, I gave her a sandwich I had made for her. Showing her gratitude, she told me to get ready for physiotherapy and she would do my washing-up. For once I was given an order with which I could happily comply.

When Maria joined me for physiotherapy she mainly did work with me lying on my front on a large ball, designed to get me bending around my pelvis and using it correctly. She was so impressed by what she asked me to do she offered me a suggestion with which I did not have to comply. Thinking the possibility of me carrying out her suggestion was remote, she never in fact phrased it as a question.

'You did that so well,' she said, 'it's a shame we cannot put you on your back.'

Quite what there was to be shameful about I never found out, since I wasn't going to allow anything prevent me getting better.

'If it does me good, I'll do anything,' I replied. I meant it as well, there was nothing I would not do on the road to my recovery, no obstacle that I would let come in my way and block my progress. Maybe against her better judgement Maria helped me turn onto my back and there I lay, extending my back over the curve of the ball, helping eliminate the flexion that causes the stoop so characteristic of many disabilities and old age.

Maria was very impressed, as was noticeable by the soft rush of air as she breathed. In fact, everyone was impressed. A hushed silence had descended over the gym, and as I scanned my immediate environment I saw faces looking back at me. Everybody was staring at me, applauding me with their eyes. For several seconds no words were uttered throughout the room; they were not needed.

Maria paused for a couple of moments then quickly recovered her composure to interrupt the flow of emotions between my heart and my brain. Trying to regain control of the situation, while also trying to aid my recovery, she gave me an exercise that I was to do while I was walking. I was supposed to walk so that my shoulders rotated in the opposite way to my pelvis, remaining antagonistic with every step I took. She called it a 'John Wayne swagger', and anyone who watches Westerns will know exactly what I am talking about. Of course, this only applied when walking in the gym in full sight of a physiotherapist and the few steps I took around my bay. I was still in the wheelchair and technically not supposed to walk anywhere. Recognising how inane this 'swagger' was I politely asked Maria why I had to use it. She said that she had noticed that I walked very stiffly and was introducing this daft walk to increase the flexion in my torso. We achieved an enormous amount in physiotherapy that morning without seeming to do anything, which, I suppose, is everyone's wish.

On the other hand, I never really achieved much during occupational therapy, although I enjoyed working in the kitchen. It did have its uses, though, as it introduced me to computers. Having given me the rundown of how the basics of the computer word-processing package worked at the start of the week, Matt now took me to the next level and showed me different fonts, cutting and pasting, moving text, and other 'complex' aspects of the program. During these early sessions I was learning several items about computing and Matt was spending time with me. Shortly, having seen that I was very good with computers and fairly competent at typing, Matt told me to have a go at writing a letter while he looked on. Not having any letters I wanted to write to friends, I started writing a journal of my experiences in hospital.

Soon I was competent enough for Matt to leave me to it, allowing him to concentrate on others. Although he did not need to help me much after this point, a couple of weeks later, he did try and teach me to touch-type – I was not very good, and did not see the necessity of this in computing. Anyway, I now had somewhere else to disappear to so that my boredom could be alleviated. From that day onwards most of my evenings were spent typing my journal.

Having all these activities – whether computing, cooking, current affairs or visiting the shops – it is a wonder I found time for anything else; yet I still needed to do my exercises. They were doing me so much good I felt as though I had to do them – I would miss them had I not done them. I would have felt empty and guilty and would have wondered why, I had to do them for my own peace of mind, so this daily routine was to continue. Looking back, had I not done them I would not have reached to the level of recovery that I attained.

One day, during my circuit training in the gym, my brother

arrived bringing various things with him and dropping them off on my bed. On returning to my bay I became annoyed that I had missed him, especially since I had all day when I could have done my exercises, yet I had the strangest, almost psychic, feeling that he was still in the building. A quick search of the unit did not reveal my missing brother. A short while later, as I was moving down from the top end of the unit, he was entering from the bottom end, as he had been searching for me outside. Our eyes met 'across the crowded corridor' from several yards away, and we soon caught up with each other and had a good chat. We continued until Mother arrived and they went home together.

As well as all these adventures, Friday of this week also proved useful to my medical progress, though the outcome was less beneficial – I was to finally see the ENT specialist at the voice clinic. Unfortunately, Barbara was too busy to come down with me, so I was taken down by another speech therapist, Fran Jackson. We went down at 9.45 and were told to wait. It was not that long before someone came around and brought us a form to fill out. This was all right for me since I love forms. The one drawback was that I was still not able to write legibly because of my accident, so Fran had to fill in the form while I answered the questions. This did not take too long and was followed by a slightly longer wait. Meanwhile I was chatting away to Fran like there was no tomorrow – although I sounded daft, it never stopped me wanting to talk. This particular wait lasted just over half an hour and was interrupted towards the end, since I was taken away and a foul-tasting antiseptic spray directed into the back of my throat to numb my vocal chords. Although this was necessary, it made it very hard to swallow and nigh on impossible to talk; Fran no doubt relished the silence since she later asked the specialist ENT therapist whether I could be told to stop talking.

'Why, does he talk a lot?' asked the ENT therapist.

'On and on,' said Fran. 'He never shuts up!'

'Excellent,' she was told. 'It is the best exercise his voice can get.'

Listening in, I smiled at this comment, as I now had an official sanction for talking continually, something I intended doing anyway.

At this stage my vocal chords gradually seemed to tighten, as though I were being strangled from the inside. I was called back in to see the next person, before this spray could wear off. This time, I was taken into a small room where the ENT therapist and a doctor waited for me, not unlike ranks of the undead awaiting their next victim. I was invited in, asked a few questions and then threatened with a long, thin tube with a camera on the end. I was asked to tilt my head back, and this fibre-optic laryngoscope was inserted and slid down my trachea in a similar way to a sword being swallowed. This endoscope was simply fed down my trachea until a clear picture of my vocal chords could be picked up in the instrument's light and recorded on video for later reference. After he had had his thrills, the specialist removed the tube and I was allowed to sit down again, awaiting further instruction.

I had now completed the reason for my coming down in the first place, and all it took was around ten minutes, though I had to wait for well over an hour. I still needed the results and the wait for these took a further twenty minutes or more. Finally I was given an envelope and, after being away from the RRU for almost two hours, Fran and I were allowed to return and I could resume normal speech therapy.

Later on Friday, Simon returned so that he could steal me away for the weekend. Before he did, I said that I would enter the day's happenings into my Dictaphone (used to record my journal before I had full use of the computer – I started to record my journal while at the Lister). However, before I started, I packed a bag for the weekend and Simon popped down to the nurses to collect my pills.

Simon returned to find me talking to myself while recording the words. As is typical of him, he decided to join in. I had begun to mention him coming to collect me. In the background this little voice piped up, '...Who was on time.' I then spoke about doing some of my packing, immediately followed by the ghostly '...Took ages.' When I mentioned taking the pills there was a faint hiss issuing from the loudspeaker as Simon rustled the bag. None of this is particularly funny, but it was very hard not to laugh at the recording, as Simon and I were giggling throughout.

When we were ready to leave, I infuriated my patient brother even more, since I saw Elaine on the way out. I could not leave without saying goodbye and wishing her a pleasant holiday, something that always took me a long time, since I talk too much. It's often kinder to simply drag me away, something Simon does with relish.

My uncle and aunt, Brian and Ruth Salter, and I had not got together since my early days at the Lister, so spending the weekend (25/26 March) with them was delightful. Joining us were Carrie and David, who had not seen me since the Royal London, and my paternal grandmother, Jane Watling. Everyone noted a large improvement and was kind enough to say so. They would not have thought so, though, had they heard my entry of the Saturday morning, recorded on my Dictaphone: '…And got here just before one, so we must have left just before… no, got here just before… oh, what! I don't know what time we… I don't know anything.' That just about sums up my brain while I was still in hospital!

> 'Although not able to write very well due to my increasing blindness, I have penned a few notes to give you my instant reaction when your father told me of your accident. My first reaction was total shock, followed by a terrible fear; what can I, a very old woman, do?
>
> 'Answer – absolutely nothing, but pray that somehow, someone (as I believe, God) will make you gradually recover, or die easily – but could you fight not to die?'
>
> Jane Watling,
> paternal grandmother

What I liked most about the weekend was seeing my cousin, Lara. I had not seen her since my first week in Royal Ward, ten weeks earlier – not that I was in a position to remember. It is even doubtful that I had, in fact, seen her at all. We had a very long talk, much as we used to when we were children. Although a few years older than me, Lara had maybe noticed a maturity in me, a wisdom not normally possible for someone my age. Although women are mature more quickly than men, meaning she should have been several years in advance of my maturity, she treated me as though I was as advanced as she was, and I always viewed her as an intellectual equal. We always got on very well and it was pleasant to be able to talk to her this time.

I was also pleased when we went for a walk in the afternoon around the nearby Campbell Park. I was (officially) still being pushed in the wheelchair, and for the most part I simply sat there; yet on a number of occasions, like going up flights of stairs while holding onto the banister, or anywhere else where I could hold onto something, I got up and walked. I probably shouldn't have done, but no one was going to stop me. Anyway, I had good reason to try and walk: the landscape around Milton Keynes is beautiful and fired my enthusiasm. This was useful since, towards the end of the walk, we went to see the new offices of Milton Keynes Parks Trust, built inside a cricket pavilion. The only way to see it was to get up and have a look – cricket pavilions are not often designed with wheelchairs in mind. Besides, it was good practice.

This idyllic weekend could not last for ever. Sunday evening came all too soon and I was returned back to hospital. I knew I would not be able to sleep, so I considered lying in bed and tossing and turning for hours on end with my brain operating in overdrive, but I didn't wish to fall out of bed again. The problems I was having with my eyes still made the effort of reading very strenuous and I decided against this. Therefore, after supper, long after sensible people had turned in for the night, I quietly wheeled myself down to the gym where I proceeded with my exercises. The place was cool and quiet at night-time and the atmosphere peaceful. It was a joy to continue with my exercises this late at night and it did not feel like a chore; it was a positive delight. Eventually I returned to my bay and went to bed, though it was probably well after midnight.

'Our reaction was predictable when we heard the news; we were shocked and very upset, feeling pretty helpless being unable to do anything to change or improve the situation. When crises happen we tend to think through, and talk about different scenarios, such as, "What if it had been at night?" or "What if help hadn't been available?" etc. Also, we are convinced the outcome would have been different if you hadn't received the appropriate medical attention so soon.

'We are very thankful that you did, and very impressed and delighted that you made such a remarkable recovery, and despite the early Welsh/Italian accent and your lack of mobility and coordination, you are the same Phil we know and love. The motivation to succeed, the enthusiasm and sense of humour was very evident, and although you had still got a lot of progress to make, we felt heartened and certainly enjoyed our first visit at the Lister Hospital. Witnessing you learning to try and tell the time again will always stick in our minds!

'Obviously the accident and the aftermath has not only had a dramatic effect on your life but has also had a major impact on your mum, dad and Simon. We feel that as they have dealt with the traumatic events with such fortitude this must have been indispensable, as you have progressed from being almost not with us to where you are today.'

Brian and Ruth Salter,
uncle and aunt

During my fourth week I had speech therapy virtually every day with one of the students, Rachel Halifax. She and Debbie had completed the test to discover how the various vocal/facial muscles had been affected by my accident. Finding no large defect, it was now down to Rachel to give me various voice exercises to help improve my speech. Before she started, though, Barbara explained the results that she had received from my ENT examination. Although no *damage* was found in the vocal chords, they were not meeting fully along their whole length and did not always vibrate in a coordinated manner. A slight chink at the posterior end resulted in the slightly breathy, hoarse tone to which most people were now becoming accustomed. I had been waiting for months to see an ENT specialist and the results found did not get anywhere near close enough to explaining why my voice was so bad. I was disappointed, but at least, I suppose, they gave me some indication.

Although Rachel was only a young student, about my age, I had never let that fact prevent me from participating in anything before, and I was not about to start now. Everyone has to begin somewhere and experience cannot be gained without seeing patients. It is my nature to help people, and if seeing me helped her continue with her studies, all the better. Besides, she was very good, I could not have asked for anyone more professional. A lot of the work she made me do was quite standard and well known. Long lists of words with different numbers of syllables, all grouped into sets with similar groups of letters remaining consistent through all the words (for example: jelly, belly, smelly), have to be pronounced as precisely as the therapist's ear considers appropriate. I had to read through short passages sounding as intelligible as possible, usually where separate sentences were phrased as questions or statements, and often using intonation where someone was angry or sad.

This said, most of what we did had absolutely nothing to do with how words sound. In order for words produced by your voice to sound accurate, and for the noise to travel a distance through the projection of your voice, in order to allow you to vary your voice due to the intonation of different words and phrases, and to have your voice sounding on the correct pitch, it is vital that the breathing is correct. Most of our energies were spent on breathing exercises, trying to increase the capacity of my lungs and help me gain control over my vocal chords. Maybe due to an increase in oxygen going to my brain because of the strange breathing, or just to an extraordinarily odd sense of humour, I used to find these exercises extremely funny – although I was assured they were not. Even so, I used to begin giggling within a few minutes of starting breathing exercises; I simply did not understand their complex detail or point of their existence. Quite often, the mere mention of doing breathing exercises had me in stitches. In between the giggles, though, my voice developed to the state where I could talk intelligibly, and the loud voice brought on by Jacqui making me shout at the Royal London was toned down an enormous amount so that I spoke softly.

Unfortunately, although quieter, my voice also developed a peculiar quality. I had never spoken with an accent, unless I wanted to, yet I started to speak with my strong 'Welsh/Italian' accent. The therapists found that I was clipping all the words that I spoke, cutting them short and making my speech sound like a foreigner talking. This was their explanation, and they made me slow my speech down – in my case not very different from holding your hand up to a speeding locomotive and shouting, '*Whoa!*' I was told to over-articulate and make a conscious effort to stretch the words, though not too much if the word ended in a vowel, I would often say things like 'evidentleeeee'.

It is at this point that I think speech therapy failed me.

Although the therapists did a fantastic job in getting me to talk and my speech improved one hundredfold, my voice deteriorated in proportion. In spite of all the help over subsequent months, I still speak with an unusual accent – for several years a Welshman and an Italian threw insults at each other until I told myself to shut up. Nowadays, often people ask where my accent comes from: was I South African? Several minutes would be spent denying everything, but maybe Jo and Sonja were right after all.

Unlike speech therapy, something I was finally beginning to understand was occupational therapy. Certainly, functional activities like 'washing and dressing' administered at the RRU were very useful for a large number of patients. Anyone who had lost an arm, for example, had to be taught how to do functional activities, whether brushing their teeth, getting dressed, or cooking a meal, using only one hand. Ever since the Royal London, I had undertaken various activities with the attitude that they could be done and nothing would prevent me from carrying them out. I am very lucky – and thankful – that I have nothing major wrong with me, and I find most functional activities fairly easy, but that is not the point. Whether you can do various processes, involving any physical problems you may have, has a lot to do with whether or not you believe you can do them. Was I able to carry out activities, and therefore believed I could, or did I believe I could do them and therefore found that I was able?

Instead I was taken down to the kitchen again and told where everything was and how all the machines worked. The therapists informed me that I would be cooking lunch for myself once every week. This pleased me a great deal since I consider myself a fairly good cook; I only use ingredients that I like and I have peculiar tastes that are not often found in other people's cooking. I would certainly enjoy this aspect of occupational therapy, though they could not teach me much as I was able to cook. Most occupational therapy never quite hit the mark, though, and made me wonder why I was attending. It was an attitude I could not shake off.

By comparison, physiotherapy was something that I still found very beneficial and was thankful when I was given it every day, often for an hour, with Theresa Heyward, my new therapist, confidently taking the helm. She was aided and abetted by Sarah Ward, a junior physiotherapist; Cath Badler, a physiotherapy helper; and a student, on various occasions when she was not available. When she was she took me through many activities, though she mainly gave me exercises on the ball, the plinth or the mat, as well as a lot of walking practice.

Thursday was a really fun day as I was told to walk down the centre of the gym while Sarah threw a ball to me from one side. After catching it, I had to throw it to the student on the other side, while continuing to walk. I was surprisingly good at this, even though my balance was not superb and my eyes were still a bit dodgy. It was not until a few weeks later I was to discover that I thought I was trying to catch two balls and I never knew which was the real one. Whether it was through complete guesswork, pure luck or a peculiar instinct, I usually caught the ball.

Another avenue of fun was the hospital newsletter. This was a short newspaper produced by the patients for the patients. The contents always followed a particular theme and contained photographs and short articles from us 'budding reporters', along with some jokes, competitions and the odd recipe. Included every week was a list of the patients and in which bay they resided, as well as the duty roster of nurses, not to mention an interesting and striking front cover. It has to be said that I loved writing the occasional article, but my forte was soon to become one of compiling the nurses' roster on the spreadsheet. It was not the easiest part of the newsletter, and most people rejected the task. However, I had the correct mentality to bend my brain around the computations, and I took a certain amount of pride in typing the roster. As the resident expert in computers, Matt was always there, as was Carol, keeping an eye on us and making several helpful suggestions.

We met twice a week. On Mondays we planned what we were going to print, decided who was going to do what, and made a start on the typing. On Thursdays we made sure everything was correct and that the artwork was completed. One particular week's theme was all about America and was the first newsletter that I worked on, even though it was my fourth week in the RRU. Since I had relatives who live in America, I volunteered to write an article. On Thursday, having completed my article, I stayed on after the meeting had finished to help compose the end product. I had an ulterior motive for staying on: I was annoying Carol!

A Winter's Tale

I have travelled to many areas in the United States, mainly the west and east coasts, to visit relatives. One of the areas I visited was the Pacific Northwest – the states of Washington and Oregon. It is called, by the locals, the Pacific North-Wet, on account of it always raining there.

One particular day Mum and I were travelling, with her relatives, in Oregon to get to a certain mountain village. We were going up a mountain pass when suddenly we were stopped by the police and told to turn back as the road was impassable. My mother's aunt said, 'Wrong time of year, carry on going.'

To cut a long story short, we should have listened to the police. Going up the pass was all right, but going down we encountered a blizzard, among other things. The moral of the story is: 'Listen to people who know more than you do'.

RRU Newsletter No. 45, 'America' Issue
31 March 1995

This week also presented me with a healthy mixture of good and bad news, starting with an appointment down at the local branch of Moorfields Eye Hospital, where they were finally going to treat my eyes. I was taken down by a porter who had no idea where he was going. He wandered one way across the ground floor of the hospital, then the other. As he came back, he came across a lift. He was just about to try it when he had an intense feeling that it was the wrong way. By now completely lost, he asked a lady at reception, who directed him out of the hospital. By the entrance, totally separate from the main hospital, he found Moorfields.

On arrival at the eye clinic, I was asked to wait, while the porter returned to the hospital. Having been asked to wait at the ENT clinic a few weeks previously, I was getting used to this hospital inefficiency – and boy, were they inefficient! I arrived at 1.30 to have a half-hour appointment, expecting to wait a short while. Although seen for a total of half an hour, I had to see three different people, with a wait before and after each one – a wait that lasted three hours.

Quite what they achieved is beyond me, though I was told to come back on the Friday (1 April) to be fitted out with a pair of glasses, but I was never told why I needed the glasses. None of the ophthalmologists looked as though they were about to cry 'Eureka!' as they investigated my problems. I had half a mind to accept this as an April fool's joke and forget it ever happened. After all, their examination was fairly simple. Mostly they asked me to read off standard eye charts. This no doubt showed them what problems I was having, though they would not tell me. One of the only things they did let me know was that there was a small amount of tension, since my eyes were weaker than would be expected for someone of my age. It does not take an expert to figure out this fairly obvious fact, especially for someone with a degree – in zoology of all things – and it doesn't say an awful lot. The information was sadly lacking.

As my wait at the eye clinic continued, time in the outside world flowed passed far too fast and my physiotherapy appointment, made for 2.30, long after my expected return, crept up on me, and then ran past at quite a speed. To make matters worse, at the end of my appointment, no one arrived to take me back to the unit. Deciding not to wait for a porter, knowing how long they take, I wheeled myself back to the RRU. I arrived back before Theresa went home at the end of her day, but only just.

As the week ended, my run of good news was to come to an end: Friday lunchtime came as normal for most people, but mine came without any food. Naturally I complained, passing a simple comment about being hungry. I cannot fully blame the hospital; my family forgot to serve me during a dinner party once, but I would have expected a hospital to be slightly better organised! Listening to my simple plea, the nurses phoned downstairs and ordered me some sandwiches. After a few moments, a health care assistant appeared with two sandwiches on offer, one of which I was supposed to choose. However, they both sounded tasty and I was very hungry. A few quiet words were exchanged between us, and both sandwiches were kindly left for me. Once more the bad luck that seemed to hang around me was turned to my advantage.

After this paltry Friday lunch was demolished (in no time at all), I went around to see if anybody wanted anything down at the shops. Finding no one, I was just leaving the last bay when I heard someone say my name. Naturally, I listened in and heard that I was wanted down at the eye hospital. On hearing this, I turned the wheelchair around and went on my way. I was by the doors anyway and it seemed silly to wheel myself halfway up the ward just to get an escort. However, as I came out on the fourth floor, Kelly, one of the health care assistants, rushed out of the staff lift calling my name, since I had left my file behind. Head injury or not, I had realised this, and did not think they would need to see it. They had seen it two days before and I knew they would remember me... we did not need the file.

As she was there now, Kelly was kind enough to push me around, and when I picked the pair of glasses I preferred she agreed with my choice, saying they really suited me. Having picked them, my prescription was filled out and the glasses were ordered. They said they would phone the RRU when they arrived; it would take about a week. According to the dispensing optician, I could probably wear them when I wanted, but he recommended I wear them when things became blurred, basically I could please myself.

A Case for Dismissal

Pinch, punch, first of the month, I thought to myself, as I scanned the empty ward for someone to apply this ancient tradition. A couple of nurses were hidden somewhere, but with only eight patients left for the weekend, they could be ensconced anywhere. Somewhat depressed at not seeing anyone, I washed and dressed, then ate my breakfast when it arrived. Although I was taken out after lunch, I spent most of the morning in the computer room and, in fact, had to be 'dragged away' when lunch arrived.

Soon after this midday meal, two agency nurses came along, pushing Melvyn Plumb and George Vella in their wheelchairs. They were just about to go outside when one of the nurses, Sam, invited me to go as well. She and the other nurse pushed a wheelchair each and I propelled myself. After forming an orderly line we headed to the main doors, when we were hailed by another patient, Norman Bembrick, who asked if he could join us. He was also intending to wheel himself so was welcomed aboard and we made our way to the lifts.

From there we went down to level four and along to the opposite end of the corridor near the main entrance where two other lifts were hidden. From there, we descended to level two to go for a spin outside past the social club and the nurses' homes. Though Norman and I wheeled ourselves we needed help down some of the trickier bits. We stopped on a sunny spot and most people turned their wheelchairs around so they faced into the sun. I declined this simple pleasure since I hated sunshine in those days.

We had a good natter and one of the nurses gave me (because I was closest?) a daisy chain she had been making. It being quite late in the day, by the time we had made our way back to the unit, we settled down to our supper and waited for any visitors. I waited patiently, but having had no visitors by 7.30 I assumed no one was coming. My parents were away for the weekend, and most of the other people I knew had probably unknowingly assumed that I had gone home for the weekend, as per normal.

Like the day before, Sunday brought Melvyn past my bay, pushed by a different agency nurse. Melvyn asked if I wanted to come to the social club, my affirmative response was accompanied with a good deal of persuasion trying to convince the nurse that I could cope on my own and did not need someone to push me.

Once outside, taking a different route to the day before, we travelled along a pavement running alongside the hospital. Unfortunately, it sloped to the side in the same direction as the rest of the hospital, and I started to slide with it. I did not go far and was not in a position to hurt myself, but it did convince all concerned that this was a bad idea. Leaving Melvyn for a moment, the nurse came to help me, telling him to apply the brakes of the wheelchair as she left him. For some reason, he failed to do this and nosedived off the pavement onto the road! The poor nurse was having kittens, but I thought she coped very well. Thankfully, no harm was done; Melvyn was fine, but quite rightly, was given a good ticking off.

The walk over (not a great surprise under the circumstances), we made our way back to the lifts. The lifts were up one hill too many and I was getting tired wheeling myself around. Whether I should or not – *not!* – I got out and walked, pushing the wheelchair back towards the lifts. I knew I was OK since I was using the weight of the wheelchair for my own stability. Once we had made it back to the lifts and I had got back in the wheelchair, we made our way up to level six and back to the unit, just in time for lunch – perfect timing.

My good friend from Willowtree, Vicki Blake came to see me after lunch, brought by her mum. Out of kindness, and because it was nearly Easter, she brought me an Easter egg and some mini-eggs. At the time I still liked chocolate and it was really kind of her to bring me some. It just went to show the friendship that we had, and demonstrates what an idiot I was going to be five months later.

> 'I don't remember much of the healing process, but every time I went to visit Philip he was better and still improving. In a record amount of time he was on his feet and walking again. He had incredible amounts of physio and occupational

therapy, more than I could stand, but he was improving, which made me feel happy that soon he could see his beloved Shannon at the stables and get involved again. It was still impossible at that time to believe that someone so used to the outdoors way of life could be reduced to almost a baby, learning for the first time what life is all about.

'Once released from hospital, he would often phone to tell me that he could finally run round the field behind his house and that at long last he could scream again without hurting his throat! All of this was improving him, but to me he did not really become a member of the Life Club again until he started riding and being around horses. Needless to say, he was soon visiting Willowtree again and becoming more himself. This process was a joy to watch as someone, once immobile, became active again. It really is amazing what the heart and body can survive and pull through all right.'

Vicki Blake, friend

Nobody else came in to see me so I decided to go down to the computer room to type some more of my journal. I first looked at my watch at about ten o'clock at night. Once I had finished my day's journal and played my one hand of patience on the computer, it was just before one o'clock in the morning! This second viewing of my watch prompted my immediate withdrawal towards my bay and the sanctuary of my bed.

The night drifted by peacefully and by the afternoon of Monday, 3 April I was to be confronted by my impending case conference. Because of this, I was up early and thought I would dash into the shower. While this impatient thought floated around my mind, Stanley Lyon, a roommate, took the initiative and beat me into the bathroom. I waited for Stan to finish in the bathroom before I cleaned my teeth and shaved, not thinking of using the sink in the room.

After a short occupational therapy meeting, and before my lunch, I had speech therapy with Rachel. This was memorable in that it was Debbie's last day, so I had a big thank you for her as she made her goodbyes. Once she had left, Rachel and I got down to some speech therapy, in which she concentrated on a lot of breathing exercises, along with the accompanying giggles that were emanating from my direction. I was forever being apologetic for my irrational giggling though my mind often returned to what

Kate told me at the Lister and I realised that it is better to laugh than cry.

Later came a very welcome lunch followed by a nurse who came round with a letter for me that had recently arrived. I read this letter, from my aunt, Laura, and decided to return to the computer room to write a reply straight away. I was halfway through the letter when Mother arrived. As my parents were both coming in to attend my case conference, they thought they would arrive early, since Theresa was due to give me an extra physiotherapy session first. Unfortunately she was unable to see me for physiotherapy and I found myself apologising for her. As my rhetoric came to a close, Dad arrived, followed by Theresa, who apologised herself. This lack of a therapist did not deter my parents, and I was dragged down to the gym where I could show them my exercises; it would also give my trigger-happy mother another opportunity of taking some photographs of me. This 'photo shoot' seemed to take an eternity, but it was probably nearer half an hour and ended promptly with the beginning of the conference.

The 'case conference' is held by the RRU so that they can let the relatives of patients know how well they consider the patient to be doing, and provides the relatives with the opportunity to ask any questions they may have. I wheeled myself to my case conference, which was attended by my parents, Theresa, Samantha, Barbara, Rachel and the consultant. Once there I transferred myself to a normal chair, since I was not going to give in to my temporary position and remain in the wheelchair if it could be avoided.

It was interesting to hear everyone else's opinions on how well I was progressing and wonderful to hear them say that I was doing better than they had expected. I looked so good that they informed us of the date they had in mind for my discharge – earlier than was normal. People are allowed to stay in the rehabilitation unit for a maximum of six months, and the therapists anticipate having made some headway by then, though each patient is expected to require most of those six months to recuperate. My discharge was to be at the start of May – two months after my transferral. This was a very welcome boost to my ego and was very gratifying. By the end, Mum and Dad were in a better position to understand what was going on and all their questions had been answered.

Physiotherapy on Tuesday, 4 April was one of the most enjoyable I have had, ever. Everything was designed to get me walking. I started work on the ball, moving up to walking my hips over the plinth while seated. Theresa then made me walk sideways with the trailing foot alternating its placement in front and then behind the leading foot. I was also asked to walk properly, both forwards and backwards, while Theresa made constant adjustments to my (still) poking chin and general posture. She was so impressed that she asked what I thought about walking on the ward. My positive answer was followed by Theresa letting me out onto the ward, where I was asked to walk up to one end, turn round and walk back again, while she kept a close eye on me. On my return she offered me the opportunity of discarding the wheelchair and walking around the ward. After nearly seventeen weeks I was finally allowed to walk by myself, although I was told I still needed the wheelchair if going on any long walks; the first thing to go when tiredness sets in is the posture. I doubt I promised that I would do this, as I do not break promises!

> 'I looked forward to the visits to hear Phil's positive reactions to his progress; his commitment to, and enthusiasm for, his physiotherapy sessions. One of the most thrilling memories was of David returning from Northwick Park with the news that Phil had proudly displayed his ability to walk four very determined, but hesitant, steps to the wardrobe. The following day I was witness to this remarkable achievement – I cried again.'

> Cynthia Matthews, family friend

Later that afternoon, Simon came for a visit. Wanting to show off, I walked with him down to the shops. He panicked constantly because I was not in the wheelchair, leading me to the conclusion that he revelled in the pleasures associated with pushing it! I can't see them myself. We arrived back upstairs just in time for supper, followed shortly by Mother – clearly displaying her old habit of arriving with the food – so Simon could take her home, leaving me happily eating on my own. After supper, my evening ended in the standard way where I did my exercises in the gym and had a quick forty winks in front of the computer before finally dragging myself back to my bay.

Wednesday's highlight, surprisingly, was occupational therapy just before my lunch. In fact, occupational therapy *was* my lunch. I was taken to the kitchen, given some food and told to cook. I was in my element in front of the cooker and loved every minute of it, having returned to a pastime I adore. Although I would not say that the hospital food was bad, it was really pleasant eating something 'home-made'. When I fried the bacon it spat at me; you have no idea how comforting a fat-burn can feel!

After I'd eaten my lunch, and done the washing-up, Simon dropped in to see me. He became addicted to one of the computer games and I was just beginning to wonder what to do on my own when Lara arrived. It was wonderful seeing her; I always enjoyed it. We had an interesting chat before I had my supper, which appeared soon after her arrival. Believe it or not, Mother then arrived, seemingly following the scent rising off the plate. Even so, I was thankful she was there, as it gave me the opportunity to eat my supper while Simon and Lara chatted with her. Mum and Simon left shortly after I had finished eating, but I continued to chat to Lara until she too had to depart.

Getting dressed that morning had been fairly easy, but by Thursday, 6 April I decided there was no real reason why I should not do activities in the same way I used to before my accident. I was not about to give in to the difficulties that now faced me, and firmly believed that the only way I could get better at doing something was to practise – a fact that various therapists had been subconsciously drumming into me for several weeks. In short, I tried to put on my trousers while I was standing. Although I realised that I did not need to do this, and there was a good chance of me falling over and hurting myself, I could see no valid reason why I should not be able to perform this feat. I would probably never need to perform this act in the future, but there was no excuse not to be able to do it. The point was not whether I needed to do it, but whether I was able to do it if I needed. My balance was still diabolical, but I knew it wouldn't get better by sitting down watching the world pass me by. Besides, somehow I knew I wouldn't fall over.

Although these acrobatics took a great deal of courage and an indifference towards my safety, I did very well. At least I now knew I could put on my trousers standing up if I had to. Stan was very impressed with what I was doing and agreed with me that everyone needs a goal to aim for, to stretch them that little bit further and give them a reason for trying. I am not suggesting hospital should be treated as a contest, but only by setting yourself small targets are you going to improve; the target can be anything, as long as you can achieve it. During our conversation, Stan confided in me, telling me about his target when he first came onto the RRU. We were talking about the bathroom and, stating that it was far more natural for a man, he said that the first act he wanted to accomplish was stand up to have a pee. I can remember my first time, and can admit to it being a wonderful feeling!

Later, all the contributors to the newsletter convened. Before we started our deliberation we were all introduced to a new member of staff. Anna Janes was a very pretty psychology student with a beautiful mane of hair and a smile that... well, you'll find out later. Anna was involved with anything that stretched the minds of the patients: she would come into the newsletter group, and introduce such things as the art class. After greeting Anna, I settled down to type the nurses' roster. Wanting to make it right, I stayed a little bit later, in fact long after everyone else had disappeared. Anna and I had a joke about this, during which she dubbed me (not altogether incorrectly) a perfectionist.

She and I would often joke about things like this. I liked Anna a lot and found it very easy to talk to her; I like to think we got on very well. As the weeks progressed and I saw more of her, and we found out a lot about each other, we discovered that we had a great deal in common. I enjoyed chatting to Anna, as our minds were alike; if there was something I hadn't thought of, chances are she would.

> 'I think I "met" Philip in the computer room; he was busy – as usual – tapping away at his journal. I can't remember why, how or what about, but (inevitably) we got talking. (I say inevitably, as two people with such a penchant for chat could hardly avoid it!)
>
> 'Although I wasn't directly involved with Philip's therapy, as such, our paths often crossed. He made a pretty valuable

contribution to the newsletter (sterling work on the nurses' roster – a pretty hefty task on the computer spreadsheet package). He was a top "ideas" man, someone with a bank of anecdotes to share with the group and stimulate discussion.

'I think Philip and I struck a chord, so to speak, for whatever reason, and as a result would often chat, about all sorts of things. One thing that came through very strongly about Philip was a downright grit and determination to progress, to overcome challenge and achieve.

'Since the accident, things on every level of Philip's life – physical, emotional and working – have been somewhat knocked for six. However, Philip has built on the changes, and one feels that he doesn't mourn for the loss of things past, so much as look forward to facing the challenges of the future. His "blazing defiance" since surviving a near fatal accident has driven him on in the face of adversity.

'Philip is a very brave guy, whose "stand-up-and-fight!" attitude should be an inspiration to us all.'

Anna Janes, psychologist

Having nothing much planned for the end of the week, I spent Friday morning packing so that Simon and I could depart quickly later in the afternoon. After packing, I retired to the computer room to continue with my journal and await my brother. I had not even been there an hour when I remembered I had been told my glasses would be ready by Friday, even though no one had phoned the unit. I went to inform the nurses and they phoned down for me to be told the glasses were there. I was asked if I wanted a nurse to pick them up for me, but since I had nothing to do, and I was allowed, I went to pick them up myself. As the members of staff were always asking me to go to the shops for them, I assumed I would receive the authorisation. I am not sure whether I was allowed to pick up my glasses or not – I just left; I never waited for permission. It was a potentially dangerous presumption and is not to be recommended. Typically, Simon arrived while I was out, but fortunately we bumped into each other as I returned to the unit. We exchanged our hellos and were soon on our way back home.

We spent the weekend with Cynthia and David, who live a little to the north of my parents near Buntingford. We also met up with some mutual friends, Peter and Jenny Hume, whom I could not remember seeing for many months. On the Saturday, as was very normal for us; we took a long walk, ending up in a pub.

David gave me a lift in the car, it being far too far for me to walk at this early stage in my recovery, and we arrived at the pub before anyone else. In fact, we were so early that we started walking back the way they would come to see if they had got lost. After five minutes we met up with Peter and Dad, and were assured the ladies were following at a slightly more leisurely pace. Feeling confident of their impending arrival, we returned to the pub to get the drinks in – or at least have one ourselves while we waited!

That evening, after supper, I showed everyone the photographs Mother had taken so far and the few weeks of my journal that I had already written. As the journal was passed around the table the laughter grew louder. It was the overall consensus by the end that 'you should get that turned into a book'. The rest, as they say, is history.

Sunday began with collecting Alison, Peter and Jenny's younger daughter, who had seen me at the Lister with Sarah, her older sister. Later, we all took an unusual walk (i.e. not to a pub!) along the mud track running adjacent to the house. It was lumpy, bumpy and wet, and I was having a bit of difficulty; no flat hospital floors there! While everyone else rushed off ahead, David kindly stayed behind to keep an eye on me. There were some very wet areas and there was a tendency for me to slip in the mud, while several other stretches had to be negotiated very slowly as my legs kept getting tangled around the brambles. Thankfully, I never fell over once, but I was exhausted. It was then that I knew what Theresa meant when she said that the posture is the first thing to disappear when tiredness sets in… but I was damned if I was going to be carried.

All in all, this had been a typical weekend, when we drank too much, ate too much and did a lot of walking. For once I was glad to return to hospital where I could have a well-deserved rest. That evening's return to hospital was doubly pleasant since I arrived before supper, and I was starving – none of my family had wanted any supper after our return from Buntingford. Conversely, returning back on Sunday evening also brought a slight complication, not helped by Mother rushing off as soon as she dropped me since she had forgotten the parking permit and did not wish to pay. I went back to my bay as usual and was just starting to unpack when an agency nurse came round to tell me that I had moved bays again. Most of my possessions had been moved throughout the day and the nurse helped me move everything else and settle in.

When I had finished unpacking and eaten, I went down to the gym to do my exercises and, as I preferred the dark, did not put the lights on. Unfortunately this simple lapse from normality made the nurses frantic, since they could not see where I had gone. One of the night nurses was sent out to find me and make sure I had not dropped off the face of the earth! After several minutes she found me, and was very relieved to do so. Knowing where I was, the nurses were much happier, so I finished off my exercises. When done, I ensconced myself in the computer room once again to type some more pages of my journal. Eventually, long after the nurses had given up any hope of getting me to have an early night, I went to bed.

Two's Company

My new location, Bay D, was a two-bed bay designed to be the link between living in hospital and living at home. Sharing with me was Melvyn Plumb, whom I had met on various occasions flitting around the outside of the hospital. Tucked in at the top of the unit, Bay D was pretty much out of the way, and these two beds were certainly the furthest away from the nurses' station, located in the middle of the unit. We may even have been viewed as being 'out of sight, out of mind'; after all, patients in these beds were supposed to do as much as possible for themselves anyway. This was no problem for me, as I was attending to many matters myself already, though some were still beyond me.

Monday morning, 10 April, brought a short, sharp shock in the form of the shower. It either came out piping hot or very slowly, something I was not able to fix, in my condition, although I did have the sense to tell the nurses later that morning. After I had finished a pathetic shower and was dry, Cath came over and wheeled me down to the hydrotherapy pool, it being deemed too far for me to walk. Getting into the pool with Theresa, I was made to lie on my back with a float placed behind my head. I had to attempt trying to keep the same posture I had when standing up, whist I was lying down and 'floating' in the water. Theresa stood behind me, supporting me when necessary, and instructed me to swing my legs from side to side, moving one over, then under, the other while the water supported my weight – not as easy as it sounds. As well as the float under my head I had one around my middle, and Cath stayed there for any emergencies. Even so, both she and Theresa agreed that I had done very well. After this paddle, I returned to the changing room and had my second shower, hoping to remove most of the chlorine. By my second hydrotherapy session I took my shampoo with me, as I discontinued my first shower!

My return to the bay was followed by that week's newsletter, all about Easter. Although not complaining, I was volunteered for the nurses' roster. In this issue I also said that I would write an article all about the pagan meaning behind Easter. Having rather strong feelings for the subject, I stayed in the computer room to finish writing it.

What is Easter?

Easter is a fundamental Christian festival. Good Friday, by tradition, is when Jesus Christ was crucified, and Easter Sunday is when he rose from the dead. There are lots of tales in the Bible from this time, one of which is that an Angel rolled the boulder which blocked Jesus' tomb out of the way. This area, where Jesus was buried, suffers from many earthquakes and even a small one could have dislodged the boulder. And what about when we went from a Julian to a Gregorian calendar? The losing of eleven days would totally mess up the meanings of the particular days.

Like most Christian festivals, Easter is borrowed from many other religions. Easter, according to the pagans (who have been here far longer than the Christians) was governed by the full moon (Easter Sunday is the first full moon after a certain day in Lent – or some such), and can vary by about a month. It is different year to year (ring a bell?).

It is a lovely festival and all the good for it. However, it should not be taken as an exclusively Christian festival, and there should be no more emphasis made on it than is necessary.

RRU Newsletter No. 47, Easter Issue,
4 April 1995

Tuesday brought the voice therapy specialist up from the ENT clinic to see me during speech therapy. Using her trained ear, she was able to give both Rachel and Barbara some tips on how to proceed with my therapy, though she thought I sounded very good, all things considered. What was even nicer was that while she was there I did not giggle once! She soon left with Barbara, leaving Rachel to continue the speech therapy for the remainder of the hour. It went very well, compared to normal, and she ended the session by giving me some exercise sheets with questions on them to help stimulate my mind as well as improve my speech.

Wednesday brought more hydrotherapy, and we did a similar routine to the one we did on Monday. It also brought occupational therapy with Samantha, who led me to the laundry room to see if I could use the washing machine, not realising I had used one at home several times by that stage. When questioned, and knowing I could use it, I suppose I was fairly flippant with her, 'Let me guess, you open the door, put the clothes in the hole and shut it. You then pour powder into the drawer at the top, closing it after you, then turn it on. After waiting until it has finished, you open the door and take the clothes out.'

She could do nothing but agree with me; I had unkindly backed her into an intellectual corner of my own devising. It was all very well me knowing what to do, and obviously I wanted to show her that, but thinking back, did I need to be quite so patronising?

I then returned to my bay and collected some chocolates for the staff. Mother had been super-efficient this time at buying them as I still had one month to go. I gave Samantha a box of chocolates to share among the therapists, and one other, handed in at the nurses' station, for the rest of the staff. Theresa then came to see me, thanking me for the chocolates and telling me that a couple of dates had been organised for me to go horse riding. The first one was to be on 2 May – something to look forward to.

With nothing left on my timetable for Wednesday, I went down to the gym to quietly do my exercises. I was putting my shoes on at the end of my routine when Karen arrived. She had arrived a few moments earlier and walked into my bay full of confidence... only to find I was not there. Fearing I had moved bays again, she asked the nurses where I might be and was told to try the gym; for once they had correctly guessed my location. Karen dragged me, willingly, down to the restaurant where she treated me to a jam doughnut, some orange juice and very good conversation.

Both Rachel and Barbara helped me during speech therapy on Thursday morning. Rachel started by going over the exercises she had given me a few days before. She then made me speak some sentences, stressing different parts and varying the intonation to make it sound like a statement or a question. While she did this, Barbara massaged the front of my neck so that she could feel the movement of my larynx as I talked. She also hoped to loosen its deathly grip on the top of my trachea in an effort to make me more relaxed when I talked and to make my vocalisation more natural. I was in a strange position in which I had speech therapists massage the front of my neck and physiotherapists massage the back of my neck, all of them attempting to relax my tight, sinuous muscles and tendons as they tried to improve my voice or head carriage. At the time I considered myself very fortunate in that they did not both perform this massage at the same time!

By the afternoon, Thursday became very enjoyable. Sometimes sharing with Melvyn proved very useful; he did not feel like eating his lunch. I can't let good food go to waste and it was roast lamb, which I adore, so I asked him if he wanted it, and if not, could I have it? He said I was welcome to it. Later that afternoon, once my food had started to be digested, came the expanded newsletter; we were combining that week's and the week afters', as Easter lay in the middle. Having checked my 'Pagan' article for spelling and accuracy, I double-checked the nurses' roster. Once the newsletter group had been disbanded, I remained in the computer room with the aim of typing some more of my journal, though I mostly chatted to Anna, finding her warm and pleasant company preferable to that of the cold, synthetic computer.

Half past four brought Simon, who came to pick me up for my long weekend home. It would be fantastic to leave the hospital for four days. At least Simon, who once wanted to train as a physiotherapist, would be there to shout at me and make sure I did all my exercises properly. I no doubt shocked him when he arrived – I was ready to go! Leaving shortly afterwards, we went home to chase bunnies and crack eggs.

Good Friday, 14 April, started with a fairly lazy morning. However, by the afternoon Rosalind Gill, an old friend from my school days, came round to see me with her parents. We provided tea/coffee and cake for them, and I dug out some of my home-made lemonade, created that morning. We chatted about old times, about Rosie's new job, my accident, and how well they thought I was doing. It was good for me to hear that the rest of the world was getting on with life, and good of them to say that they had not noticed any major difference in me from before my accident. They even said that my atrocious voice wasn't that bad! Mind you, nobody, not even me, can remember what I used to sound like before my accident. I found this sort of kindness in people very rewarding.

After our tea break we took them on a little tour of the grounds of the manor house next to my parents' humble abode, the walking being good for me anyway. It was really pleasant to see Rosalind as it had been a couple of years since we last met, and at least five from last seeing her parents.

'I received a letter from Philip's mother in the New Year of 1995. There weren't that many details given but it was enough to knock something out of me. I don't think my imagination could actually cope with the full horror of it and therefore did not flash terrifying images before my mind's eye, but what I read then and heard in telephone conversations with both Philip and his mother confirmed that this had been a most horrific experience for everyone concerned.

'I finally managed to see Philip in the spring, around the Easter period. By this time he was walking around albeit rather stiffly. Given the context of his accident, the fact that he was on his feet at all was a miracle. Philip told me that initially the consultant had said he wouldn't be able to walk again – but he defied them and had worked to get himself mobile – the result was plain to see.

'This terrible accident has brought out all the best qualities in Philip, his determination, his desire to live life to the full once again.

Rosalind Gill, friend

After we had said our goodbyes and a couple of photographs had been taken, they returned home to Radlett and I awaited my next visitor, having quickly arranged the trip before lunch. Towards the end of the day, Sam Selvadurai came for a short visit. Sam was someone I had known from secondary school. We met up, aged eleven, at The King's School in Chester. I remained there to complete my O levels while Sam disappeared after only one term. A long while later, following a job move by my father, I left to take my A levels at St Albans School. Strangely, it was the school that Sam had entered! It was also there that I met Rosalind, who went to St Albans High School. Often our two schools would meet up so as to partake in joint projects, like current affairs or drama. I am not sure quite where we met, but as Rosalind and I got to know each other better we used to meet up for lunch, nearly every day.

Having not seen much of Sam since we left school in 1989, with me to go to university and Sam to take a year off visiting Moscow before going to university, it was great to see him, and we chatted for quite a while; not on anything important, mind, just the ramblings that old friends have when a long spell exists between meetings.

Easter Sunday dawned early for me, and the whole world was quiet (or at least my little corner was). Later, I made a few phone calls – to Vicki, Leigh and Becky. The trouble was that I still did not have full control of my fingers. No matter how hard I tried, I could not punch in the correct number, and my father had to dial for me. Nevertheless, it was delightful to hear from them all again, and visa versa, I'm sure. Most important of all was a phone call I made to Melissa Price, as it had been her birthday in the middle of March and I had simply forgotten. To some people this wouldn't be a big surprise, but to me it was a shock, accident or not. Consequently I had to wish her happy birthday. She was very glad I'd phoned and very pleased I'd thought of her, even though it was belated – at least it showed her I cared. She hoped that it would not be long until she saw me again.

By Tuesday, 18 April, Easter seemed a long way behind us, even though I had only just returned to hospital the night before. Melvyn, however, did not return, as would have been expected, further baffling me by not turning up on Tuesday morning either. This enabled me to have my breakfast in peace, followed by Samantha accompanying me down to the bus stop. Even though she knew, she told me, for the sake of therapy, to ask the first bus driver I saw which bus went to the supermarket.

Having completed this arduous task, we boarded the correct bus and I was then asked to pay for the bus tickets with hospital money. We then drifted through the centre of Harrow until the bus reached its destination: a bus stop next to the supermarket.

We spent a few minutes wandering around the store collecting various items from the hospital list she had brought with her before I had to go and pay for them at the till. Completing this really difficult session we returned to the RRU, where I went straight to the computer room to write up some more of my journal, having nothing else to do until lunch arrived.

After lunch, Jane White came along, providing me with the opportunity to talk with someone, if only to thank her for more jelly babies. It was great to see her and we chatted for hours, something we have no difficulty in doing. Usually it involved me, unknowingly, impersonating her Liverpool accent. She stayed talking as I ate my supper, but left shortly afterwards, it being a long way back to South-east London on public transport.

After Jane's departure, I was happily abducted by Anna, since she thought that I was part of the Art Club. I was not and I do not particularly like painting, but I went along with her anyway. I sometimes think I will do anything for a woman with a pretty smile, but that is another story. Joining her in the day room, I did a rather morbid painting of an imaginary landscape being attacked by a horrendous thunderstorm and several missiles. Mushroom clouds were forming, showing them to be nuclear. It was not very good... not that it needed to be.

Towards the end of the week, as I was whiling away the hours in the computer room, Samantha grabbed me to go and do some cooking for my lunch. I had known, it was down on my time-table, but I had let the minutes slip by once again. I boiled some spaghetti, fried some bacon and, adding a slosh of milk and some cheese and cracking an egg into the mixture, I turned the concoction into my version of *spaghetti alla carbonara*. The plate was pilled high with food, but I did not mind, it was wonderful.

Returning back to my bay, I was soon confronted with Samantha's suggestion of cancelling the hospital lunch on days I was cooking, as the hospital food was brought to me as well. Silly me had forgotten. Unfortunately, it was roast lamb and, naturally, I felt obliged to eat my helping as well; better in the human dustbin that is my stomach than the bins out the back of the hospital!

After this scrumptious extended lunch, I went around and

asked everyone if they wanted anything from the shops. I had to go anyway because a future roommate, Kelvin Connett, wanted some batteries, and no doubt Elaine would like her regular *Evening Standard*. Chris and I had been visiting the shops for the unit staff ever since his arrival during the previous month. The occupational therapists had anticipated this simple, but valuable, effort on our parts to finish after Chris went home at the end of this week. In our time together, though, I had noticed how much people appreciated someone going down to the shops for them; it was often one less detail for them to worry about. Though not on my timetable after Chris's departure, and having no need to keep it up, I decided to continue going down to the shops anyway as it helped the people who were helping us. Besides, the walking would do me good, and it might work off some of the extra weight if I ate any more large lunches! Although Chris had not yet left, his departure was imminent, so I decided to go down to the shops alone, for practice.

Unfortunately, unlike the previous two days, everyone I asked wanted shopping – and of course I timed it too late, so the afternoon shift was coming on before the morning nurses had left. I found myself buying goods for everybody, and with no Chris to help me! I returned to the RRU with five minutes to spare before speech therapy, and I remembered to buy everything – everything, that is, except Kelvin's batteries! At least it left me a job to carry out on the next day, Chris's last.

Although I had bought most of the items that people wanted, as speech therapy was imminent I did not have much time to give out the goodies. Those people I saw as I walked from one end of the unit to the other received their goods; the hunting around for everyone else had to be left until later. At least some people were able to have their goods early, though I had no time to sort out the change and they all had to wait for that. It did not take me long, though; Rachel was delayed at the start of therapy, giving me enough time to calculate who got how much change. She came along soon enough and we went through the questions/statements exercise that I did on the previous night, and I practised reading some more sentences using the correct intonation and stress.

Later I had physiotherapy with Elaine once again since Theresa had now gone on holiday. Unfortunately, she needed five minutes first before she could see me. Using this time to my advantage, I went and dished out all the shopping and gave out the change. I knew Elaine would not mind if I was a little delayed, since I had bought her her paper.

When I arrived at physiotherapy proper, Elaine checked out how I was moving my arms and shoulders in all the positions I tended to find myself in and then looked at my walking. As I was walking she kept calling me and I had to look at her over my shoulder. I started by turning my shoulders, practically facing her, but she told me that was wrong; I was just meant to turn my head. I was feeling so plucky I even took a few paces as I turned my head over my shoulders – until she told me to stop walking when I looked back. I was glad of this, because walking while looking backwards, and not falling over, was one manoeuvre too many! Besides, it took a while for my eyes to refocus when looking backwards, leaving me with a few moments of disorientation; a feeling best coped with standing still rather than walking. All said and done though, Elaine was very impressed, especially when you consider that when she last saw me I was still in a wheelchair.

By late afternoon on Thursday, we had our regular meeting for the newsletter. In this unusual week, though, we did not have our earlier meeting due to Easter Monday. We were thrown into turmoil, as we had not discussed anything. Undeterred, we used this Thursday meeting as a discussion; printing would not be done until the following Thursday. It didn't matter too much, as this week's events had been included in the Easter edition of the previous week.

We decided to do a newsletter about animal conservation. It is a subject that touches my heart and I said I would write an article about elephants, my favourite animal. As I had a week to write it, and as I am always at my best when a few days have been spent rolling some thoughts around my brain, I got on with doing my (by this stage) normal function: the dreaded nurses' roster. Chris's normal function was to draw the newsletter front cover. Though his last day – Friday, 21 April – was approaching far faster than I had anticipated, he fortunately found time to complete this small task before he left. Unfortunately, his move did leave me doing the dubious excitements of shopping for the staff all by myself. If I wanted, I could refuse; after all, I was not expected to go, but I think some of the people at the hospital were getting somewhat reliant upon me.

On that Friday morning, with Easter a week behind us, I spent five minutes persuading myself to get out of bed, and this slight delay was my undoing. Both Melvyn and I wanted a shower that morning, and since our shower had not seen the repairman for some time, that only left the main hospital shower for us to fight over. As Melvyn had beaten me in getting up, I was polite and let him go first. I thought about getting scalded in our shower, but soon discounted the idea!

Melvyn drove his electric wheelchair down to the nurses' station, where he waited for someone to help him with the shower. Later I heard him complain that he had been waiting for an hour and no one was helping him. I was concerned that time dilation was affecting my corner of the universe, since I had only been waiting half an hour, but then we all know about my concept of time! During my half-hour wait I had cleaned my teeth and shaved, eaten some food and had had a long drink of water, my thirst being highly noticeable that morning, before settling down to some daydreaming.

After what seemed like hours I took a quick look outside the bay to see where Melvyn was. To my utter disbelief he was in the same place as he had been half an hour before – still in his wheelchair by the nurses' station, waiting for help to arrive. If only I had known, even I could have had a shower in less than half an hour... well, probably. A long while later, Melvyn had finished in the shower and I was able to go down and partake in some aquatic delights before lunch.

As the nurses brought the food, I joked with them saying that I would only have one lunch. Unfortunately, Melvyn was in a funny mood. He had recently opened a carton of Ribena, which seemed to have mysteriously disappeared as his food arrived. He had a jolly good moan about the inadequacies of the staff throwing his drink in the bin, stating that he did not want his food since his drink had disappeared. Grasping this heaven-sent opportunity as dinner flashed into view, I asked Melvyn if he wanted his food... it ended up in the dustbin – the human dustbin, that is!

As soon as lunch was over I wandered around the unit asking people if they wanted anything from the shops, and I was inundated with pleas. Kelvin had been brought some batteries from one of the nurses (and people say they are sweet on me!) but he wanted some shortbread fingers instead. I was very good, I got everything... everything except the shortbread fingers; they did not sell them. Thinking I would stick to nurses and therapists only, in the future, I went off for my next therapy session.

This Friday's speech therapy was interesting as Rachel and I went through limericks and discussed their merit. Apparently they are useful tools in speech therapy as they have a precise rhythm that is the same whatever the limerick. I practised reading one and was not too bad. In fact, I was so good Rachel suggested that I wrote a limerick of my own that I could read out during the following week. Mentioning that I tended to be very childish or, at best, very strange when I made words rhyme, I hesitantly agreed to try and write one.

Speech therapy was followed by a break for half an hour, so I went to the computer room to write some more of my journal. When my half-hour was up I went back to my bay to get ready for Cath's arrival, basically to collect a pair of sunglasses. When she arrived she took me out for a short walk, in brilliant sunshine. It was sensible for me to bring my sunglasses along since I hated sunshine, or at least it hated me. One of the staff nurses found out that I used to hate sunshine (and mirrors!) much preferring the dark and the cold... he was convinced I was a vampire! Braving the sunshine, I accompanied Cath on a short walk to a bench overlooking the entrance to the hospital, where we sat down to have a chat. Therapy took many guises.

After Simon collected me, as per normal on a Friday, and took me home, we passed a quiet night before I woke early on Saturday morning. Dad disappeared soon after to play his routine game of golf and the peace and quiet it left us in enabled us to do our own chores. Mother and I went shopping while Simon remained at

home to await Claire, as she was coming back from a holiday in the USA. He could make her feel at home since she would be staying with us for a couple of days. Afterwards, she would go back to university in Loughborough with Simon. It was good for him to see her and wonderful for us to see the beaming smile return to Simon's face. Unfortunately they did not have much time together: she spent most of the morning asleep trying to recover from jet lag. He did have some more time with her that evening, though, as Dad took us out to a restaurant.

The rest of Saturday was spent tying up loose ends. Vicki had asked me if she could have any photographs of me from the Trauma Unit, something I happily sorted out for her. Going through all the photographs that Mother had taken of me over the past few months was a voyage of self-discovery and always fascinated me. I found several spare photos that were suitable. Getting into the mood, I also started to sort through old keepsakes from my childhood, during which I was reminded of a question Barbara had once asked me: did I have any recordings of my voice? Looking at our old-fashioned spool-to-spool tape recorder, I remembered fooling about with it many years earlier. On listening to it, I did find a recording of my voice still on it; we obviously hadn't used it for many years, though, as the recording dated back to before my voice broke!

On Sunday afternoon Mother drove me back to the Lister. I knew there would not be any therapists there, but for some reason I felt that I needed to go back. I was probably only burying ghosts; other than the nurse, Heather, there was nobody there whom I knew. It was good going, though; Heather was very pleased to see me and said that she thought I looked a lot better with the extra weight I was carrying from my few weeks in the RRU, saying I was dreadfully thin before, even though I ate like a horse.

It is one thing that surprised me as people generally lose weight in hospital. For years I weighed 9st 7lb reaching a maximum of ten stone until I broke up with Alison. Then the starving that I inflicted on myself reduced my weight back to 9½ stone, where I levelled out again. At the time of my accident I had once more reached ten stone, but within days I was down to about seven stone. I was only a couple of stone heavier by the time I was at the Lister, but by Northwick Park, I piled the weight on, whether I wanted it or not. When I left I was 11st 7lbs, but within a few months stabilised at around eleven stone – a weight I am happy with, even though a lot of my clothes are a bit tighter now!

Waking up late on Monday 24th, having returned to the RRU the night before, I rolled over and, in the half-asleep state I was exhibiting, panic welled up and threatened to choke me. I knew physiotherapy was due to start at 8.30, and that left me all of half an hour to get ready – I 'ran' around in a senseless stupor as I tried to make myself ready in the rapidly dwindling minutes.

Luck played her hand favourably once more, and I realised that physiotherapy's early start was not until Wednesday and I had made a mistake. I was up, though, and thought that I might try and turn this perverse luck to my advantage. As the repairman had still not been, I decided that our shower was off limits and the main hospital shower held much more favourable prospects – and I now had plenty of time to use it; I thought I had, anyway, but just before I went into the shower, I noticed the food trolley at the bottom of the unit corridor and it was slowly heading in my direction. Undaunted, I had my shower, enjoying the pleasure as the warm water cascaded off my shoulders, but time was ticking away and the food was gradually nearing my bay. I hurried my shower along and then rushed back to the bay, where I was able to find time to have a shave and clean my teeth. I even managed to be practically dressed by the time breakfast arrived.

Not having much in the way of therapy that morning, I went to the computer room, finishing just in time for lunch. Wandering back to my bay, I was struck by the barrier of heat that was hanging over the room just inside the door. Melvyn, the rotter, had hidden a heater in the room and it was blowing out hot air on this very hot spring day! I could not see it to turn it off and I was not about to scrabble around on the floor looking for it. I understood that Melvyn felt the cold – continuously – but this heat was unbearable and he was nowhere to be found. While Melvyn was out, however, I opened the windows in an attempt to let out some of the hot air.

Suddenly he burst into the room saying he was moving somewhere else and the bay was all mine. I thought all my Christmases had come at once, though I was not sure whether to believe him – no one has this much luck! Besides, even if he were moving, the bay would only be 'mine' until the next person moved in.

Lunch was finished by one o'clock and I was cheerfully faced with an hour-long session of speech therapy starting after a half-hour break. Using this time to my advantage, I quickly circled the ward, asking people I saw before disappearing to go shopping. Only two people wanted something: Cath wanted some mints and I was asked to get a sandwich for the consultant. I was lucky they were the only people who wanted anything as I arrived at speech therapy with only seconds to spare. Why I rushed though I do not know, there had been a slight glitch and I was scheduled for something that did not exist.

As it was supposed to be speech therapy, I decided that I'd better talk and I ended up chatting to a fellow patient in the corridor. Unfortunately, we had to be there in the corridor; the nurses were busy in his bay and I had recently found Melvyn fast asleep in our bay. He had shut the window and I spied the heater – under my bed! Why the several blankets he had wrapped around him on the bed could not suffice, and he had to inflict his ferocious heat on everyone else, was beyond me. How selfish can you get? I fail to see why me liking the cold was any more unusual and incorrect than him liking his near-tropical weather conditions; yet I am constantly told to adjust to heat so that 'normal' people do not have to adjust to my cold. At least, I hoped, it would not be long before Melvyn vacated my bay to move into his new premises.

Quite what they did to my timetable nobody would tell me, not wanting to admit to the error, but speech therapy had been moved until after physiotherapy, rather than before, as previously timetabled. When it arrived, Rachel, whom I was to see for the last time before she left, said that we would go through the limericks that we had been preparing since the previous week. She happily presented hers with a hint of complacency in her voice, as though she did not think I had prepared anything. With great pleasure, I brought my limerick out as well. I then practised reading them both aloud, making sure the intonation, stress and other vocal operations were correct:

'There was a young man from Soweto,
Who wanted to take a wild photo,
So he went outside,
And hid in the hide,
But nothing came in to the ghetto.'

OK, so it is not Shakespeare, but then I don't think he wrote limericks...

Last thing at the start of this week was the Monday newsletter group. I double-checked the nurses' roster that I had typed on the Thursday before and then hurriedly typed my article on the conservation of elephants and rhinos. When it was all done, I helped arrange everything and compile it into the format of the newsletter. I didn't mind staying behind to help them finish it off, as I was going to stay there anyway and enter the previous few days of my life into my journal on the computer. I would then retire to my bay – by now cooler! – where I was going to curl up in front of the television.

I made my way to physiotherapy by nine o'clock on Tuesday morning, though I knew Theresa would not be returning from her Easter break until Wednesday. I wandered down to the gym, wondering who had the pleasure of my company that morning. Cath said that she had been roped in to look after me, but was sorry, as she was busy with someone else. She said she would not be able to see me, and told me to get on with my exercises, firmly shoving my ego back where it belonged as she did so. This was annoying since I had already organised my day, fitting my exercises in towards the end. By doing them now I was opening up a gap in the afternoon, although there was nothing to stop me doing them again if I wanted.

After physiotherapy, I paraded around the unit asking the nurses and therapists if they wanted anything from the shops. Anna said that she wished to have a bottle of water, though she told me not to bother going unless someone else wanted anything. Telling me this caused changes to occur in some plane of etheric existence, in the same way that it always rains when you hang the washing out or wash the car. Put simply, nobody else wanted anything. So what did I do? On the basis that the walk would do me good anyway, and seeing as a very pretty woman had asked me for something politely with a smile on her face, I went down to the shops to buy a bottle of water. What I would not do for a woman with a pleasant smile! And for Anna, I treated it as doing a favour for a friend, rather than a chore for a therapist. Besides, I had to keep my customers satisfied.

Long after supper, having no visitors come and brighten my small corner of the world, I went and made a few phone calls. Having become used to seeing Vicki every Wednesday and not having seen her for a number of weeks, I decided to phone her – my best friend. I was still five months away from falling out with her, and in those days before the changes that radically altered me became firmly imprinted on my soul, she welcomed the phone call. It was very wonderful chatting to her, something I would miss during that long year without her friendship.

Unfortunately, in the months to come I was to say something to her that would drive her away. Much how I hated it taking place, it was a very important lesson that I maybe had to learn in order to leave the emotional devastation that my accident brought me, while I learnt from the mistakes that I made along the way. Somehow the mistakes had to happen in order to allow me to evolve into the person that I have become.

'I lost touch with Philip about a year ago when we had a dis-agreement, but I have received a birthday card every year since, and now we have spoken to each other on the phone and written letters, catching up on the last year of our lives. Shannon is no longer alive, but Philip has managed to secure himself a flat with two cats and a wildlife sanctuary just down the road. It's been a long hard haul for everyone involved, but most of all for Philip, who has had to bring himself back from the brink of possible brain damage and even death, but he has made it and so have we all. As far as I'm concerned Philip is just the same as he was; he's had a tough learning process, but now he can be thankful he survived and I'm sure the animal population of the world will be glad too. He is a true animal lover and they, like us, haven't lost him, as was feared.

Vicki Blake, friend

Horsing Around

I was correct in thinking that I would only have my own bay until the next person arrived, an event dawning far sooner than I anticipated. Staying in bed may have been an advantage; I might have imposed squatter's rights and not been moved – wishful thinking! There were empty beds in the unit, but only in male bays, and the new arrival was a woman. Although such an arrival on a male bay may have helped their rehabilitation in a big way, it was decided that hers might have faltered to a similar degree. As Melvyn had already left for a new bay, I was the only obstacle to her arrival. Having no choice in the matter, I was moved again, my third relocation, my fourth bay, my eighth week (and I would only be there for ten). Unlike my other moves, this time I was told to move, whereas before I was helped. I had to pack all my clothes and possessions, scattered around the cupboards and drawers of this larger bay, and move them down to Bay B, cramming my belongings into a smaller bay.

Having moved, I started to unpack and arrange my possessions so that I knew where they all were and could easily reach them. I was just beginning when a couple of visitors arrived. Jane came in to see me again, bringing good cheer, the indispensable packet of jelly babies, lots of talk about the horses I loved so much, and news that she was pregnant, the baby being due in December. This good news pleased me a great deal, but was not the only surprise she had in store for me. She had brought a little visitor – her four-year-old daughter, Sammie-Jo, who, apparently, had been asking how well I was for several months, though this was the first time she had been able to come and see me. It was lovely seeing her, and even more cheering seeing the admiration in her face as she gave me a big hug and kiss. Jane had a habit of presenting me with 'objects of desire', and seeing Sammie-Jo made my day, as I am sure Jane knew it would.

Jane and I had just begun our conversation when Cynthia

arrived. Just as my mother would always arrive when dinner came, visitors often seemed to arrive together. To further complicate matters, a new member of staff was having a problem in the computer room and I was asked if I could go and investigate. Temporarily leaving Jane and Cynthia to chat about me behind my back (?) and to collect my supper that was just starting to be brought onto the ward, I went to try and sort out Sara's problem, though why they took me for a computer expert I will never know.

Finding the error, I was explaining how to sort it out when Sara started to panic about my dinner, its smells by now tickling our nasal hairs. She was afraid that it would get cold – if only! – or that I would miss out on it completely since I was helping her. Not wanting the latter to happen I returned to my bay to eat my food, which had now cooled to a respectable temperature, when I was confronted by a nurse telling me about a phone call. After a few seconds it dawned on me she meant right then, so I hurried off to get the telephone.

Mother almost had an excuse coming to see me during my supper, it coinciding with her leaving work, but she could have picked any time to telephone me. Annoyed with her bad timing, I said my hellos and left her to (try and) have a quick chat with Cynthia while I ate my food in peace.

Eventually, towards the end of my meal, these two gossips had, surprisingly, finished chatting – someone probably needed the phone! – and Cynthia went home. I spent a few more minutes with Jane and Sammie-Jo, but soon they had to go as well. They had been with me for nearly three hours and had to return on public transport back to South-east London.

When the small corner of this bay I could call my own was returned to me in its entirety, I finished my unpacking before returning to the computer room to type some more of my journal, making sure the way was clear first! Arriving unhindered at the computer room, I found the door locked. Annoyance laced with a mild form of panic started to bubble up inside me before I remembered that a key was held by the nurses. Having spent many an evening chatting to the night nurses, and slowly obtaining a previously unknown confidence, this did not distress me in the slightest. Borrowing a nurse, I got the door unlocked for me, allowing me to continue with my journal for the next three hours before I left to watch television at midnight.

Having looked at my timetable the day before I knew that physiotherapy began at 8.30. So why was it that I woke up at eight o'clock? A mild form of panic arose as I rushed around trying to get ready in the time left to me when I noticed my clock, the small hand of which was languorously approaching the number six. Rubbing my eyes in disbelief, I flinched as the reality hit me. Now with over two hours to make myself ready, I had my shower and was finished long before the arrival of breakfast.

After physiotherapy and speech therapy, the two activities on my timetable that morning, I went back to the gym, where I was going to do my exercises. Almost as if she knew I was coming, Sarah Ward greeted me graciously and started chatting to me. Stupidly, I mentioned that I had nothing to do. It was then that Sarah smiled at me, and that was my undoing. It was warm and inviting, and I was captivated. I started to notice how lovely and mischievous her smile was when... it was too late! She had me, 'hook, line and sinker', and when she asked a small favour of me I dutifully carried out her wishes. All I had to do was return a wobbleboard to the physiotherapy stores near the hydrotherapy pool. I did not fuss, I did not complain, and she gave me a hug on my return. Some rewards are worth paying the price in the first place.

My other, self-inflicted, duty of the morning was to go down to the shops for any of the staff that wanted. That Wednesday I didn't mind; I had to go down as I was to cook potatoes on the Thursday and someone had to buy them. The fact that I had just returned from a walk past the shops didn't seem to bother me. Predictably I turned up empty-handed from my rotation around the unit, nobody else wanted anything! It was worth going though, it helped fill the time leading up to my current affairs. Other than this pleasant distraction, and popping down to the shops to buy the potatoes, I spent most of the afternoon buried in the computer room. This was fortunate, since most of my time was needed sorting out other people's problems. At least I found time to do some of my own work.

The rest of my day was spent eating (what a surprise!) and waiting for any visitors. I had just reached the conclusion that no one was coming in when I was told I had a phone call. It was Mother telling me that she was not coming in. About five minutes later there was another phone call for me. Mother again, telling me she would be in on the next day. What wonderful conversations she and I have... at least I was not eating!

As Thursday dawned, I awoke at seven o'clock and, lifting my lethargic body from the bed, I dived into the shower. In the same manner that I had started a couple of weeks before, I ate my breakfast, then put my trousers on, doing both while standing. Following on from this 'simple' exercise, and wanting to make life hard for myself, I tried to put my socks on while still standing... a precarious ordeal at the best of times. Continuing in this madcap scheme, I also put on my shoes while standing up – surprisingly easier than socks. When dressed, I cast a glance at my timetable and noticed that the morning was thankfully a good deal busier than most mornings had been that week. It would all begin with computers at ten o'clock. I spent most of the time on the computer finishing my article for that week's newsletter. Like most computer sessions, I naturally assumed that it was at the end of the day and there was nothing to prevent me from staying in the computer room.

With this in mind, once the article was typed, I settled down to typing the most recent day's happenings into my journal. I had just started, and the creative juices were beginning to flow, when I had a very strong urge to be somewhere else. So real was this feeling that I went to check my timetable, in doing so proving how correct these intense, almost psychic feelings had been. Theresa had recently returned from her trip abroad over Easter and it would have been a bad way to start physiotherapy with her if I never turned up – I arrived with seconds to spare. Once I had arrived, she and I carried on with my exercises, changing some of them and putting in harder ones. She said I was now too good for a lot of the exercises they gave people, and if I wanted to get better, it was up to me. Get the right attitude and everything falls into place. It was something that took me several more months to figure out.

As soon as Theresa had released me from this morning's 'toil' in physiotherapy, I met up with Samantha in the occupational therapy kitchen, where I was introduced to an occupational therapy student, Jessica Johnson. I was told to cook something, and, fancying a fry-up, settled down with some sausages, bacon and eggs, some baked beans and the potatoes I'd purchased from the shops the previous day, which I mashed. It was in my normal proportions and was huge; nobody who saw the plate could believe I could eat it all. In fact, I had all of my meal, and half of the one provided, once more having forgotten to cancel the hospital food the day before. This immense meal was followed by half-an-hour of digestion before my next therapy, so I did my duty of going to the shops to buy the few things for the nurses and therapists. I checked everyone, from the consultant down. On my return, I handed out some of the goods at the nurses' station, where a gathering of hospital staff was taking place. Suddenly one of the nurses took it upon herself to complain about me, saying she was astounded that I had the cheek to interrupt someone as esteemed as the consultant, and I should basically leave her alone. After hearing this outburst, I was shocked. If she wanted to be left alone, all she would have needed to do was tell me; meanwhile I was doing her a favour. Natasha agreed, siding with me. She thought it was great that I had the confidence to ask the consultant, whereas most people would be too shy. She is only human and she may have wanted something from the shops, as she had a few days previously, just as this nurse who moaned at me might... it would have been rude to ignore her. It is for confidence like this that my thanks go to Northwick Park. If nothing else, it helped this useful quality grow inside me.

After Cath had taken me for a walk around the hospital for physiotherapy, I went along to the last group meeting for that week's newsletter. Being the person I am, I spent most of the time chatting to Jessica and Anna. Although I would have preferred talking to them the whole time, I had my duties so managed to find some time to double-check the nurses' roster. I also found time to talk to someone else. Anita Stratford had arrived on the unit a couple of weeks before I did, and one of the first times I saw her, she was walking around seemingly 'normal' while I was painstakingly propelling myself in a wheelchair. I considered myself to be far below her – why would she want to know me? Needless to say, in the first six weeks of my existence on the unit she did not know me. By the seventh, I started to walk and this new found mobility changed my outlook into one that was far more positive, why should she not want to know me?

This change of heart may have altered the same etheric plane that Anna had previously, asking for a bottle of water – in other words, she did get to know me. We, in fact, became quite good friends, or at least as close a friendship that can be created with someone you hardly know, under far from ideal circumstances. Our senses of humour were very similar; we were always playing at verbal fencing in the same way that Catherine and I used to, in what now seemed like a lifetime ago. Our verbal fencing continually pricked each other's sense of humour, only drawing laughter. She was a devil, though, and would forever try to grab my chest, always doing so with a big smile and a giggle – a giggle that cheered me up and helped smooth any bad points that my recovery may have brought. I was forever joking with her that if she kept fondling my breast, I might fondle hers. This was continually met with mock ignorance. She was lucky hitting on me then rather than now. In those days I was still lacking in the confidence that I have since found and was always far too polite to retaliate.

After the newsletter group had been resolved for the week, I stayed in the computer room to type some more of my journal. I remained there until my supper arrived. Predictably, Mother had to drag me out, her arrival happening to coincide with that of supper, her timing once more revolving around the smell of the hospital food, which, although very tasty, was, as usual, far too hot for me. As she was there, Mother was able to take home many of my possessions; with only two weeks left to go before my discharge it seemed like a good idea. The rest of my evening consisted of sitting in front of the computer and occasionally typing something, doing my exercises, and going to sleep some time in the early hours of Friday morning.

Beauty and the Beast

It is amazing what we do 'for beauty', and yet still call ourselves civilised. Admittedly, a lot has to do with the world's rising population. When the population was quite low, we could carry out our business to not much ill effect. Since it increased (and being very set in our ways), what we used to do before now has a much larger effect. Take ivory, for example. A few centuries ago, there were lots of elephants and the demand was quite low; it was made into everything from jewellery to piano keys. Since then our demand (percentage) has stayed about the same. Unfortunately, the world's population has gone up exponentially, and is now far above the estimates. Hence, the overall world demand for ivory has gone up, and we can't manufacture it. Since the normal African can earn far more selling ivory on the black market than he can in a 'legal' job, many people have turned to poaching. Consequently the elephant population (both African and Indian) has taken a hammering, and is fast approaching the point of no return.

The same is true for a lot of the world's animals. Be it killing mountain gorillas to make their hands into ashtrays or their teeth into jewellery, killing leopards to turn their coats into clothes, or killing tigers to turn their bones into Chinese medicine, it is murderous and disgusting. Rhinoceros horn, for example, is carved into intricate handles for daggers in Yemen. Rhino horn is replaceable. If cut off – when the animal is still alive – it will slowly grow back. However, it is far easier for the poacher to kill the animal and hack off what they came for. The populations of both rhinos and elephants have started to crash in the past few years, and if we don't do something soon, we will lose both of these fantastic species for ever.

RRU Newsletter No. 48, Conservation Issue,
28 April 1995

After the few hours' sleep I seemed to be able to survive on in those days, I awoke on that Friday to find, once more, that physiotherapy threatened at 8.30. Everything went normally; I ate breakfast while standing and dressed in a similar fashion. I also started a new regime that morning that I would continue with every mealtime throughout the duration I had left on the unit.

Once I had finished my breakfast, rather than waiting for a nurse to take my tray away – something I knew they could do – I carried it back to the trolley myself. It saved them a bit of time, time I had available to waste (not that getting better can ever be viewed as wasting time), and helped work on my balance. Providing I did not drop a tray this exercise would benefit everyone.

In my short physiotherapy session after breakfast, Theresa tried to tie up some of the loose ends; any major advances made from now on depended solely on me. If only this simple fact had dawned on me at this early stage rather than surfacing several months later during the little physiotherapy I had as an outpatient. Following this half-hour in physiotherapy there was a two-hour break before my next therapy, so I stayed in the gym and did my exercises. When finished, I walked up the ward, then down it, pacing inanely trying to waste a bit of time. When enough time had been wasted, I met up with Barbara for speech therapy. I was shown a very funny play about this American tourist who had been pulled over by a policeman since he had been driving on the wrong side of the road. The story, which involved both of them talking allowing me to practise lots or intonation as they exchanged questions, was a play on words. The American could not understand why it was not right to drive on the right, but was right to drive on the left. Going right left him bewildered. It was a very funny play. When we had read it through once and I had been able to grasp where all the stresses and all the funny parts were, we read it again. I was far better the second time around. This speech therapy, an appropriate sandwich filler, was then followed by more physiotherapy, in which Cath took me for a walk before computers. Afterwards, as she had shown an interest in the photographs that Mother had been taking of me following Jo's suggestion within the first few days, Theresa met up with me in the computer room, and I took her off to my bay to lend them to her. Unfortunately, I do not know what she thought of them. Barbara, who thought they were amazing, brought them back.

The week concluded with a very lazy, boring and highly for-gettable weekend before everyone was faced with the notable joys of May Day on the Monday. I had spent the whole weekend in hospital and did not even go home on the May Day bank holiday.

There was a very simple explanation for this as well. Due to the VE day celebrations the following week, the bank holiday was being postponed. With nowhere to go and having no visitors, this two-day break seemed interminably long.

When the weekend was finally over and we were presented with the joys of May Day, we were confronted with an outbreak of highly contagious MRSA on the unit. Kelvin, who was the latest victim, had to be isolated while our bay was ruthlessly cleaned. As a precaution, another roommate, Arthur Yettigoda, and I were sent to another bay to eat our lunch, which had arrived while they were cleaning the bay. It was hardly joyful, but at least it was memorable.

After lunch I made my way around the unit asking people if they wanted anything from the shops. Naturally, as I had no pockets in my tracksuit trousers, everybody wanted something and, as I only received the correct change, I was laden down with money. It was spent quickly enough, though, and by 2.30, having returned and given out everything I had bought, I had occupational therapy with Samantha. She spent the hour telling me all about the 'work visit' I was having on Wednesday and asking how I thought I was doing.

After this really strenuous activity, I wandered up and down the corridor, as I wished to have a word with the consultant who was busy on the phone. Soon Anna collared me and told me to go straight to the newsletter group, as I would be late. Although I did not think so, I dutifully carried out her wishes. I think she smiled as she told me! So quick was I at getting there, that nobody else had arrived; but, unconcerned, I started work immediately, my progress being more important as I would not be there on the Thursday. Consequently, I went ahead and typed the following week's nurses' roster onto the spreadsheet.

The rest of the week was to be mainly concerned with horses. Before it began, though, I started with a neuropsychology assessment with Clare. I wanted to know which parts of my brain had been most damaged and whether I would have lost much intelligence because of it. On hearing that I am a member of Mensa, Clare was very annoyed that she had not known earlier; she had never seen anybody from Mensa professionally. She gave me various tests, many of which were in a similar style to those I am used to. One I remember was having to repeat to her a sequence of numbers after she told me them, getting harder each time as they slowly increased in length by one digit. After I had completed the test, not stumbling at all, she told me I was very good and was sorry that the test stopped where it did, saying that I could probably have gone on with strings of numbers two of three digits longer. Astounded, she repeated the test, asking me to recount the numbers backwards, and here I met with a problem. Once or twice I repeated a sequence backwards with a couple of digits lying the wrong way around. Shocking! I then said I was having problems with my eyesight. Giving me a short eye test, she said that whether I was having problems or not, my eyesight was better than hers.

Feeling relieved, I went to computers and then down to the shops for anyone who wanted bits and pieces. Returning, I had a hurried lunch before Theresa and I took a taxi to Penniwells Riding for the Disabled yard in Elstree. We were met by Sue, the organiser, before Sarah Hayes took me for my lesson on Tosca, who was waiting patiently, having already been tacked up. Although I had not ridden a horse for nearly six months, my trip to Willowtree in February had fired my enthusiasm, and all I wanted to do was sit on a horse again – I loved every minute.

Asking Tosca to walk and trot, change the rein and perform circles and serpentines was essentially very easy and unexciting. However, I had not ridden for such a long time and my body was not in the same state as it had been six months earlier – it wasn't far short of a miracle that I could sit there without falling off! Although sitting on a horse was a very strange sensation, it felt natural, as though I belonged there. When you consider why I was at an RDA stables in the first place, I coped very well, although I was nowhere near as good as I had been. Luckily Sarah proved very good at nagging. 'Chin!' she would often shout, the echoes reverberating through my mind. I wonder where I've heard that before, I thought.

Not surprisingly, I did not look my best; my posture was all over the place. Mind you, when you consider how bad my accident was, this did not matter, but I couldn't help feel a little embarrassed at how badly I knew I was riding, as Theresa was recording it all on the hospital camcorder. In fact, looking at the cassette now, it is amazing how well I was riding – not for an expert, no, but far better than an able-bodied person riding for the first time. I couldn't wait until I returned and improve on what I considered was appalling riding.

Horses continued to occupy my thoughts on Wednesday, as I was taken for a work visit. Before I could think about returning to work (which is what I was expecting to do in those far-off days) my workplace had to be checked by the occupational therapist to make sure facilities like the toilet were accessible. The physio-therapist also had to assess the kind of work that I would be confronted with and decide whether I could realistically cope. After I'd quickly (excitedly) eaten my lunch, Theresa fetched her car so that we could leave for South-east London, placing Samantha next to her as map reader, while I and Jessica, who came to observe in order to further her studies, sat in the back of the car. I will happily chat to anyone, but so few people talk back with equal vigour. Often I find myself chatting away, totally unaware that the other person has stopped listening. Occasionally I meet someone who enjoys talking as much as I do, and when that happens the world can continue on its merry way and we can remain oblivious. Alison, Leigh and Anna were people like that; Jessica was another. We spent most of the journey talking.

My excitement at revisiting Willowtree had heightened my awareness so that, while talking, I did manage to pay attention to where we were going. Although I trusted the therapists, to know which way they were going, they took a long, winding route to the stables and I had to help them towards the end. Even so, we arrived at Willowtree in good time. It was wonderful to be back, even if only for a few hours – I relished showing everyone round the yard. They were blown away when they saw it, noting that it 'was a small area of greenery surrounded by concrete'. They could not believe that such a place existed, when nearby Kidbrooke was known as the 'concrete jungle'.

Especially gratifying was the way they reacted to the horses. It warmed my heart seeing their response as I showed off Shannon, and I also introduced them to the rest of the horses, as well as my little ponies – not unlike a proud father showing off his children. It was so good to see Shannon again, at least it cheered him up for another month before I was to return for good. They all, therapists and horses alike, seemed to enjoy themselves; I could see a strange light in the therapists' eyes as they looked around, fascinated. It seemed as though they thought I should go back there even if I might not have been able to. I do not think they wanted to find any obstacles to prevent my return.

Karen Lawley, being the wonderful friend that she is, had popped down to see me. While my therapists and my mother – who had also come down – and the Masseys were discussing me, I chatted to Karen and Jane. Lots of hugs and kisses were exchanged, both between us and given to the horses. It was wonderful feeling the admiration, especially from Shannon, and so pleasant simply stroking him on the neck. Only by being blessed in temporarily finding myself in such a position was I able to understand quite how severely handicapped children respond to horses. I think if I ever forget these feelings I will become less of a person than I am now.

It was lovely seeing Jane and Karen again, not just the horses. At least they could talk and I could ask questions! More than anything though, it was good to be back 'home'; I certainly felt far more relaxed there and it was one of the few places that I could 'tower above' the therapists.

When we left the yard, Samantha and I changed positions. Although Theresa used to live in New Cross Gate, I was the only person with experience of the maze-like road network of South London. Whatever the risk of any failing memory, I sat in the front, entrusted with giving Theresa directions back to the Thames, using a more direct route to the one we came by, while Samantha and Jessica sat with Mum in the back. After a much simpler return home, we arrived back at hospital, though it was after four o'clock by this stage. Mother came to my bay, shortly before going home with most of the rest of my possessions, leaving me to do my exercises, eat supper and work on the computer before going to bed.

Horses were on the list again on Thursday, as I was to return to Penniwells. Thinking back, a year later, I could not imagine it, but that Thursday was incredibly hot, so hot that Tosca could not come out as she was suffering from the heat. A big horse, Arthur, was brought out instead. He was a friendly horse, but had less impulsion than Tosca, and I did not have the energy to keep him going. More to the point, I did not have the balance to stay on his back while squeezing hard with my legs – it was one or the other. I rode far better than before, though, and felt much more in harmony with the horse. I really enjoyed this second ride of the week, and I think Sarah could see this; she also agreed that I rode better. She certainly did not shout as much!

My ride was followed by a taxi journey back to the unit. While we drifted through the backstreets of Harrow, it occurred to me that on the Monday before, I had typed the *previous* week's nurses' roster into the spreadsheet. Fearing nobody would notice the error, I gave Anna further proof of my perfectionist nature and went along to the newsletter group before they finished, so that I could redo the roster. The end of the newsletter meeting could not come soon enough. The hospital was heated and I had been on a horse. There must have been some smell rising from my person, although of course I could not sense a thing, as I was used to that rural perfume. Not having had a moment to wash before, at the end of the newsletter meeting I had time to go and have a well-deserved shower before my supper arrived. Once this was voraciously eaten, I settled down to a normal evening, filling it with my exercises, riding the exercise bike for ten minutes, and typing an up to date copy of my journal, to include the past couple of days.

The end of the week brought further psychology with Clare, while Anna joined us for her own experience. We mainly went through the results of the tests from the start of the week. Apparently I was normal, or above normal, in everything apart from one area. There was nothing that would prevent me leading a normal life, and people would probably not even notice I had been involved in an accident. The one area that was slightly abnormal for someone my age was my visual perception, something that continues to evolve throughout one's life and is not vital; though quite how Clare figured out that my warped visual perception was abnormal due to my accident I will never know. Basically, I wasn't too concerned.

Monday, 8 May 1995 was fifty years since the end of World War II, when Europe celebrated victory over the Nazis. To commemorate those lost in the war a bank holiday was introduced to celebrate the Allied Victory in Europe – VE day. In the neighbouring manor house, the local residents' association decided to hold a 'street' party in honour of this great event. In spite of my Dad complaining and trying to hurry us along as we were late, we arrived five minutes after the evening officially started – the fact that nobody else was there was not the point!

After everybody else had arrived we all settled down to a barbecue. When this had been eaten a strange noise come rushing to our ears. A doodlebug was coming down to crash, and we all had to put on gasmasks (cardboard cut-outs) and run to the designated 'air raid' shelter. 'Last one there is a sissy!' – and, no, I was not last. Of course, being by chance the closest person to the shelter did help. Having survived this mock 'air raid' we settled down to playing a more civilised game of croquet, followed by an entertaining game of rounders. Although surviving the 'air raid', my team lost the game of croquet, and I never even hit the ball in rounders. Even so, I surprised myself at how well I played, all things considered. Once in the game of rounders, I was running – if you could call it that – between the bases. Arriving at the second base I was not able to run any further, so I softly applied my brakes in an effort to stop. I did stop, about five metres after the base… on my knees! I quickly jumped up from my collision with the ground, looking somewhat embarrassed and hoping nobody had seen me. Although I'd still not fully recovered from my accident it did not seem to matter – I enjoyed myself. It also gave Ann and me plenty of time to have a chat, usually in the middle of the pitch, and we were on opposing teams!

Returning to the RRU on Tuesday, I did little in the morning, but Mother came to take me to Penniwells in the afternoon. Not knowing the route as well as the taxi drivers, we left very early. It was surprisingly easy to find and we arrived in plenty of time. Having at least half an hour to wait for my ride, I offered Penniwells my services. Pleased to hear this, they happily let me tack up one of the horses. It was, perhaps, amazing that I could still do it, but more remarkable was that they let me. When I had finished tacking up, I settled down again to riding Tosca, who had recovered from the horrendous heat of the week before. As the lessons at Penniwells continued over these two weeks, my enjoyment leapt to new heights, and I could noticeably ride better than when I started. Before leaving, I thanked Sarah for all the wonderful nagging that she had dished out!

Though I walked outside with Theresa on Wednesday, my most exciting event during the day was occupational therapy, which I had, unusually, been looking forward to all morning. Jessica accompanied me to the kitchen and stayed with me while I cooked something. Technically, my macaroni cheese was not perfect; the sauce was too thick and the macaroni was overcooked. As well as the slight faults with the cooking, there was far too much – enough for three adults, when there was only me. I should be proud though, I had cooked a fair cheese sauce after five months and a head injury. It was very tasty and I managed to eat all of it, much to everyone's surprise.

> 'One of my first meetings with Philip took place in the occupational therapy kitchen. Here, we assessed any problem that patients had with carrying out activities in the kitchen. Philip had already had some sessions in the kitchen and was now at a stage where he was requested to plan and prepare a meal independently.
>
> 'Having purchased rather large proportions of macaroni, cheese and bacon, he progressed to pile the ingredients in a saucepan and somewhat haphazardly cooked a meal, which I thought was fit for at least three people.
>
> 'Having serious doubts about his ability to eat all this food, I questioned him as to whether he thought this was realistic. He insisted that he always ate such an amount.
>
> 'At this point I began to wonder whether his head injury had possibly left him with a problem of "disinhibition". I was then even more concerned that he had actually eaten it all, and wondered if he had a thyroid problem!'
>
> Jessica Johnson, occupational therapist

On the Thursday I awoke at seven o'clock, questioning the early hour especially given the busy two days before. A rough calculation showed that the early hour helped mark the ninth hour in bed asleep – out of the past forty-eight! Being completely ready a good half hour before breakfast normally arrived. I decided to go for a short stroll about the unit. Quite why I did on this particular day when I normally sat in my bay waiting I am not sure, but it was a good job I did. I wandered down to the bottom end of the corridor, where the front doors were, expecting them to open as I approached the sensor as per normal. As I neared the doors though, nothing happened. I was puzzled, but not concerned, yet I kept an eye on the doors.

As each person arrived outside, a nurse had to retrieve the key from its hidden location, unlock the automatic control and punch in the security number on the keypad before the doors could be opened. Having watched the busy nurses continually rush to let therapists and other people in, I decided to be polite and sit by the doors, unlocking them whenever someone wished to gain access. Quite why they trusted me with the key to the doors and the security code I will never know, but I wasn't going to argue. I had nothing to lose, since I knew unless someone unlocked the doors breakfast would be stranded outside. Once breakfast appeared I even ate it sitting by the doors, having nothing pressing until speech therapy. While sitting there, eating, I noticed the poem by Walter D Wintle (included at the start of the book) attached to a notice board in front of me. I found it fascinating, since it summed up exactly how I was treating my accident.

When most people had arrived and everyone was up, I thought about returning to my bay to get ready for speech therapy. While I was thinking Barbara came to get me. Once more my timetable had not been entirely accurate and speech therapy was booked half an hour earlier than it appeared on my schedule. It began immediately. It did not last long, though, and then I buried myself in the computer room until physiotherapy, which arrived at 11.30. Accordingly, Theresa and I went for a long walk around a football pitch next to the hospital. I walked in a dead straight line (I was told to imagine I was walking along a thin path between two lanes of a motorway) and, while continuously checking my posture, Theresa kept badgering me to walk faster, to the point where I was practically running.

Walking had one slight problem: as I had very little feeling in my right foot, it had no idea where the ground was. For every step

I took, the ground came up to meet my foot with a thud. The unexpected jars were like little explosions going off inside my head. Even so, I enjoyed the walk, which lasted for nearly an hour. I was happy to return, however, and go straight to the newsletter group. As nobody had been there on Monday, we had no theme, so time was spent talking about possible topics. While everyone discussed a theme I managed to compile the nurses' roster, and I wrote an article for the newsletter. It would be my last one, and I felt I ought to be decent and say goodbye to everyone, so that is what I did.

I woke before six o'clock in the morning on Friday, 12 May, in spite of – and probably because of – it being my last day. After getting ready and having breakfast, I went to my last session of speech therapy. Like the physiotherapy later on, we did not do that much, and most of the time was spent having a chat, giving me exercises to continue after my discharge, and making sure I was ready for the outside world. Most of my packing was done, so I finished off what was left before Matt took the discharge video of me showing the 'after' stage, to complement the 'before' stage in the admission video, taken two months earlier. We did similar activities to test my progress: a short walk, a memory test, and I took off my shoes, socks and my top (thankfully without buttons) before putting them back on again. Only taking ten minutes it went very well, in spite of managing to get knots in my laces – at least it showed Matt I could undo them. Before I attacked the computer while I waited for collection by my father, I tried to see as many people as I could to say goodbye, and was able to take photographs of most of them as well.

Where There's Life There's Hope

Northwick Park is more than a hospital, more than just a name. It's a group of dedicated people who happen to be in the same building. The hospital has a reputation of being good at what it does, and returning people to society very much improved. And there is a good reason for that. It is that it has impeccable physiotherapy. Its best is not the best I have found in my three hospitals, but on a whole, it can't be beaten. The speech therapy is also very good. When I came here it was very difficult to understand anything I said, yet now it would be hard to distinguish me from any normal person. Like everything, though, it has its faults. Occupational therapy here is probably excellent. However, I have washed my clothes and cooked for years and there is little they can teach me. I may be a bit slower, but I have been out of practice for five months and it will take a bit of time. And I have been doing washing and dressing for the best part of four months. After one session there was little my therapist could give me to do. There was, in fact, very little to keep my brain and my hands active. But I'd say this hospital is pretty good if that is my only gripe.

On a personal level, I have been fairly subservient while in hospital, yet the 'laid-back' attitude here made me come out of my shell and gave me a lot of confidence, even more than I had to begin with. This is a very roundabout way of telling all of you to keep trying, never to give up. I know as well as any, having admired the woodworm on Death's front door, that it is often a lot worse than people make it out to be. However, it can't be as bad as all that. You must never give up.

When you read this, I will have already gone home, my time out of the world being up. So I will thank all of the patients for being there, the nurses for being friendly, and the therapists for being helpful. I am bound to be back at some point for a visit, but for now, 'Goodbye.'

RRU Newsletter Issue No. 50,
12 May 1995

A Diversion into Self-expression

My accident, though serious, was to leave me very like the person I was before, except for the few physical problems that continued to irritate me. Thankfully my memory and intellect were intact. I have often told people that I am the same as I was before. No malice or ill humour developed, as would have been expected after surviving such an ordeal. I am as much the carefree, happy-go-lucky person I have always been. Many people, both friends and family, certainly say so, but kindly, all freely admit that I have somehow been left better in many ways. They say that I am more considerate and more caring – Mother has even said that my driving is better!

Having said that, I changed, there is no way I can deny it. I changed in ways that took me countless months to discover. Most were small corrections to my behaviour, be it making my bed in the morning or eating an orange without laboriously peeling off all the pith. Other traits were more enigmatic. Some of these would cause major misunderstanding, some would be beneficial; the fact that I do not like chocolate very much now is probably a good thing!

However, there are some differences that are hard to fathom. For years I have kept out of the sunshine and hidden behind sunglasses. Now, though, the sun does not affect me as much; I wander around outside without wearing a hat or sunglasses. I appear to be more tolerant of the bright light and did not suffer from sunstroke, like I always did before, during the very sunny summer of 1995. Before this time I had been known to roll up my sleeves and occasionally wear shorts, but most of me remained covered – within a few minutes I would invariably turn a livid shade of red, making me indistinguishable from a lobster! Yet now I walk around uncovered when outside and do not really burn; I am brown all over, a natural wash of colour that only makes its presence known when brought up against unexposed skin – the colour looks as though it should be there. Maybe I should fear skin cancer; but, unhealthy or not, I do not fear anything now.

'Corrections' brought about by my accident like this may ultimately kill me, but that does not seem to bother me. I believe that in some way I died in the accident anyway. By some fluke I have been given a bonus life that I can treat in any way I want. If I die tomorrow, I would say people are lucky to have had me for the period since the accident – they should not mourn that they have lost me, but rejoice that they had me for longer than anyone would have dared consider possible. Maybe I only say that to justify what I do now, thinking that nobody can touch me and I cannot cause harm to anyone else.

Although many of these changes would not alter me that much, some of these modifications were very profound and would completely change who I was; I started to realise that I could still cause harm to other people. Those whom I hurt along the way were cast off to one side to lie dying, not unlike the accidental massacre of flying bugs smashing into the windscreen of a car speeding down the motorway. Only by learning from the accident, and evolving out of the darkness, was I going to extract any benefit from the experience and let goodness lead the way; and learn I did: the experience taught me a lot. I began to see how people related to others and how I wished to react. By providing me with confidence, it gave me the ability to determine how I would treat people.

That most human of certain mental attributes, *confidence*, changes from person to person and adapts constantly throughout your life, altering the way that you view life and how you treat it. Ultimately, the confidence that is reflected on the world will determine the way that you are treated by the world and by the people in it. It must also be noted that there are two distinct forms of confidence.

The first and most obvious variation is confidence that is shown to other people – in mystical terms, one's aura. More than anything else it defines how people react to you, and can determine the sort of person that you are able to become. People with such confidence can also be viewed as having a very objective slant on life. It was the sort of confidence that did not come easily to me.

The second form is a much more subtle kind of confidence and has nothing to do with anyone else. You truly believe in yourself and have faith in whatever you are doing; nothing will stand between you and your objective – you will not let it. Put simply, it determines how you can relate to the outside world from a purely subjective viewpoint. No one else takes a part in the way you view life, and the arrogant opinions you voice are very self-rewarding and often deprecatory to other people. This self-confidence came very easily to me, and may very well explain how I was able to recover as well as I did.

Variations in these two forms of confidence provides us with several groups of people. Some are naturally confident, and they can travel through life knowing that they will get on with everyone and that they will be well loved by all around them, and even that they can do what they like without suffering from the consequences of their actions. As they are confident, they believe in themselves; by believing in themselves they naturally feel confident. This belief in themselves is so strong that others find they believe in them as well. Certainly, those people blessed with a large amount of such charisma find the ability of liking people and being liked comes far more readily to them than to the average person.

At the other end of the scale are those unfortunates who have little or no confidence and who travel through life trying to hide away from other people's quizzical natures, while ignoring everyone and hoping not to be noticed. They believe they are as low on the evolutionary scale as you can go and see no reason why others should not treat them like the worthless scum they believe they are. They view themselves as not being very far removed from biological sludge, and the pitiful 'face' they show to the world will only reveal their timidity and self-doubt. Of course, most people exist somewhere in the twilight zone between the light and the dark.

Being the archetypal Gemini that I am, I display both of these views equally and the person I am consists of an equal mixture of these two entities. The belief I have in myself is so strong that nothing is ever too big an obstacle to my progress; not even the few hiccups that punctuate life are able to disrupt me as I steamroll through. So strong is this faith in myself that there is no room left for anyone else, and the visits by the chaplains made no difference to my life.

As far as this self-confidence goes, I have more than my fair share. Only by using this innate ability was I able to return comparatively undamaged from the hellhole I had become lost in, back to a world where I was able to play a significant part. This subjective nature plays a large part in who I am, predetermining the strength, fortitude and sheer stubbornness that I was able to utilise in helping me achieve the level of recovery that I reached. Quite simply, so strong was my belief in getting better that I would not let anything stand in my way. I could walk again not because I regained the physical ability, but because I never once thought that I couldn't. On seeing how well I had recovered, most people summed it all up in one word: determination.

When it came to innate confidence though, it is fair to say that I had none. I displayed a great deal of potential in the way that I was able to totally relax around people I knew and, although I never thought it at the time, a certain amount of charisma in the way that people naturally liked me, allowing me to make friends very easily. I was too socially immature to realise that at the time, and the manner in which women constantly said they wanted to marry someone like me, yet no one would go out with me, acted very powerfully in making me believe that I was unattractive to the opposite sex. Although I accept that there is someone in this world for everyone, it did not matter how many times people told me, I would not believe it. What little confidence I had took somewhat of a hammering, leaving me very insecure, especially around strangers. Put in a simple word to explain what I was feeling, I was shy – a common complaint. So peculiar is this mix of self-confidence and shyness that it left me with the improbable task of being an introverted extrovert.

When I was first in hospital, I would not say boo to a goose. I was quiet and meek and tried to go through what was left, for some strange reason, of my life, without disturbing anyone, trying to hide in some dark corner and act invisibly so that nobody would notice me. Although this is remarkably difficult in hospital, I had a very good shot at making it succeed. I would not moan, no matter how bad the pain was (it certainly helped not feeling any pain), and did not look at people, thereby inviting them to ask me a question. I talked only when spoken to and would, under no circumstances, interrupt two nurses if they were talking to each other.

The trouble is that this mask of politeness is not wanted in hospital; it runs by the exchange of knowledge and information, and patients are expected to inform nurses of any problems. Under these conditions, shyness is bad and is not helpful. You are expected to ask questions, even if that means interrupting nurses' indispensable conversation. Yet I remained quiet, not screaming out, no matter how much I needed help, merely lying there hoping someone would look at me, thereby inviting me to ask *them* a question. One morning in Royal Ward I was desperate to go to the toilet; I remember sitting further and further up in bed – it was somehow more comfortable and less of a strain. I edged my back higher up the wall, until it reached the point where a nurse had to come and see me before I fell out of bed... again! She could also take me to the toilet!

I learnt very slowly – so slowly that I was totally unaware of it – but by the time I was ready to leave the Royal London, a change was already apparent. It all started at the beginning of January when friends began to come in to see me. Somehow, over the past several millennia, humans have come to appreciate that a kiss can cure all manner of ills. Being in the situation I was, people exercised this thought a great deal. Every visitor felt obliged to give me a peck on the cheek. I did not think to refuse, as I once would have done, and by the time I knew what was going on I had already started to understand the significance and even to like the concept.

Before I left Royal Ward, I wanted to show Ros the previous night's miracle of being able to straighten my right arm. Although I had no therapy on my last day, the physiotherapists came up to the ward anyway to see the people too ill to go to the gym (at least I was not in that category). I was busy watching them walk around the room, biding my time while I waited for the moment they would come over to say goodbye to me. I was absent-mindedly scanning with my head across the foot of the bed when a nurse, who was checking my notes, suddenly smiled at me.

Throughout my life this show of friendship was always treated in the same way: an embarrassed thought, My God, I've been caught! This was instantaneously followed by me rapidly averting my gaze and pretending as though the whole incident had never happened. On this occasion something remarkable took place that I will remember for years to come. *I smiled back.* I had never done that before and maybe had not even realised I did it then – but the fact remained, I did.

It was only a simple gesture and may well have been written off as a strange quirk brought on as a result of the severe bang to my head. However, when I was finally discharged on 12 May, this thought remained with me and dictated the way in which I would relate to other people from that moment on. To begin with though, very little happened; I did not go to many places or see many people. I treated those I did see with a natural courtesy laced with my cheeky sense of humour; but more than anything, I was able to talk to them without exhibiting any shyness. I treated everyone as though they were on the same level as me, as though they were equals and did not deserve to be viewed with any special privilege. It was a remarkable change, but I had only just ventured onto the lower slopes of the mountain I was to climb.

It would take several months to scale this peak, and it took several more months to complete my transformation and fathom the complexities of these changes. Most people have their whole lives to figure out who they are and understand the different qualities that fashion their make-up. Certainly, I understood who I was; but now I was not the person I was. A lot of the new me I could understand, but some of these changes were so radical that I did not discern them immediately. It took over a year from my accident before I would start to learn the intricacies of the person I had become. My evolution was continuous, but it still took a very long time. Even so, I was able to learn with everything I did. As the weeks drifted by I slowly began to understand the muta-tions that were running rampant within me, but although I started to see small parts of the picture, the whole image was still wrapped in fog. I took numerous wrong turns, hit many dead ends and made several mistakes before the correct route out of the maze was shown to me.

Less than two months after I had been discharged I was invited to go for a small holiday to Normandy along with my uncle, Andrew White, and maternal grandparents. We would stay there with my aunt, Laura, and her three children. It was here that the enormity of my transfiguration was really brought home to me.

Laura's parents own a château near Alençon in Normandy, and when she was there, during the school holidays, as many people as possible were invited to visit. We stayed for two weeks and probably saw somewhere in the region of thirty visitors, and the French, being French, gave everyone a kiss on each cheek. My mentality had changed to the extent that it did not matter to me what people did or what their viewpoint was, and I did not care that all these strangers were kissing me; after all, strangers are just people you do not know yet.

At the château worked a student, Anne-Frédérique, hired as a maid, an ordinary servant, and not any part of the family. She knew her place and, under no circumstances, would she go around kissing members of the family or their guests. I did not accept this point of view and saw before me a very attractive lady, about my age, whom I liked very much. The fact that we spoke little of each other's language did not seem to matter. Not caring about other people's opinions and having no fear from the effects of my actions I started to kiss her in the normal French style – I gave her two pecks on the cheek, one on each. I think I somewhat surprised her, but she did not mind, so much so that one day when she saw me before I saw her, she came and kissed me.

Her acceptance fired my enthusiasm and one morning I suggested, in my stilted French, that we give each other four kisses, two on each cheek, as I had learnt on a trip to Paris several years before. She saw no reason to object, and so we continued in this manner for the few days I had left at the château.

> 'Philip has taught Colin, myself, and our children a lesson: never to give up! His tremendous will power towards a full recovery impressed us all and despite the occasional slur in his speech, which is faster than ever, he is back to his old self,

with a gentler touch to his personality. One could have expected Philip to come out of this accident slightly bitter for what it did to him, and he therefore deserves to be praised for his present outlook on life.'

Laura White, aunt

When I returned to England I made a conscious decision to continue with this style of greeting. I enjoyed it and could see no reason for not doing it nor why anyone should object to this harmless kiss. Certainly, few people I kissed afterwards showed any great cause for complaint – many women, in fact, welcomed it, accepting it with great fervour. Quite who I was 'allowed' to kiss took a long time to work out. To begin with I went around and kissed everyone I knew, young or old, whether I wanted to or not. As the time since my accident increased and I learnt more about these changes that were slowly transforming my inner self, I began to be more selective. There was the occasional person who resented my kiss (after all, people had become used to me being one way, and now I was totally different), and these people I did not kiss. Of those who were left, you could tell the ones I liked because I kissed them. Some preferred a hug, perhaps believing it to be less intimate than a kiss; but a hug means far more than a kiss. Perhaps it was this they realised. The kiss of greeting, after all, is just a peck on the cheek and means nothing in itself. Some close friends took my harmless peck on the cheek one stage further. The peck was still given, and there was no intention meant for anything beyond two close friends greeting each other. The cheek was bypassed, though. Two sets of closed lips clashed gently, and then the moment passed. It was nothing heavy; a peck is just a peck. The target for such innocent affection did not reveal a level of close intimacy, merely the closeness of the friendship involved.

I have often wondered at the improbability of my transformation. Why was it that I treated hospital as a place to learn and develop, and came out far more confident than I went in? This oddity is more pronounced when taken with my gain of both weight and strength, features that are not normally known to develop when in hospital. How is it that my misfortune has enabled me to increase in these attributes? It may be enough just to be grateful that these qualities are now within me. I should simply be glad that I have a strange ability to utilise any bad luck I am confronted with, turn it back on itself and learn from the experience. Yet, somehow, that is not enough. Without knowing 'why', I have learnt nothing.

Maybe it is an ability that only I possess, but I think not. This ability has certainly become well developed in me, but it is available for all to use. I do not suggest that everyone goes around with an endless supply of confidence, since that is just not possible. Keep an open mind to any possibility, really believe you can achieve whatever you set out to do, and you will be surprised with what you actually attain.

The Land of the Living

The week following my discharge was one where memories play no part; the time brought such a culture shock that I have no recollection of it. Even so, one memory is very vivid in my mind: when phoning people, even those whose number had been (and still was) committed to memory, I always got a wrong number. No matter how much I concentrated, my fingers would not press the correct buttons on the telephone! Still, that did not matter. I was out of hospital – after a mere five months – back home where I could be who I was and do what I wanted. None of my family or friends could believe my return home happened quite so quickly. Nobody who met me could imagine the extent of my head injury, as I showed very little sign of it. Even when I look at my photographs it appears unreal, almost as though the person lying in the bed, wrapped in the warmth of the sheets, with tubes emanating from every obvious place, was someone else.

I tried looking for evidence of their falsification. None could be found. Somehow the person lying on those crisp, white sheets was me. As I lay on the sofa at home I considered this presumption possible. Then I got up to fetch a glass of water and the image of it being me lying on that bed disappeared in a puff of logic. If it was so improbable, how was it possible? Yet there were witnesses. Several people had seen this inanimate object rouse itself and transform, slowly starting to talk, to walk and to feed itself. It seemed there was no doubt that some force appeared to have been at work: life was followed by death, yet I had been given a second chance. I ought to go out into the world and right the wrongs that slowly flow through society.

Somehow I was not ready; I still had to undergo changes before a new person would show himself, not unlike a phoenix rising victorious from the ashes of its own failed existence. To begin with, though, I spent days at a time simply resting, watching television – basically doing nothing that required any effort. I used up enough energy in pushing the buttons on the remote control! I think I ate, but I do not recall actually helping prepare any of the meals.

Then it all changed. I am an active person, and it was too difficult to stay with my parents and not do anything. Although I had spent the previous few weekends doing various jobs at home, much of my recent life had been spent doing nothing – although, yes, a great deal of effort on my part had been put into surviving and recovering to the point I find myself at now. That was not effort, though, as my survival instinct is very strong; now it was about time I progressed and did something constructive.

Before I could do anything, though, it was decided that I really ought to see a GP, just in case. As I had been living in London when my parents moved to Stevenage, my doctor was still in St Albans. Though I was now out of his catchment area, Dr Michael Croft was the only medical person to have known me from before my accident. I needed to see him first. He was pleased to see me and very sorry to hear about my accident – the worst calamity to have happened to one of his patients without them dying. He was very helpful and seeing him again was worthwhile.

After I returned from my day trip to St Albans I started to settle down to living back at home. Before I could, I baffled my parents by revisiting Northwick Park. I chatted to a few people, including Anita (in her last week there) and I took further photographs for the album, but there was no need for me to be there. Institutions, be they hospital, the army or even prison, have such a strong hold on the individuals involved, that to break away entirely is very strenuous and required the kind of fortitude that was coming close to breaking point in me. By taking one step at a time, the break was less of a strain, and I found it much easier to cope with. Everyone I knew, my friends and my family, were overjoyed at my discharge and could only see it from that viewpoint. From where I was standing, coming from a society where someone else does your thinking for you, and arriving somewhere else where you have to cope with every small detail, was a little bit daunting. At least I had spent many weekends home with my parents in the previous three months and the change was not that radical.

I had no sooner returned from my visit to Northwick Park when I revisited the Lister – a hospital I had, by this stage, grown to like. Two days every week I travelled the several miles to hospital to attend physio and speech therapy, either catching a lift off my mother or from one of two neighbours, Eileen Conley or Anne Styles. Anne was a fellow author who had sent me large amounts of home-made chocolate fudge brownies while I was at the Lister. I returned home sometimes by catching a bus, or occasionally by being very lazy and taking a taxi. More often than not I walked. It took me so long to walk what I thought was four miles that I was delighted when my father told me it was nearer six – I was walking faster than I thought!

Audrey Canadas, my speech therapist from February, took me once again. My voice had certainly developed over several months, I spoke slower and my accent became less obvious. Audrey had one less obstacle to contend with in that I could speak. Nevertheless, in my opinion my 'voice' sounded terrible: there was no presence, and the articulation around certain syllables caused a distinct slur – even though allegedly I was not dysarthric. I also had a slight stammer over vowels at the beginning of words – especially over the word 'I' at the start of a sentence – or the first few words spoken after a rest for a few minutes. I was not able to project my voice. This was unfortunate, since before my accident a whisper from me could be heard by everyone, and now anybody listening was far too easily distracted. I often likened my bad voice to trying to talk without any harmonics.

My physiotherapist was Nicola Russell. I had travelled a long way down the road of my recovery by the time I saw her and I was coping very well. I had a few minor problems, but there was nothing distinct, nothing that could be put forward to blame for these problems. There was nothing that really could be corrected; I just needed monitoring. Even so, Nicola did try to find lots of exercises for me to do and anticipated making them a little bit harder, since I didn't have any problem with the easier exercises. Here we came up against a little obstacle. There were many exercises I was still unable to even attempt, and without the ability to attempt them there were not many ways that she could find to give me exercise. Press-ups were far too easy, for example, from a kneeling position, but the correct feeling had still not returned to my right leg and without it I was unable to curl my toes under my foot to do a proper press-up with my legs straight. Until the feeling returned and I was able to do this, press-ups had little purpose. My head injury was affecting me physically in ways I was still discovering.

Although in the early days physiotherapy was fantastic and the type of therapy I needed badly, I had now reached the point were it was not doing very much – due, strangely, to the far-reaching complications of my initial head injury – and occupational therapy was becoming far more important. The only drawback was that I had not been referred for occupational therapy. As this therapy came easily to me at Northwick Park, why bother?

I cannot be certain this was the reason, but it makes sense. Occupational therapy at the Lister was different, though, and was much needed. After a discussion with Kathy Freedman, the head therapist who would be taking me as an outpatient, I telephoned the consultant at the RRU to ask for a referral. Eventually I was able to start this therapy.

I was also able to take up woodwork, something the occu-pational therapists had advised back in February, since it would strengthen the right side of my body and help me to use both sides of my body independently while keeping the symmetry. The technician, Tony Coxall, was very helpful, and I was able to build several objects, starting with a spice rack for Mother. Several items later, I worked on restoring a turn-of-the-century hat stand bought for me by my mother and Cynthia at an antique's shop. I cleaned and polished it, repaired places where the wood was splitting, and attached a new section that had disappeared completely. My lifelong ambition of owning a hat stand was realised.

Occupational therapy itself followed a similar course to February's. However, mostly tests on my memory and measurements of my finger/wrist/hand strength and speed were taken. Discovering that there was little feeling in my right hand, it was arranged for me to join the 'hand class', where I would use different tools to help make me become more aware of what my hand was doing. One test involved feeling coins in a bag and saying what denomination they were. This was very hard, and I was not as good as I expected. Mind you, when Michelle had a go and found she was no good either, I felt a little bit better.

Later in the year, two other former head-injury patients and I met once a week to start up a new group, the 'head class' (an arbitrary name, as the class was so new it did not have one). One of them, Helen Allardyce, was a very talented artist; the other, Clea Fletcher, I had met a few weeks previously during speech therapy. I had heard that she had read my article in the *Daily Express* about HEMS and was very interested in meeting me. How could I deny her this opportunity as my fame spread?

In the 'head class' we practised activities ranging from planning and cooking a meal to games of table tennis. Everything we did was devised so as to increase our reactions; our awareness, not only of what was going on around us, but also of our own 'handicaps'; and our confidence in, for example, asking total strangers for information – not at all daunting for me any more. I was also given many activities to try at home to help improve any occupational skills; no doubt my mother loved the therapists for this! Whether I would have done anything or not, I was told to help with various tasks ranging from cutting vegetables and assisting with the cooking to sweeping the outside path and helping with the housework. Within a few weeks I had increased this workload until I could practically look after myself properly once more.

As I went to the Lister twice a week, I would see the same group of people each visit and would begin to get to know them. I was able to practise my social skills, heightened since the increase in my confidence, learnt over the previous six months. A good example occurred during July. As I was walking through the X-ray department, taking a short cut to therapy, this very pretty nurse smiled at me. Reacting in a traditional manner, I continued walking, wondering why I had been granted such a smile. Within a couple of steps I 'slammed on the brakes' and backtracked a little.

'I recognise your face,' I said, 'but I can't remember where from – who are you?'

'Katrina!' she replied. 'You must remember me, I was on your ward.'

At last I knew something the old me would have pondered over for a long time, but would have done nothing about. Strangely, though I recognised her face, I couldn't remember Katrina herself; something I still find surprising. I mean, how could anyone forget somebody as beautiful, warm and caring as Katrina? Mind you, I had had a head injury!

I only saw Katrina once after that, the week before her impending birthday; but that didn't really matter, I had asked who she was. I even went and bought her a birthday card during lunch. All praise to the alterations running rampant throughout my system.

Other than going to the Lister, I spent most of my time horse riding. After my discharge, Penniwells RDA, referred me to Digswell Place RDA about ten miles away from my parents. I started by going there on the days I was not at the Lister, although I eventually stuck to Mondays only. Mother gave me a lift there in the morning, alternating with two of my neighbours, Steve Conley and Mike Styles.

Spending a half day there was an inefficient use of my time, so I decided I would stay there all day, and at some point had my ride. The rest of my time was spent helping; so good was I that after a time I was regarded more as a helper than a rider. I cleaned as many horses as I could and helped tack them up. After all, I probably knew more about horses than most of the helpers (head injury or not), and it would have been unfair, and very difficult, not to help them.

I thoroughly enjoyed riding horses again and it got me out of the house all day. It also meant that I was able to do some shopping if I wanted as I had to pass the Welwyn Garden City shops on my way to the train station before I could return home, at which point I was often picked up by another neighbour, Innes Garden, on his way home. Going shopping was useful: living five miles away from the town centre, and 1½ miles from the nearest bus stop, I was not able to go shopping from home that often.

Horses took me from the house a great deal. Having the time, I often went down to Willowtree to see the people there, and to spend time with Shannon. By the end of July I decided to go down for the whole weekend. I was there for both days, spending the night in one of the caravans at the yard, something I was used to from my previous life. Occasionally, I expanded my small excursion to include Thursday and Friday so as to be able to see Mrs P, Fiona, Melissa and all the other riders whom I used to look after six months previously. It was great fun being down there, seeing all the people and the horses I knew, and important spending time with, and looking after, Shannon.

I continued spending most of my weekends at Willowtree until the end of September, at which point the weather turned really miserable. It became so cold in the early morning that Mr M banned me from coming down for both days and spending the night. The importance of spending all this time at the yard was only revealed to me at the beginning of 1996 when Shannon was sadly put down, after surviving a couple of heart attacks and having endured laminitis for many of his twenty-five years.

Horse riding was not the only social activity with which I was involved. On the last Sunday of every month, until the final meeting at the end of November, I went along to see Becky, a keen horse rider herself, and attend my regular Mensa games meeting. It was great seeing everyone again, and I never tired of talking about my recent experience. Recovering as well as I had, I never minded talking about it and was even quite proud. It was refreshing seeing the surprise in people's eyes when they found out, as I knew it meant they otherwise would not have known anything had happened. After all, only a small amount of evidence existed to show that I had been in an accident, little proof that I had a problem. I even joined in a game of Trivial Pursuit once, me verses five teams of two people. It was an advantage to them being a pair, since if one did not know the answer, their teammate might. Conversely, it was an advantage for me to be on my own. When I knew the answer, I didn't have to convince anybody else first. It may be an arrogant attitude, but I won the game!

At the end of June, I stayed the night after the Sunday meeting as I often did, and took the train back to Stevenage early on Monday morning. I was walking towards the hospital for Monday's therapy, travelling along the cycleway. I was about half a mile away from the Lister and was crossing the top of a grass bank when it happened. My right leg – the feeling of which had still not returned to normal – stepped in a dip, causing me to tip over forwards. Although I should have collapsed to the ground, stopping immediately, I tried to keep upright. I managed down most of the slope – even with my appalling balance – but as it levelled out at the bottom onto the coarse stone of the cycleway, I fell over; my trousers were ripped, my knees were grazed, blood was everywhere, my legs hurt and nobody was around. Not wanting to sit there and hope that someone might pass by and offer assistance, I had to complete my journey. Any limp that was evident before was now obvious, but I just had to grit my teeth and get on with it. The occupational therapists were superb, sitting me down, cleaning the wounds and applying antiseptic cream and plasters. They then told me to lie down, read my book and take it easy. Annoyingly, they gave me no work to do.

The reason I fell over was all due to the lack of sensation in my right leg. Whether this was down to the whack it had received from the car, or caused by the left-hand side brain damage as my head hit the side of the bus, did not matter. The head injury on its own made me 'disabled', and there were many people who said I was, though I showed little sign that they were right. At least that is what I thought. Certainly I never thought of myself as disabled and didn't recognise my shortcomings – though it seems that is one by-product of my 'disability'! I might not have minded, were it not for the stigma attached to being disabled – other people's attitudes are very prejudiced and discrimination is rife. It was a paradox that was to cause far-reaching complications.

Although I spent several days a week as an outpatient, at the RDA school or visiting my stables, most of my time was spent writing letters. Much of this task was pleasurable. I sent one to my old landlord, John Nippress, from when I lived in East Ham attending London University. I had told Mother to phone him when I was in the Royal London, thinking I still lived with him. I had heard nothing, and knowing that he would not have ignored her message, I wrote to him. It was lucky, since he had lost my phone number – typical of John! It was also good in that we renewed our friendship, one that had developed over my two-

year stay with him in East Ham while attending Queen Mary and
Westfield College.

> 'The first I heard about your accident was when you wrote to
> me many months after the event. Your mother had rung here
> but I was on holiday at the time. When I read your letter, in
> which you laid out the details of the accident and the immedi-
> ate period of hospitalisation and ongoing treatments, I read
> each word, but they were not being absorbed as I found it
> hard to believe what I was reading.
>
> 'Only on reading the letter immediately again did it seem
> to be factual. I felt quite drained, for quite awhile I just sat
> there, and read the letter again.'
>
> John Nippress, friend and ex-landlord

Unfortunately, most of the letters I had to write were ones I did
not think I needed to, but I was forced into the position where it
became necessary. Up until 28 June, Mr M had been paying me
money because of my ill health. When this statutory sick pay ran
out, the Department of Social Security (DSS) should have taken
over and paid me Benefits. After waiting a few days, I was so
distressed at hearing nothing I was forced into writing to them.
Almost immediately they sent me an incapacity benefit form,
which I quickly completed and returned.

After I'd waited until 12 July, the tenterhooks were finally
removed and I was turned down for incapacity benefit, with the
suggestion I apply for income support. I was given no reason why
I was turned down, and this was odd since it was obvious that I
was incapacitated. Furthermore, nobody would answer my letters
or my telephone calls asking for an explanation – or, indeed, the
phone call made for me by the Citizens' Advice Bureau. Dutifully, I applied for income support right away, needing some
money on which to survive. In the manner of the farce that this
was fast becoming, I was turned down for income support on
25 July. It was obvious to me that I needed help, but my only
experiences of social workers came from the Royal London.
Though my social worker in the Trauma Unit was excellent,
while I was unconscious, the one from Royal Ward was somewhat
disturbing; so bad that I never even saw her, even though by then
I was conscious. I am told she saw me before walking off saying I

looked all right. She did talk to my mother, but all she was concerned with was giving her the address of a solicitor so that we could get compensation from the driver and the address of the charity *Headway*, where Mother could receive counselling.

Although *Headway* would prove invaluable to me in future years, for Mother the counselling was not necessary and possible compensation was not possible unless I could prove, beyond a doubt that the driver was at fault. At this I was troubled: how could I prove what I cannot even remember? What we needed was help, but were not given any assistance in wading through the quagmire of red tape and bureaucracy that is the DSS. Meanwhile, I had no income, and the government was giving me no money, money I might have needed to survive. I was beginning to wonder whether anybody was going to help me. I even tried telephoning the DSS helpline, but did not receive any help; in fact the person I spoke to was positively rude! Although the knowledge that I had so little evidence of my 'disabilities' was satisfying, I was still not able to work; I was surely entitled to some form of sick pay from the government or it would make a mockery of the taxes I had paid when I did work.

This seemingly obvious fact slowly made its way through the system and by the third week of August I was given some income support. Although they did have the decency to backdate it to mid-July, it took them a further three months to do this, and even then they missed out the first fortnight. By then it might have already been too late – I could have been lying alone on the streets of London, my withered hand clutching onto my cardboard box as I fought to stay alive, my tired lungs gasping for air as I hoped and prayed, my dying breaths fading into obscurity... Phil Collins did this sad existence justice in his song, 'Another Day in Paradise'. I was one of the lucky ones, though, with my parents stepping in to fill the void.

On Halloween, the date still haunting my life, I was sent a letter from the DSS stating that I would now be entitled to income support; the fact that I had been receiving it for the previous three months did not appear to be relevant. It was a simple letter, but it summed up the immense problems with the DSS. Quite simply it is such a big organisation, looking after so many millions of people, that sometimes information can be overlooked or repeated.

Although, I had been turned down for incapacity benefit I guess the DSS eventually realised they should cover their bases and determine whether I was entitled to this benefit or not. I was sent for a medical examination in Luton to find out whether I was physically entitled to incapacity benefit. Not only did I later discover that the problems I had made me exempt from the medical in the first place (and I still have ataxia), I had to wait until 23 January 1996 before I was asked to see a doctor. This was over a year since my accident, and I had improved – what about all those months when I was at Death's door? Even though I was half blind, spoke atrociously and, having significant problems with my right leg, was even on crutches... the doctor decided that I was fit for work! Can you imagine mucking out stables on crutches?

Six months followed. I sent pointless letters and made irate phone calls. I even turned to my MP for aid, who also got nowhere. I sent the DSS as much proof as I could that I was disabled. They wrote back saying that my entitlement to benefit had '...nothing to do with how disabled you are' – yet they would not tell me what it *had* to do with! I got nowhere. People like me can slip through the net.

In spite of my continuing problems with the DSS, I was not about to let any of them get me down. July was a fabulous month. My aunt, Laura, had invited her parents-in-law over to her parents' château in Normandy. After several weeks of indecision, and with the help of Colin's brother, Andy, they were finally persuaded to cross the Channel for a holiday, if only because they could pick me up on the way. Whatever the truth of the matter, I had a ten-day trip to Lonray for my summer holiday. On arrival, we were confronted with Laura, two of her daughters, Natacha and Antonia, and the dog, Quassia; Laura's husband, Colin, and their other daughter, Lavinia would be arriving at the weekend. Lots of the children's friends and even the odd parent came to visit at this time. Little was done that first day as we spent much of it moving in and unpacking, but that did not seem to matter; it is a beautiful old house and we were on holiday.

After the accident, ten-year-old Antonia (with whom I had had a special relationship) sent me a card which, in her own childish writing, expressed exactly what she felt and brought a tear to my eye. The card very simply read: 'I want you come back.' Poor Antonia did not understand where her Philip had gone; the Philip who was here was different. It will take a long time to rebuild our special relationship, though it will probably never be the same.

> 'Later, we had the opportunity of seeing you again, when you had reached the state of recovery to be able to ride on horseback, which thankfully increased our awareness of your improvement.
>
> 'Your interest in horses has always given me something to think about, having many of my ancestors being keen huntsmen or farmers – not to mention your three cousins Lavinia, Natacha and Antonia. So don't give up your interest in horses.
>
> 'Marie and I send you our best wishes for a continued improvement in your recovery.'
>
> Gordon White, maternal grandfather

In the mornings I was up about six, washed, dressed and downstairs soon after. The first item on the agenda was to feed the dog and let her out. I then emptied the dishwasher before my breakfast. Three hours later most of the others rose for their breakfast. Laura tended to be up in the meantime to visit the shops and buy the day's bread, sometimes taking me along so that I could practise my French!

We filled our days with standard activities; I played with the children and Andy helped construct a fence around one of their many fields. In the few days I was there I also went walking, I rode horses and went swimming in the moat – the first time I had been swimming since before my accident. Occasionally, my grandfather joined me on a walk, though more often than not he would venture out on his own, something he no doubt would not have done had he remained in sunny Dorset. I think he felt young and vigorous again following his second hip replacement operation and wanted to make the most of being in these beautiful surroundings; while my grandmother, a month short of ninety, simply rested.

The most important part of the day, though, a time when we could all get together and discuss what we had been doing, was lunch. Like the supper in the evening, it was a time when I was increasingly helpful. After every course, the maid, Anne-Frédérique, came and took the plates away and brought the next course. At the end of the meal, all the diners put their arms back and rested while Anne-Frédérique cleared away the dishes. Feeling adventurous like my grandfather, and purely from an occupational therapy viewpoint (the fact that she was very pretty *never* crossing my mind), I helped her clear the table. We took the plates away to the kitchen and removed the serviettes, place mats and cruet from the table. We did talk, but I know little French and she spoke no English; our conversations were often reduced to '*Bonjour*' and '*Ça va*'. At the time that did not matter, she had a lovely smile and it said a thousand words... all of them French, though!

Although a great number of the changes in me, including the increase in my confidence, occurred in hospital, this trip to France helped close the lid and cement these changes to what was left of me. I could easily have been viewed as a very innocent, impressionable youth whose soul lay bare like a blank page, an unwritten masterpiece, for others to write upon. Unfortunately many of these changes were alien to me and it took many months for them to be understood, and along the way mistakes inevitably happened.

Quite how badly what I said to Vicki was taken I am not sure, though it was bad enough to totally destroy what little confidence she had amassed in her short life; it seems that whatever I thought I said was taken far worse than I could ever have imagined. Precisely how it was perceived though is not important. I made a horrendous mistake; I drove away my best friend of five years. God knows I did not really mean what I said, and I am very sorry, but it's too late; the past cannot be altered.

The end of July brought more excitement. For the first time since my transfer to the Lister, I was to revisit the Royal London Hospital. Mother had organised the day out through the HEMS

Rehabilitation Coordinator, Julie Baldry Currens. She met up with us in reception and recognised my mother immediately, but had not seen me without any tubes or even standing upright. It took her a few moments before she recognised me, but the way her face lit up when she did was ample compensation. I had not heard much about Julie, but what I had I liked, and I was very pleased to make her acquaintance. Although she would take me back to Royal Ward and show me around the casualty area, the main part of my visit was to see the helicopter, my saviour, up on the helipad.

We were met on the helipad by Alastair Wilson, Clinical Director (A&E) and Paul Rudd, Production and Operations Director of the *Daily Express*. It was really interesting seeing the helicopter and I was able to chat with a lot of the crew and staff who were there, though unfortunately Phil, Gareth, Ian and David, who had dealt with me, were not. The team on duty showed me around their office and gave me several of 'my' printouts that they had been collecting from their computer. I think seeing me cheered them up as much as being there had me.

The other aspect of the day that was interesting was the alarm sounding and the crew rushing forward as HEMS was activated on another call. Although fascinating to watch, the knowledge that any call-out could have been to someone else like me gave me a bitter taste in my mouth and I was relieved when the helicopter came back empty. A false alarm; perhaps the unlucky person was not as bad as was first thought.

During the previous weekend I had seen a news story on the TV in which it was stated that the helicopter cost far too much money and should be closed down. Fools who do not think things through properly wanted this lifeline to the whole of London cut off, meaning people like me would be left at the roadside to die. Incensed, I wrote a letter and handed it to Paul Rudd to see if it could be printed in the *Daily Express*. The timing was good as well, as they were mid-way through a series of articles saying how much HEMS was needed. Within a few days I even had a photographer come round to take my photograph for the paper, my letter winning £25 as the Star Letter.

I Owe my Life to Express Helicopter

The car hit me. That was bad. My head hit the bus. That should have been fatal. Indeed, a trip on the road, by ambulance, in London's rush-hour traffic, over the bumps and potholes (once the ambulance had made its way to me), would have terminated my visit to this planet.

Even when I got to hospital, the nurses in the Trauma Unit told me that I was a fraction of an inch away from death on arrival.

But I was one of the lucky ones. I was 'rescued' by the Helicopter Emergency Medical Service, sponsored by Express Newspapers. If it was not for HEMS I would almost certainly have died.

It is expensive, though. I am not rich, I am not famous. Have I justified my life having been saved?

I will answer that question with another. How much is a human life worth? What is the price you would put on one?

At the moment there is only one helicopter to cover the whole of London. More time and effort should be spent on creating similar life-saving services.

Daily Express, Monday, 31 July 1995

Returning back to hospital, Julie took us along to Royal Ward and the physiotherapy department off Sophia Ward. Unfortunately, other than Jackie Newitt, whose hair was shorter but cheeky grin was still the same, I did not meet up with anyone I knew. Julie was quick to point out that I now had an excuse to have another trip, something I was to do several times. Weeks later I received a letter from Doug Jones that I think summed up the way a lot of the nurses and therapists felt:

'It was excellent news to hear of you looking in such good health when you visited the ward last week. You are still much remembered and the huge progress you have made gave us all great pleasure.'

Doug Jones, staff nurse

Although July had little else in store for me, that period of transition as summer began to end and autumn loomed on the

246

horizon was to mark a time for two very important birthdays. In the middle of the seasonal change, Lisa turned twenty-one; a party in her honour was held on the first weekend of September to which I was invited. No more than one week before that, a party was organised at the Savoy in London as my grandmother reached the grand old age of ninety, years young! The whole family was there: her three children (Colin, my mother and Andy), as well as all of their three families, including six grandchildren. After eating a very good meal, my grandparents took to the dance floor as the band played 'Happy Birthday'. I took to the dance floor as well, with much trepidation – the first time I had danced since my accident, and I didn't want to step on any toes!

Birthday parties excluded, the most pleasurable detail now I had left hospital was my freedom. After my five-month incarceration following the serious injury I was able to go anywhere I wanted, and do whatever I pleased, in my own way, without the constraints of having to cope with any physical problems – a reality for which I will ever be thankful. I certainly kept very busy during the end of 1995. I was feeling fit and well and all the parts of my body were working properly – well, all except my eyes.

Yes, for some reason Moorfields Eye Hospital, the best in the country, was having a big problem with me. When I went for my first appointment at the branch opposite Northwick Park Hospital as March came to a close, complaining of double vision, I was tested and was found to be short-sighted (only in the right eye, not that I was told), and prescribed glasses. From a vision point of view my left eye was uninjured and it became dominant. If I closed it, the glasses worked for my right eye, but with my left open the glasses were essentially useless. Even so, I was told they would cure my vision problems.

They did not, and in my six-monthly check-up in October I told them so. After looking at me again, they found the double vision was being caused by a weak muscle in the *left* eye. Many months of puzzlement followed before I remembered my education. Though affecting vision in my right eye, the damage to the left-hand side of my brain would cause damage to the peripheral vision of my left eye – hence the double vision. To try and cure this somewhat annoying problem, a prism was put on the glasses to bend the light rays and prevent the double vision. The prism gave me a headache, made it harder to see anything, and caused a lovely starburst effect that interfered with my vision.

By mid-November I was seen again, by someone totally different, who treated me like an intelligent adult, acknowledging my degree and looking past the head injury I was supposed to have. She told me that no prism could be made weak enough to cure my problems, and anything in front of my eyes would be irritating. She pointed out that the problem I was having with my eyes was so slight I probably would not notice it – even the right lens was practically clear glass! Apparently there is a minor operation that could help, but what would be the point? I was unknowingly compensating for the double vision by tilting my head slightly to the right. This adaptation meant I could see clearly, and it did not leave any scars! Initially, it caused tremendous problems with my posture and balance, but these too adapted to the slight head angle given time.

Checking my eyes again, the consultant was surprised to see that they were still improving when they should have stopped months before. She also agreed with my theory about my shortsightedness – that the muscles in the right eye connecting to the lens were weaker, and the lens could not be pulled to the correct shape to focus on faraway objects. This was understandable, as all the muscles on the right became weak due to the damage done to the left side of my brain from the accident. Unfortunately, it was unlikely that those in my eye would ever strengthen.

Like so many of my problems, my eyes encompassed one more curiosity to baffle modern science, leaving me with the impression that experts do not know everything and I am better off looking after myself. Either that or I am different – an enigma – but I am not sure if I am arrogant enough for that!

As November started to give way to December, one particular date became very obvious. Although I had only been discharged for seven months, 9 December 1995 marked exactly one year from my accident, and I thought that I ought to try and get my driving licence back. Though I later found out the Phenytoin was not started until 19 December '94, the 9th was one year on from the accident. I asked the DVLA for my licence and they gave it back, no questions asked; it shows what can happen if you are upfront and honest right from the start, as I was.

Overjoyed at this, and to mark the occasion of my accident, I decided to have a party. It was not a negative commiseration for a death almost occurring, but a very positive celebration of a life having been given back. It was a terrible time of the year to organise a party, but I am not getting knocked down again in the summer for anyone!

Even so, about fifty people were able to take a day away from their Christmas shopping. Most of my family and old family friends came. Having seen me in all three hospitals, Cynthia and David were not going to miss out on this meeting so, like Peter and Jenny, the other couple who had been friends of my family for over thirty years, they came bringing love, support, and more of the ever popular jelly babies!

> 'Time passed, progress was made, Phil's determination and stoicism can only be applauded. His celebration party was the bringing together of everyone whose encouragement helped bring Phil so far, perhaps undoubtedly the largest contribution coming from Phil himself; but the love, support and complete dedication of Rose, Nigel and Simon must be a marvel to us all.'
>
> Cynthia Matthews, family friend

Several neighbours and newer friends came as well, including Mrs P with Fiona (Melissa having flu); Liz, who brought Lisa, and Karen, who came bearing a card, the inscription in which was very touching:

> 'I know how hard you have worked and how much courage it has taken to get this far. I also know that you will keep on until you are fully recovered. You are amazing and an inspiration to all who know you.'
>
> Karen Lawley, friend

Some professional people turned up to my party as well, several of the teachers from Digswell Place RDA; Michelle, Georgia and Kathy from the Lister; as well as Sonja, one of my two main nurses from the Trauma Unit, whose presence made the whole event worthwhile. Much to my surprise and jubilation, Ian and

David, my two HEMS pilots, also came. I had a lovely time, and even though I made some of them work, everyone enjoyed themselves. Mind you, I did not make them work very hard. On the driveway leading up to the manor house where my parents live, several trees had been blown down in the 'hurricane' of 1987. As well as being 'in remembrance', I thought it would be ecologically sound to plant some more to replace them; so three beech trees were planted. A shovelful of earth was put on by Ian and David for the HEMS tree; Sonja (with some assistance from me) helped plant the Royal London tree; and my three loyal occupational therapists from the Lister helped plant a tree for my second hospital.

Those trees will outlive me, but at least now, anyone reading through the garden records of the manor house will find out about my accident, the wonderful helicopter and all the care that I received.

Rebirth

My life began again: no, it never really stopped, but it certainly seemed that way. Quite what took place after the party I am not really sure – most of the following days concertinaed into one and I am not sure what occurred when. However, before my move on 26 October 1996, when I managed to escape to live on my own again, a lot happened. In fact many of the things I did would change my future for ever, making changes that were fundamental to my existence. Unfortunately a great deal of that time was also spent being very frustrated. I knew I was able to care for myself, but found it hard having Mother clucking around me doing her motherly bit – mind you, she might not have cared at all, so I shouldn't complain too much. Thankfully, it only took my parents a couple of weeks before they pretty much left me to my own devices.

The major change in my life, something that may never have happened had it not been for the accident, was finding my mother, Elizabeth. 'Hey! What's going on?' I hear you all cry.

Well, I am adopted. It's something I have known all my life (adoption was my first word!) as do most of my friends. I talk about it quite freely and generally assume I have told most people, since it does not bother me at all, to the extent that I forget who doesn't know.

My accident gave me the realisation that I might have died without meeting her (initially all I wanted to do was see her face, look into her eyes and know who I am and where I came from). I knew that I would have been very unhappy and missed something had I not searched for her. It also occurred to me that if she ever found out about 'her son's' death, she might have been upset as well.

I thought about what to do for a long time. Then, on an RDA holiday at Bradbourne Riding and Driving Centre in Sevenoaks, Kent, in July 1996, I was talking to one of the helpers there, Liz

Turner, who had herself been adopted. She had looked for, and found, her birth mother. Though they did not have much time together before her mother died, she said it was the best thing she had ever done, and impressed upon me the need to do the same saying that I would never forgive myself if I did not. Realising this to be true, by the autumn I wholeheartedly went about looking for Elizabeth.

I got in touch with the agency that oversaw my adoption, had a meeting with the 'post-adoption worker', Val Payman, and looked at all the paperwork, most of which I already had (I'd done a lot of research for many years). Going through the papers we discovered that on my birth certificate there was an address for Elizabeth's parents. Maybe they were still there, twenty-four years later. After finding they were, by using the electoral register, Ms Payman offered to very carefully write an inquiring letter. A few days later she telephoned me saying Elizabeth had just phoned her and taken down all my details.

Elizabeth and I exchanged letters and photographs, and spoke on the phone. All was going very well; I even 'psychically' knew it was her when she phoned. It was going so well that, on 12 December 1996, we arranged to meet. 'Getting on like a house on fire' would be an understatement! We spoke like we were old friends and happily chatted, without ever being at a loss for words, for several hours. Since then we have met again, exchanged further letters, and have had more telephone conversations. Who knows what the future will bring.

Finding 'my mother' was, perhaps, one of the greatest events in my life; I saw what she looked like, she found out that I was OK and had had a pleasant childhood... all that she initially wanted to know. We both agreed that anything else would be a 'most definite bonus'. We are pleased with the bonuses we have had, but I hope for the 'star prize', i.e. getting to know my 'family'. Who knows? We have years ahead of us.

Another change that may never have happened were it not for my accident has a lot to do with other people's accidents. I was given two 'armfuls' of blood in hospital, so I thought it only fair that I should return the blood. Getting carried away and not minding needles I gave back three units instead of the two I had been given. Once started, giving blood is the kind of habit that is hard to break. My next 'bloodletting' is in a couple of weeks and I intend to continue.

Though for most of 1996 I was able to drive Mother's car, a relatively new automatic with power steering, I was relieved by the autumn when I obtained an older, heavier, manual car with no power steering. I knew the car was there, I knew I was in control; the 'panic state' that came over me from being taken for a drive by Mother's car was alleviated to a great extent and I felt comfortable once more. Mother, of course, never thought the day would come when I would be able to drive a manual car again, but perhaps strangely, I am better at driving than I was; I'm certainly slower.

With all this good came some bad – as I have said initially, my new life was very frustrating. Therapy had reached the point where I did not seem to be improving. Though I knew I could and would (and did!) get better, the therapists could not do much to help me. In outpatients, by Christmas 1995 the physios, who could do nothing constructive that I could not do myself, and the speech therapist ('you can speak, what's the problem?') had both discharged me. My friendly occupational therapists held on to me until Easter '96, but even they were 'fed up' with me by then. I had convinced everyone (but myself) that I was OK.

I knew I would improve and was never satisfied with how I was. It is perhaps for this reason that I did improve. After all, as I ceased to be aware of the small changes to my person, I never really knew whether I was improving or not. Even so, by the summer of 1997, I realised that I was stronger and fitter than I had been before my accident. Though my left arm was still stronger, my right arm was quickly heading back to normal – in fact, it would be were it not for the slight problems with my once dislocated right shoulder.

Before that summer, on 6 March 1997, I was to return to the helipad on the Royal London Hospital. Along with a dozen or so HEMS patients, I was invited back to meet Richard Branson. After eight years (far longer than they initially promised) the *Daily Express* was giving up sponsorship of HEMS, to be taken over by

Virgin. We were all able to meet Richard Branson and thank him for his commitment; many of us would not have been there were it not for HEMS. When asked what she thought on ITV Carlton's *Newsroom South East*, Lucinda Dymoke White said, 'It's good, 'cos it saved me.'

Another talented artist, Lucinda was someone I met at Northwick Park's RRU a few weeks before the Virgin launch while visiting Lisa, who had returned for an operation. She had also been knocked down by a car and had had similar problems to me. She had been affected more though (a GCS of 4 and several weeks in a coma), but had recovered very well, coping with her difficulties in much the same way I had. Though they initially may seem daft, perhaps my methods are not altogether wrong?

Coincidentally, I had just written another article, published in *The Link*, the staff newspaper for The Royal Hospitals NHS Trust.

I am able to ride a horse, drive a car, and live independently, yet my consultant had told my parents that I would not be able to do any of these. He even had serious doubts as to whether I would ever walk again – something I am happy to say I am able to do, though it does bring a small amount of pain. Mind you, given my serious car accident, not to mention smashing my head into the side of a bus, I am not altogether surprised at his questioning attitude.

A lot of my recovery can be put down to sheer determination and stubbornness, but I am also very lucky still being able to live life normally, and thankful that my mind and my memory have been left unaffected. Certainly, luck did play some small part, but if not for one glorious, shining light all the will in the world would not have been enough. Although it's unlikely I would have died, having a score on the Glasgow Coma Scale of 5 (out of a maximum of 15, though 3 is dead), my quality of life would have been seriously compromised. As it was, I arrived at hospital not being able to walk or to talk, my sight was very blurred, and nothing was remembered for the following five weeks.

The Helicopter Emergency Medical Service (HEMS), a miraculous, yellow 'bird' came swooping down to land near where I lay in the middle of a busy road, at the height of that morning's rush hour. It deposited a doctor and a paramedic who stayed with me for over half an hour before I was considered stable enough to be taken anywhere. If left to the ambulance paramedics (themselves a fabulous team of people) I would have been taken away in a far worse condition and it could have been a long time before I saw a doctor. As it was, my doctor was with me in less than five minutes after receiving the call.

When we did eventually leave, I was taken back to a hospital (the Royal London), which has one of the best trauma units in the whole of the country, and probably Europe.

No, being hit by that car and headbutting that bus may not have killed me, but if it were not for the unique qualities of HEMS, its speed and the presence of a doctor, I might not be able to talk or to write, to cook a meal or even to eat it myself; I could well be reliant on a wheelchair.

Even if I was not going to die, HEMS helicopter saved my life!

The Link, Issue 35,
March 1997

My RDA holiday in July 1996 was fantastic; I was up at 5 a.m. every morning to muck out some of the beds. I was never told to, and maybe even advised not to, but I was awake and had to do something. Besides, it was work I was used to and I loved every minute of it – had I not wanted to do it there was no way I would have. Even better, we were able to ride twice a day, to include cantering and jumping as well as the normal walking and trotting, under the watchful eye of Peter Felgate.

By the end of the holiday, having read bits of my book and noting that I had a basic skill, Liz asked me if I would write a short article about the week to be published in their RDA Newsletter – something I was happy to comply with:

A Leg to Stand On

'Slow down!' he said.

What a wonderful idea, I thought as Ernie was speeding up around the corner.

We were jumping – not just any old jump either; a double, the likes of which I had not attempted for a year and a half, before my accident. Ernie, an ex-show jumper, was in his element; he was enjoying himself. He was an RDA horse, but did he know that? He was not acting calm and docile like most RDA horses. I had been riding for several years, had many years' experience under my belt, and had worked with horses. He could probably tell, an assumption that explained his carefree attitude, it certainly mirrored mine.

What a week, though: we rode twice a day, an hour at a time, usually once inside and a hack outside. The weather was the complete opposite of the sunshine from the week before; yet we were lucky. Although it did rain, we managed to time the hacks so that we did not get wet. The riding started with an assessment on the Monday so that Peter could see if he had picked the correct horses for our riding ability and, if not, which horse would be more suitable.

Mostly we walked around, though Peter did give us a quick trot. He also gave us a few dressage manoeuvres to carry out. They were not very hard; the most difficult was probably the turn on the forehand, something which in itself is very easy. We all did very well, but what was the name of the exercise again? Making sure we had all been listening, Peter asked Sandy what the exercise was called. Later, he claimed to have misheard, as he confidently said, 'Jimmy!'

Obviously Peter knew the name of every horse and we all had a good laugh as the exercise 'turn on the Jimmy' was quickly christened.

Lunch was cooked for us by Lisa and Clare, though thankfully Liz took over when she came on Tuesday. Evening meals were often courtesy of Lisa's mum, providing main courses and some lovely cakes. We had a Treasure Hunt on Monday, Dean (Nicky's recently honeymooned husband) cooked us a barbecue on Tuesday, while Babs took us each for a drive (in a horse and trap!) throughout the week. On Wednesday we visited an oast house owned by Jill, while we visited Anne's converted barn on Thursday. Friday started with an assessment ride in the morning, followed by an afternoon of rest as we visited Whitbread Hop Farm and had a horsy quiz.

When outside we mainly walked, although we did have a couple of trots towards the end of the week. When inside we trotted, cantered and jumped, mainly because it was safer inside. This was very fortunate as was to be shown by Lionel midway through the holiday. His horse, Cindy, spooked a little in one of the corners, and Lionel wobbled. His leg got detached, becoming caught on the saddle. Cindy jumped in surprise, and Lionel came off. The few moments of incredulity passed quite quickly as

Shirley calmly approached Cindy and removed Lionel's artificial leg from the side of the saddle.

The Bradbourne Group *Newsletter*, Issue No. 16,
Autumn 1996

Much to my delight, I have been invited back in July 1997, doubly pleasing since I had ceased riding with the RDA in Digswell at the end of spring 1996, when they closed over the summer holidays.

By the autumn I could not go back to Digswell either. On 26 October 1996 I was offered a rent-free flat, provided that I acted as the caretaker for Campbell Park Pavilion, home to Milton Keynes Parks Trust, which I had visited (as noted) on a weekend excursion from hospital, back in the spring of 1995. The pay was only enough to buy a Lottery ticket, but that did not matter given that my accommodation was included. The work was not hard either, a quick inspection in the evening before bed, and I was there if there were any problems overnight. Consequently, I had all day to try to find a job that paid money. Although the DSS had eventually started paying me income support it was barely enough to survive, there being no income for it to support! I needed a proper job with proper wages. All I had to do was find one that I was physically capable of doing, and the people there would trust that I could do it. Once more we end up back with discrimination and prejudice.

The move to Milton Keynes, though, did open my eyes, and introduced me to several activities. I started going to the monthly Mensa meeting, and it was not unknown for me to go out, even if it was just a solitary trip to the cinema. Through Mensa I met Colin Zealley, who invited me along to his weekly game of Dungeons and Dragons, a game I loved, but stopped playing when I was about seventeen due to another of my father's job moves. I also joined an archery club and started to enjoy a sport I have been interested in for many years. It was enjoyable playing a sport again, especially as most ball games are simply too difficult now – it is hard playing a ball game when you cannot see the moving ball! I was even given several compliments for my shooting skill, and surprised many people when I told them about my accident.

Voluntary help was also given at the local 'monkey sanctuary'. PEACE (People Establishing A Caring Environment) is a charity set up by Monica King to care for animals that are ill, illegal importees, or simply those pets bought by silly people who could not look after them. The difference with this sanctuary was that it looked after exotic animals. Though this meant mainly monkeys, they had also had an arctic fox, Lucy; a beautiful caracal lynx called Royal; a horde of small mammals; some parrots: Alfie, who was very talkative and outrageously rude; Sam, who squawked annoyingly if he saw you eating; Pepsi, a killer parrot who would bite anything encroaching too close... and three rabbits!

They almost did not have me, though. My first working day, I was being shown around the cages and introduced to the monkeys. One of them, a Black-cap Capuchin called Billy, got too close for comfort. The bite was so bad I believe I should have blacked out, but for some reason I did not. Even so, blood oozed from the wound for the next two hours. (I refused to go to hospital – I was invincible!) In spite of this harsh introduction, all I could think was, Hooray, I could feel it!

The bite was to the ring finger of my right hand, a hand with 'no' sensation... and I could feel the pain. I was so pleased I did not think of reprimanding him. Now, over six months later, Billy and I are best friends.

I went down to PEACE most weeks to help with cleaning the cages and preparing the food. Having a degree in Zoology, it was good to get back to basics. I was also able to run an 'experienced' eye over much of their paperwork and even wrote letters about them to the local newspaper, *The Citizen*.

Whether I believe I died in my accident or not is unimportant. What is important is that I am still here now. Only this morning, my father was thinking and then said, 'It's so nice to have you here; I am so grateful that you are still alive and are physically and mentally well. I have a lot to be thankful for.'

And, you know what? I have a lot to be thankful for as well.

Philip Watling BSc, 6 July 1997

A New Beginning...